THIS IS NOT A BORDER

Reportage & Reflection from the
Palestine Festival of Literature

Edited by

Ahdaf Soueif & Omar Robert Hamilton

BLOOMSBURY

NEW YORK · LONDON · OXFORD · NEW DELHI · SYDNEY

Bloomsbury USA
An imprint of Bloomsbury Publishing Plc

1385 Broadway	50 Bedford Square
New York	London
NY 10018	WC1B 3DP
USA	UK

www.bloomsbury.com

BLOOMSBURY and the Diana logo are trademarks of Bloomsbury Publishing Plc

First published in Great Britain 2017
First U.S. edition 2017

ISBN:	PB:	978-1-63286-884-8
	ePub:	978-1-63286-885-5

Library of Congress Cataloging-in-Publication Data is available.

2 4 6 8 10 9 7 5 3 1

Typeset by Newgen Knowledge Works Pvt Ltd., Chennai, India
Printed and bound in the U.S.A. by Berryville Graphics Inc., Berryville, Virginia

Acknowledgements

PalFest's founding board of trustees were Victoria Brittain, Alison Elliot, John Horner, Brigid Keenan, Sheila Whitaker and myself. Suad Amiry and Fiona McMorrough both did time on the board. The current trustees are Omar Robert Hamilton, Nathalie Handal, John Horner, Brigid Keenan and myself.

PalFest has the immense good fortune to have many friends, some it started out with, some it collected along the way. It's not possible to list them all, but we are grateful to each and every one of them for the various ways they've contributed to the festival.

Some of our friends are no longer with us. Henning Mankell, who died in October 2015, was visibly angered by what he saw at PalFest 2009. He made a generous donation to the festival the following year and was on the Gaza flotilla that included the *Mavi Marmara*. We hold him in our hearts. Taha Muhammad Ali, who honoured us with one of his last public appearances. Rawda Attalah, who introduced us to Nazareth and Haifa, adopted us and hosted us in her home.

We would like to thank all our friends in Palestine for their support and advice. Tania and Hanna Nasir, Islah Jad, Suad Amiry and Selim Tamari for their delicious food, their company and the comfort of their beautiful homes. We thank all our partners in Palestine: the Khalil Sakakini Cultural Centre in Ramallah, the Municipalities of Ramallah and Nablus, Paola Handal, Dar al-Nadwa and the Reverend Mitri Raheb in Bethlehem, the Hebron Rehabilitation Committee in al-Khalil, Project Hope in Nablus, Morgan Cooper and the Palestine Writing Workshop, the Freedom Theatre, the Qattan Foundation, the Arab Culture Association in Haifa and the Universities of Bethlehem, al-Quds, an-Najah, al-Khalil, Birzeit and Jenin.

Najwan Darwish has been a superlative comrade and literary adviser to PalFest, and we have benefited also from the advice of Wafa Darwish. Omar Barghouti of PACBI and BDS has provided solid and cogent information and ethical guidance, as has Ray Dolphin of UNRWA.

We are grateful for the solidarity and input of our friends in Zochrot and that of Angela Godfrey-Goldstein.

Safwan al-Masri of Columbia University has godfathered connections which made PalFest viable over the last few years; we treasure his friendship and support. We are also grateful to Caroline Moorehead and to Amal Ghandour for their thoughtful and selfless generosity.

The British Council has been an excellent friend, partnering PalFest from the start; it was a privilege to know Susie Nicklin and every country director we've worked with has provided crucial logistical help. It was our great pleasure to work with Alan Smart, and Suha Khuffash has been the most support- ive point person on the ground. We value all this, particularly as the political positions PalFest has felt it necessary to declare have sometimes not been at one with British Council policy. We value the Council's belief in constructive disagreement and their commitment to the support of cultural work.

We thank the Bank of Palestine for much-needed financial support for the last three years and the Sigrid Rausing Foundation, which provided support in an earlier three. We thank our network of friends – from the group of young financiers who gave PalFest its initial start to the diaspora Palestinians who have steadfastly provided the funds we have managed on: Samir and Malak Abdulhadi, Fadi Ghandour, Maher and Randa Kadoura, Hussam and Tina Khoury, Zahi Khouri and Amal Nasser, Nabil Qaddumi, Rana Sadik and Samer Younis, and our most constant friends Zina Jardaneh and Hossam and Madiha Abdalla. For Riad Kamal a very special tribute; his friendship and support have seen PalFest through some difficult times, and it's been a great comfort to know he's always there for us.

Raja Shehadeh, Penny Johnson and Ritu Menon gave the proceeds of *Seeking Palestine: New Palestinian Writing on Exile and Home* to PalFest. Ru Freeman's authors in *Extraordinary Rendition: American Writers on Palestine* also donated their fees to PalFest. Nada Hegazy and her young team in Cairo have gifted PalFest the translation of authors' extracts distributed free at the festival.

Ismail Richard Hamilton gives his time, charisma and organisational skills to market and sell PalFest books and bags off the Internet throughout the year and, with Léa Georgeson-Caparros (to whom he is engaged to be married), is responsible for sales at all our venues during the festival.

PalFest's logo was the gift of Jeff Fisher.

Because of the circumstances under which it operates, PalFest is more or less structured afresh each year. We can never be certain which spaces or roads will be open to us or what the difficulties we'll face will be. Sometimes our events are closed down or made very hard to get to. We also never know exactly what our budget will be and, despite the goodwill of our partners, we operate on a shoestring. The delivery of a successful festival every year is completely dependent on our small and dedicated team, who have always had to be empathetic, flexible, inventive, quick-witted.

Eleanor O'Keefe organised the first edition of the festival (2008) together with Carol Michel. She was ably succeeded by Cristina Baum (2009/10) and Adania Shibli (2010).

But PalFest, as it is today, is very much the work of Omar Robert Hamilton. From the start he was responsible for the production of the events. His fingerprint grew more clear over the years until it was obvious that he was directing the festival. His vision has made PalFest young and contemporary, with more music, more performance, more merging of forms. He has collected for PalFest the amazing team of talented and committed people which delivers the festival every year: Yasmin El-Rifae, his partner (now in life as well) in conceptualising and running the festival; Muiz, who has forged our visual identity with his stunning artworks year after year; Beesan Ramadan, who coordinates the festival on the ground; Maath Musleh and Hussam Ghosheh, on whose ideas and invention we rely annually; Rob Stothard, whose photographs showcase the festival to the world; and Murat Gokmen, whose short films convey a true sense of PalFest to those who've not been.

PalFest was immensely lucky to secure the patronage of Harold Pinter in 2008. The speech he felt moved to make at our launch in the home of Ghalia and Omar al-Qattan in London was tremendously moving, and it is a matter of lasting regret that we did not record it. The messages of two more of our patrons, Chinua Achebe and Mahmoud Darwish, are reproduced in this book. We were also honoured with the patronage of Seamus Heaney and John Berger, and are most grateful to Philip Pullman and Emma Thompson for their continued support.

The most enormous thanks to my friend and publisher, Bloomsbury's Alexandra Pringle, herself a PalFestivalian, for encouraging this work, and to Madeleine Feeny, Angelique Tran Van Sang, Callie Garnett, Vicky Beddow, Rebecca Thorne and Sarah New for seeing it through the publication process and beyond. Eternal gratitude to my friend and agent, Charles Buchan of the Wylie Agency, who saved Omar and me from sinking under the administrative and legal burden of a book with forty-seven contributors.

Finally, everybody who contributed to this book gave their work for free – unless it becomes an international best-seller, then they'll want their share.

Ahdaf Soueif

CONTENTS

CONTENTS

CONTENTS

CONTENTS

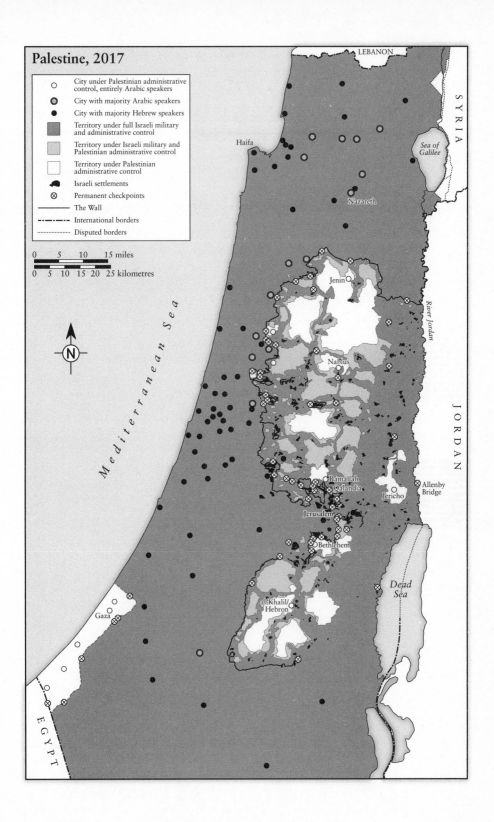

Palestine, 2017

○   City under Palestinian administrative control, entirely Arabic speakers

◉   City with majority Arabic speakers

●   City with majority Hebrew speakers

▨   Territory under full Israeli military and administrative control

▧   Territory under Israeli military and Palestinian administrative control

□   Territory under Palestinian administrative control

▰   Israeli settlements

⊗   Permanent checkpoints

──   The Wall

─·─·─   International borders

·········   Disputed borders

0   5   10   15 miles

0 5 10 15 20 25 kilometres

LEBANON

SYRIA

Sea of Galilee

Haifa

Nazareth

Mediterranean Sea

River Jordan

JORDAN

Jenin

Nablus

Ramallah
Qalandia

Jericho

Allenby
Bridge

Jerusalem

Bethlehem

Dead Sea

al-Khalil/
Hebron

Gaza

EGYPT

INTRODUCTION

Ahdaf Soueif

In an elegant Ottoman villa set in a garden a few metres away from the centre of Ramallah, on a pleasant evening in October 2003, I did a reading. I was in Palestine for the *Guardian*, following up on an earlier visit, and Palestinian friends had asked me to do an event. It was set up overnight and the room in the Khalil Sakakini Cultural Centre was packed. Halfway through we heard a tremendous explosion somewhere outside. I stopped. People waved me on. It's nothing, they said. It wasn't nothing of course, and they knew it; they had simply wanted this 'normal' evening, talking about books, to continue.

We – Omar Robert Hamilton (my son) and I – spent a portion of that night perched on a friend's roof, watching Israeli soldiers smash in the door of an empty house across the otherwise quiet, residential street.

Then there was a message from An-Najah University in Nablus inviting me to go and read there. Nablus is only thirty-six kilometres north of Ramallah, but the city had been under Israeli closure for three years. Not a problem, said the university; we'll send someone to get you. They sent a Samaritan in a white mini-van who took us also to visit his home in Mount Gerizim. He showed us pictures of himself in traditional Syrian dress. The Samaritans self-identify as 'Palestinian Jews' and carry both Israeli and Palestinian documents. Israeli checkpoints open for them. We arrived in Nablus to find that – on the occasion of the beginning of Ramadan – Israel had intensified its siege of the city. Students who lived in neighbouring towns and villages were stranded; the chancellor was providing Iftar for them all and they were going to camp out in the university. I did a seminar next door to a student photography exhibition. Picture upon picture of young men blindfolded, wrists bound behind their backs.

In Palestine almost every situation you can be in is layered. Nothing, not a single thing, is free of the occupation, its instruments, its outcomes. In the same gaze you take in the row of gracious early-twentieth-century Palestinian houses, the Palestinian refugee camp set up in 1948, now rooted and solid, and the young Israeli settlement bristling on top of the hill, waiting. You can see the stony terraces and the centuries that coaxed them into fruitfulness, the Israeli wall severing them from their farmers, and the settlement road cutting through the sky above them, its supports digging deep into their soil.

On my first visit, in 2000, the thought had kept coming to me that I wished people – lots and lots of people – could actually see what I was seeing. From 2003 I had a second wish: that when a Palestinian audience ignored explosions for the sake of a literary event, when a university took the trouble to smuggle a writer through a military checkpoint, they would get more for their efforts than just me. The Palestine Festival of Literature made both wishes come true.

In the first decade of this century literary festivals were springing up everywhere. Could we organise a small group of writers to travel to Palestine, experience the situation there for themselves and do literary events that Palestinians want? 'We' in this case were my family and friends – two specifically: Victoria Brittain and Brigid Keenan. Victoria had long been a supporter of the Palestinians; indeed we first met as patrons of the Palestine Solidarity Campaign. Brigid and I had met at a London fundraiser, Visions of Palestine, in 2004 and become fast friends.

In 2007 a series of happy chances pulled it all together. Brigid in her diary piece for this book describes how she and I spoke of a literary festival in Palestine and how Eleanor O'Keefe came on board to organise the first edition. Eleanor invited John Horner, who became PalFest's invaluable treasurer. At a London Book Fair lunch a chance seat next to Suzanne Joinson, then working for the British Council, won us the Council's support. A friend in finance secured me a meeting with some of his colleagues – all young financiers of Arab origin – and I walked away with a good portion of our first year's budget.

We were in constant consultation with our Palestinian friends, and all were unhesitating in their encouragement. Mahmoud Darwish's letter, with which we open this volume, was PalFest's entry into the cultural landscape of Palestine.

We stated PalFest's mission as 'to bring world-class cultural events to communities that otherwise would have no access to them'. Over ten years PalFest brought to Palestine some of the finest English-language novelists, essayists, dramatists and poets. We also brought publishers, agents and cultural producers. Their brief was to conduct literary events, workshops and seminars, to network, to scout for new talent; for one week they would meet and interact with Palestinians on their home ground. This book – marking PalFest's tenth anniversary – contains some of the writings that were born out of this undertaking.

For some, PalFest was a doorway. Suheir Hammad, who was changing the face of American performance poetry, had her own constituency, particularly among the young. Rachel Holmes and Jeremy Harding both went back repeatedly to do writing workshops. Henning Mankell joined the following year's flotilla to Gaza. Many of our participants, like Remi Kanazi, Nathalie Handal, Haifa Zangana, Omar El-Khairy, Robin Yassin-Kassab, Jamal Mahjoub, the WildWorks Theatre Company, Sabrina Mahfouz, Molly Crabapple, Nancy Kricorian and others either stayed on after the festival or returned at other times. Haifa Zangana has gone back every year to teach. But I think that for everyone, whether or not they returned, the week they spent in Palestine became part of their inner landscape.

It was important for PalFest that it should try to travel in the same manner as its Palestinian audience. Palestinians under the occupation are issued by Israel with one of two types of pass: a Jerusalem ID or a West Bank ID. If you have a West Bank ID you cannot enter Jerusalem or go beyond the 1948 line without a special permit. This means that, in effect, you are not allowed to use Ben Gurion Airport and must travel in and out of the country via Jordan, over the King Hussein (or Allenby) Bridge. The bridge, therefore, became PalFest's entry point for the festival.

Israel has never agreed to an official delineation of its borders. However, it controls all access routes into historic Palestine. So even though the bridge connects Jordan to the occupied Palestinian territories, it is under Israeli – rather than Palestinian Authority – control and is the first point at which the visitor is subject to Israeli procedures. And so it makes an appearance in many of the pieces in this book.

An aspect of the occupation that is quite difficult for non-locals to get their heads around is that the majority of the barriers – the wall and the checkpoints in their varied manifestations – are not in fact borders; they do not separate 'Palestine' from 'Israel'; mostly they cut through occupied Palestinian land, separating communities from each other, from their land, from their markets, their universities, their schools.

Another imperative for PalFest was to make it possible for Palestinians to attend our events without undue hardship – in other words, people should not have to cross checkpoints to come to a PalFest event; PalFest would cross the checkpoints to reach its audiences. And so we became a 'cultural roadshow', packing our bags every morning, getting on the bus, pulling our bags through the metal grids and turnstiles of the checkpoints and back on the bus to get to our next university, our next municipal garden, our next event. There are fast roads built for the convenience of Israeli settlers who live in the occupied areas in violation of international law, but PalFest, confining itself to roads that Palestinians are allowed to use, does its best to avoid them.

The physical hardship that this entails is another reason we're grateful to our international guests – some of them not young – who gamely enter into the spirit of the festival, dragging bags, eating sandwich lunches on buses and delivering their events with spirit and panache.

To date there are some 170 PalFest graduates, and naturally not every one of them is in this book. We hope, however, that the ones who are here reflect both the diversity of PalFestivalians and the contours of the journey that ultimately bound us all together.

Fate has not permitted PalFest or this book to be placed before Edward Said. But Said's all-encompassing humanism, his intellectual standards, political astuteness and moral rigour have been our guide and our example. One of Said's recurring themes was the issue of personal responsibility in the face of world events and directions. In *The Reith Lectures* (1993) he says, 'Certainly in writing and speaking, one's aim is . . . trying to induce a change in the moral climate whereby aggression is seen as such, the unjust punishment of peoples or individuals is either prevented or given up, and the recognition of rights and democratic freedoms is established as a norm for everyone, not invidiously for a select few.'

We hope that it is to such a change in the moral climate that *This Is Not a Border* might contribute.

Cairo, December 2016

Welcome

Mahmoud Darwish

Dear Friends,

I regret that I cannot be here today, to receive you personally.

Welcome to this sorrowing land, whose literary image is so much more beautiful than its present reality. Your courageous visit of solidarity is more than just a passing greeting to a people deprived of freedom and of a normal life; it is an expression of what Palestine has come to mean to the living human conscience that you represent. It is an expression of the writer's awareness of his role: a role directly engaged with issues of justice and freedom. The search for truth, which is one of a writer's duties, takes on – in this land – the form of a confrontation with the lies and the usurpation that besiege Palestine's contemporary history; with the attempts to erase our people from the memory of history and from the map of this place.

We are now in the sixtieth year of the Nakba. There are now those who are dancing on the graves of our dead, and who consider our Nakba their festival. But the Nakba is not a memory; it is an ongoing uprooting, filling Palestinians with dread for their very existence. The Nakba continues because the occupation continues. And the continued occupation means a continued war. This war that Israel wages against us is not a war to defend its existence, but a war to obliterate ours.

The conflict is not between two existences, as the Israeli discourse claims. The Arabs have unanimously offered Israel a collective peace proposal in return for Israel's recognition of the Palestinians' right to an independent state. But Israel refuses.

Dear friends, in your visit here you will see the naked truth. Yesterday, we celebrated the end of apartheid in South Africa. Today, you see apartheid blossoming here most efficiently. Yesterday, we celebrated the fall of the Berlin Wall. Today, you see the wall rising again, coiling itself like a giant snake around our necks. A wall not to separate Palestinians from Israelis, but to separate Palestinians from themselves and from any view of the horizon. Not to separate history from myth, but to weld together history and myth with a racist ingenuity.

Life here, as you see, is not a given, it's a daily miracle. Military barriers separate everything from everything. And everything – even the landscape – is temporary and vulnerable. Life here is less than life, it is an approaching death. And how ironic that the stepping-up of oppression, of closures, of settlement expansion, of daily killings that have become routine – that all this takes place in the context of what is called the 'peace process', a process revolving in an empty circle, threatening to kill the very idea of peace in our suffering hearts.

Peace has two parents: Freedom and Justice. And occupation is the natural begetter of violence. Here, on this slice of historic Palestine, two generations of Palestinians have been born and raised under occupation. They have never known another – normal – life. Their memories are filled with images of hell. They see their tomorrows slipping out of their reach. And though it seems to them that everything outside this reality is heaven, yet they do not want to go to that heaven. They stay because they are afflicted with hope.

In this difficult condition of history, Palestinian writers live. Nothing distinguishes them from their countrymen, nothing except one thing: that writers try to gather the fragments of this life and of this place in a literary text, a text they try to make whole.

I have spoken before of how difficult it is to be Palestinian, and how difficult it is for a Palestinian to be a writer or a poet.

On the one hand you have to be true to your reality, and on the other you have to be faithful to your literary profession. In this zone of tension between the long 'State of Emergency' and his literary imagination, the language of the poet moves. He has to use the word to resist the military occupation. And he has to resist – on behalf of the word – the danger of the banal and the repetitive. How can he achieve literary freedom in such slavish conditions? And how can he preserve the literariness of literature in such brutal times?

The questions are difficult. But each poet or writer has their own way of writing about themselves and their reality. The one historical condition does not produce the one text – or even similar texts, for the writing selves are many and different. Palestinian literature does not fit into ready-made moulds.

Being Palestinian is not a slogan, it is not a profession. The Palestinian is a human being, a tormented human being who has daily questions, national and existential, who has a love story, who contemplates a flower and a window open to the unknown. Who has a metaphysical fear and an inner world utterly resistant to occupation.

A literature born of a defined reality is able to create a reality that transcends reality – an alternative, imagined reality. Not a search for a myth of happiness to flee from a brutal history, but an attempt to make history less mythological, to place the myth in its proper, metaphorical place, and to transform us from victims of history into partners in humanising history.

My friends and colleagues, thank you for your noble act of solidarity. Thank you for your brave initiative to break the psychological siege inflicted upon us. Thank you for resisting the invitation to dance on our graves. Know that we are still here, that we still live.

8 May 2008

WHERE DOES PALESTINE BEGIN?

Yasmin El-Rifae

I'm sitting in my office in New York, lingering over the draft of an email I need to send to the staff.

It explains my complicated trip through Saudi Arabia and Germany and Egypt, finally to Palestine for the festival. I feel that I am not straightforward enough for these colleagues, most of whom are three or four hours away from home, their families a city or a state away instead of scattered across continents.

But I know that this is not exactly the source of my hesitation. It's the word *Palestine*. But what else could I call it? The Territories? The West Bank? Do I need to hide it, the way I hide it at the Allenby Bridge crossing? Do I need to soften it for this audience by placing it next to the word *Israel*? Can a word be made so absent without people becoming alarmed when it does appear?

What else are we hiding when we hide Palestine?

I send the email. Two people mention it to me, in separate conversations, before I leave. One registers her surprise, calls it brave. Another is excited because he has found an ally in a cause he has not been able to express his passion for to any other colleague.

This is a press-freedom organisation.

A manager, whom I respect and am friendly with, crosses her arms in front of her chest and keeps them there, hurries me out of her office when I come in to say goodbye.

The political choices that we make about language, about names, are more than tools for use in a broader effort. They are the effort, and the battle.

Can you have a literature festival in Palestine without *including* Israel? Without inviting Israeli writers, without going to Israeli audiences?

There is often confusion when talking about Palestine as a geographical place. Most people don't know that Gaza and the West Bank are as unreachable from one another as two places can be. You cannot reach either one without going through a border or a checkpoint controlled by Israel. Sometimes you can reach Gaza by going through Egypt, Israel's ally in its siege.

You cannot be in Palestine without saying your grandfather's name to Israeli officials at the border or the airport. You cannot eat in Palestine without buying or dodging Israeli products. You cannot buy anything at all without using Israeli currency.

In Palestine, Israel is everywhere.

We drive through Ramallah, capital of politics and finance for the would-be Palestinian state. Here you buy your Jawwal or Wataniya SIM card for use in the West Bank. Palestinian phone operators have not been allowed to provide 3G, although we hear that might change now.

Some people manage to buy Israeli SIM cards, either in Israeli cities or from rough neighbourhoods near the separation wall, where they are on sale along with other contraband such as drugs and weapons. Communication is a serious offence. The options are Cellcom and Partner, which used to be called Orange until Orange pulled out after campaigning by the Boycott, Divestment and Sanctions Movement.

These SIM cards will pick up 3G from settlement communication towers sometimes, especially in the hillier parts of Nablus and Ramallah, near land with the densest settlements. If you are looking for a West Bank settlement, look for a tower. They go up first, poking out of the hills like flagpoles, and the settlers follow.

We go to shattered, buried Palestine in the old city of Hebron. We look up, and Israel lives above the wire mesh which catches its rocks, its garbage, although not its urine. Israel is in the upper floors of houses taken over and occupied by settler families, or turned into watchtowers for the soldiers who protect them. Palestine on the ground floor, on the street level, and Israel between the wire mesh and the sky.

We drive north to look for Palestine in Haifa. We have hidden our Palestinian friend in the back of the bus. Hidden is too strong a word here perhaps. She sits in plain sight, sunglasses on, flanked by white writers on either side.

The bus is stopped at a checkpoint. A man with a machine gun and a baby-blue shirt gets on the bus, a woman in khaki behind him.

He asks for the group leader. Omar gets off the bus with him. They are gone for about twenty minutes, standing nearby, talking. On the bus the writers are filled with questions; some are worried. Our Palestinian friend is calm.

They come back on the bus, angry that one of the writers had been taking photographs out of the window. The man with the machine gun asks to see the phone, and to delete the photos. The offending writer wants to know what authority he has to see his phone or his passport.

The man tells us he is a civilian. He shows us a card to prove it. His machine gun is the width of the aisle between the seats.

Eventually the writer backs down. He knows that he can recover the photos instantly.

We continue our drive. The traffic had grown worse during our hold-up at the checkpoint, and we will be late to Haifa. But we are late to Haifa every year; one year we were so late that the writers had to be hurried into borrowed bathrooms in which to collect themselves after the three-hour drive before going immediately on stage half an hour late.

The road to Haifa becomes coastal, and it is poster-perfect: designed landscapes, the plumper, softer light of the seaside, the sky paler near the water. The wall is far from here.

When we reach Haifa the bus makes two stops. We have split the group between the only two Palestinian-owned hotels in the city. At the first hotel I call out the names of the people who should disembark now, tell them to get their bags and check in, tell them where and when the next meeting point will be. It is now the fourth day of the festival, and I can feel them getting annoyed, wanting to break free and have a beer by the sea and walk around this pretty town and not have to deal with the slowness of a group splitting between hotels, one of which doesn't provide breakfast. Can't we just stay in the Marriott?

At night our audience finds us. Young and cool, arty and multilingual. After the event we go to Masada Street, where the cafes and bars are open to a mixed crowd of Jewish Israelis and Palestinians in the daytime. At night the socialising is segregated. We stick to Eleka and a couple of other Arab-owned bars.

A week after the festival has wrapped a drunk man in Ramallah says, Don't be enchanted by Haifa. Haifa is corrupt, her beauty is a cheap mask. Go to the abandoned villages, go to the Muthallath, go to Um el-Fahm; there you will find Palestine.

So then where are we now?

He orders another Heineken.

What of the Palestine of camps, of exile, of statelessness?

When a house gets demolished in East Jerusalem, does it stop being Palestine? When, in which moment? When the first brick drops or when the last is cleared?

When the Palestinian Authority arrests teenagers days after the Israelis have released them, do they leave the same absence? Where does Israel stop and Palestine begin in the network of incarceration?

When you are driving into Ramallah, there is a sign that warns you are entering Area A. It is forbidden by Israeli law, and it is unsafe, the sign says. On the other side of the checkpoint children sell cassette tapes, pillows, kitchenware.

There is no security check for those going in to Ramallah. Anyone can drive in or walk through. Going the other way, leaving Area A and going into Jerusalem, is a different story.

So we go through areas A, B and C, a rambling bus of privileged-passport holders, popping up with events which we

14

can only run with the help of patient friends who show us their Palestine and share their stage.

We do not schedule ways to engage with Israel, because Israel is everywhere in Palestine. It may not be the version that Israeli officials and cultural actors would like seen. But perhaps the role of literature and art should be to look for what is hidden, what is obscured, what is made harder and harder to reach.

There is a point when you are entering Bethlehem where you can see the wall's curve through a field of olive trees. The scene has it all: the idyllic beauty of the land, the concrete abruptness of its severance, the two together surreal. Every year I try to snap a photo at the right moment as the bus drives by but it always appears too suddenly, and blurs.

THE GAZA SUITE: GAZA

Suheir Hammad

a great miracle happened here
a festival of lights
a casting of lead upon children
an army feasting on epiphany

i know nothing under the sun over the wall no one mentions
some must die wrapped in floral petroleum blanket
no coverage

i have come to every day armageddon
a ladder left unattended
six candles burn down a house
a horse tied to smoke
some must die to send a signal

flat line scream live stream river a memory longer than
life spans
the living want to die in their country

no open doors no open seas no open
hands full of heart five daughters wrapped in white

each day jihad
each day faith over fear
each day a mirror of fire
the living want to die with their families

the girl loses limbs her brother gathers arms
some must die for not dying

children on hospital floor mother beside
them the father in shock this is my family
i have failed them this is my family i did
not raise their heads i have buried them
my family what will i do now my family is bread
one fish one people cut into pieces

JERUSALEM
Ahdaf Soueif

I was not prepared. Who could have been?

Remission Gate. There were two Israeli soldiers in the gateway. It was December 2000 and the second Intifada was in full swing and there were soldiers everywhere. At least here they were on foot; at Damascus Gate they'd been mounted. I walked through the gateway into the Sacred Sanctuary of al-Aqsa – and a few enclosed acres became a world. At my back the city behind the walls, but in the great sweep ahead there were tall, dark pines, broad steps rising to slender white columns and, beyond them, a golden dome and the biggest sky I had ever been under.

A sanctuary on a hilltop. Around it the earth fell away.

Palestinians are masters of terracing; they built Jerusalem on a hill and the old city slopes gently towards the south-east, towards the Sanctuary, and there the central and biggest of twenty-six terraces is for the Dome of the Rock. From the south twenty steps lead up to it, from the north just nine. You can see the Dome from the surrounding hills, but you cannot see it from the city. Only when you come very close to one of the great gateways, when you are almost through it, is the Dome revealed: light, almost floating, framed by necklaces of slim colonnaded arches and attended by other domes and pulpits and fountains each of which, alone, would have commandeered your attention. But in the Sanctuary they are modest, demanding nothing, content to be here.

From the gateways behind me, through the trees and across the grass, women were coming in from the city for sunset prayers. They crossed the white piazza and passed through the canopied doorway in the blue-tiled wall. Girls paused to slip simple white cotton skirts on over their jeans. I followed: up the wide stone steps and under the laced archway and stopped. Right there, in front of me, was the blue octagon, and across the gold of its dome birds dipped and swooped and wheeled low in their last flight of the day. At the far end of the Sanctuary a reticent wide building under an austere grey dome was the Southern Mosque. And in between and all around I seemed to recognise the scattered, smaller pieces of architecture. I sat down on a low wall of white stone; I was at home, among friends.

I kept going back, that first week. It was the first time I'd come right up close to the story I'd been following all my life, the first time its pieces had come together. The women befriended me, took me to their nearby homes. I realised that the north and west walls of al-Aqsa are not walls at all; they are a porous urban border that houses people, schools, libraries and archives. And all these institutions, and the Aqsa itself, were charities supported by a vast waqf system; a system of trusts and endowments. The Sanctuary has for thirteen centuries been a charitable Islamic waqf at the centre of a matrix of endowments and funding. In 1948, many of the lands and properties and businesses supporting the al-Aqsa Waqf fell under Israeli control. The administration of the waqf was assumed by Jordan.

My new friends' homes were each growing out of the other, al-Aqsa was their neighbourhood mosque, its court their own front yard. They told me how East Jerusalem had stood firm after Israel occupied it in 1967 and demolished a whole neighbourhood in the Old City. For two decades the Israelis had been unable to get a foothold in the place. Then one man had succumbed, vanished overnight, taken his family and his new dollars and put an ocean between himself and his old neighbourhood; Ariel Sharon had secured the first settler house in the Old City. Barbed wire went up, Israeli flags were hammered into balconies, eaves and porches, searchlights and cameras were trained on the streets, on the neighbours.

That was thirteen years earlier. Now, a woman showed me, a new settler family had moved into rooms in the building next to hers. From her stoop we watched the settlers obstruct pathways, blast settler music from the windows and throw rubbish into their neighbours' yard. When the neighbours remonstrated the settlers summoned the soldiers. One night, I was told, they'd blocked an ambulance and someone had died.

The Arabic root, 7/ll, is to arrive in a place with the intention of staying. It can lead to i7tilal: 'occupation' and i7lal: 'substitution'. The Palestinians say that the Israelis in East Jerusalem have moved from the phase of i7tilal to that of i7lal. We can deal with them living here alongside us, they say, but they want to live here instead of us. This is 1948 all over again.

Within three days of the end of the 1967 war and with a massive deployment of bulldozers, Israel demolished 140 houses just outside the west wall of the Sanctuary – the 'al-Buraq Wall', and forced the displacement of 650 Palestinian residents. In their place Israel created 'Wailing Wall Plaza', later 'Western Wall Plaza'.

In 2000, on that first visit, in a street near Wailing Wall Plaza, I came upon a hole-in-the-wall outlet displaying ill-printed leaflets that spoke of 'The Third Temple'. The millennium was upon us and the world was full of crazy ideas.

But from the western wall the Israelis were digging under the Sanctuary; digging since 1968. They claim the dig is for archaeological reasons. The Waqf Authority says that the tunnels are undermining the foundations of al-Aqsa. The cliff-face under the Sanctuary's southern wall is now a puzzle of excavational entrances and archaeological walkways. Tunnels deeper underground come out in Silwan, the pretty, green village just outside the southern walls. And there, through demolition orders, fines, taxation, police raids, closures, stop and search, detentions, banishment and attacks or provocations by settlers, the Israelis are clearing a space to construct an alternative reality. Instead of Silwan, a theme park: the City of David.

q/s/a: to become far. From this root the emphatic 'qassa' is to narrate – and also to cut. A story can cut the distance between us and what is far.

IN 1187 AD / 583 AH A BATALLION OF YOUNG VOLUNTEERS from the Maghreb fought alongside Salah al-Din al-Ayyubi to liberate Jerusalem after eighty-eight years of Crusader rule. Victorious, Salah al-Din re-established the pact that Omar, its first Muslim ruler, had made with the city when he took it: everyone had the right to leave the city or remain under the new rule, their safety, possessions, churches and crosses guaranteed. With this Salah al-Din reinvigorated Jerusalem's links with its past and breathed new life into it. And in recognition of the young Maghrebi volunteers, the state, six years after Hattin, established a charitable waqf for the benefit of people from the Maghreb 'regardless of gender, faith or purpose'. The Sidi Abu Madyan Waqf covered some 45,000 square metres immediately to the west of the Sanctuary, starting at al-Buraq Wall. It included houses, schools, mosques, bath-houses and lodging-houses. This became known as the Moroccan Quarter.

'One of the most pleasant features of the al-Aqsa Sanctuary is that wherever a person sits within it, they will feel that they have found the best position with the best view,' the Baghdadi encyclopaedist, Yaqoot al-Hamawi observed. Nine centuries later I heard his words and lingered. A building led to its builder, to its patron, to a story. One dome is Mahd 3eesa, Jesus' Cradle, other domes are named for Solomon, for Joseph, for the Prophet's Night Journey and for the Scales of Judgement. With Mi7rab Maryam, Mary's Chamber, the Sanctuary embraces the story of the Virgin's seclusion as she awaits her confinement. The Prophet David gives his name to a gateway. The multiple narratives of Jerusalem are accommodated here, made room for, honoured.

Within its walls and its eight hundred metres of cloistered galleries, al-Aqsa has seven individual mosques, four minarets, twenty-six terraces, ten domes, twenty-five wells, fourteen fountains, eight colonnaded arches, as well as museums, libraries, archives and court registers and twelve schools. Many are exquisite works of art. Most

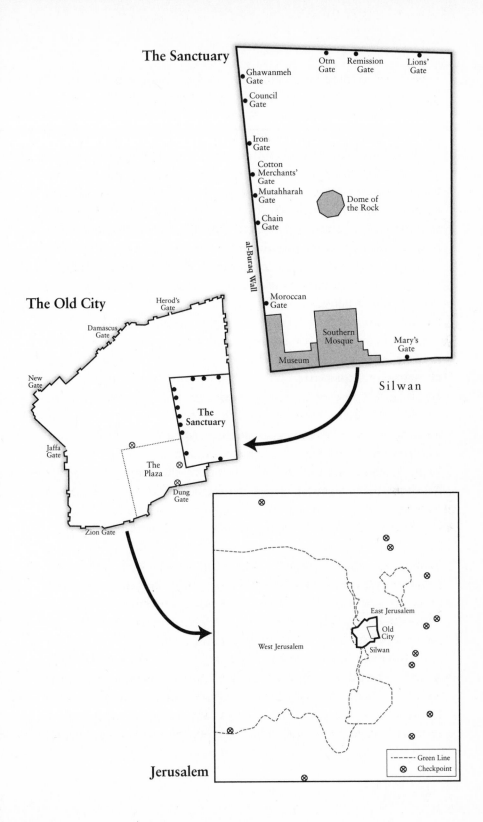

The Sanctuary

Otm Gate
Remission Gate
Lions' Gate
Ghawanmeh Gate
Council Gate
Iron Gate
Cotton Merchants' Gate
Mutahharah Gate
Chain Gate
al-Buraq Wall
Dome of the Rock
Moroccan Gate
Southern Mosque
Museum
Mary's Gate

The Old City

Herod's Gate
Damascus Gate
New Gate
Jaffa Gate
The Sanctuary
The Plaza
Zion Gate
Dung Gate

Silwan

East Jerusalem
Old City
West Jerusalem
Silwan

Green Line
Checkpoint

Jerusalem

have been restored or adapted or augmented over the centuries. They demonstrate in stone that aspect of Muslim artistic and scholarly practice that we see so clearly in music and in thousands of manuscripts: the newcomer comments on, embroiders, riffs off, develops, competes with, refutes, rejects – but always sees their work in relation to what has come before. Every piece is unique, a layered treasury of the materials, the styles and practices of different architects, patrons, builders and periods. Many are at the centre of a network of endowments and financial instruments and social relations that spread across the entire world. Here, stone by stone over a millennium and four centuries, a civilisation constructed a layered and harmonious work of civic and sacred art.

On our first PalFest, in 2008, I was eager to bring our authors to the Sanctuary. I wanted them to see all this, and to have that moment – the moment I kept coming back for, the moment when you step in from the noise and the trouble, from the soldiers and settlers and guns, into this open space of thoughtful clarity. I chose my favourite of al-Aqsa's nine great open doorways: Bab el-Qattaneen. We strolled the length of the covered Cotton Market to get to it. In the gateway the two laconic Israeli soldiers asked if we were Muslim. There were twenty-five of us. Some are and some aren't we said. Non-Muslims, the soldiers said, are not allowed into al-Aqsa; the Muslims will not permit it. That's not true, I said, I've never heard of such a thing. I appealed to the Palestinian caretakers behind the soldiers: what do they mean the Muslims won't permit it? The rules of the Israelis, they said. I could see the white terrace rising to the Dome, the white columns. I argued and argued and the soldiers just repeated 'Moroccan Gate'. We raced through the streets. We asked for Moroccan Gate and were taken aback at the curtness with which people waved us onwards. We raced past Mutahharah Gate and Chain Gate and then were halted by an Israeli checkpoint: glass and steel and show your passport and put your bags through a scanning-machine and we emerged into Western Wall Plaza – and into a different city; a city that's pretending to be Jerusalem. Gone now the houses growing out of each other, the soft-cornered Jerusalem stone, pinked and mellowed and glowing with age and life, the barber-shops, the bakeries with crooked doorways and trays of fresh pastries and sweets. Here were new buildings: towers, sharp-edged and bland, made of steel and concrete and clad with thin slivers of Jerusalem stone, stern carvings on their fronts declaring them gifts of patrons in North America and Europe for the Jewish Community. There were purpose-built walkways and observation points, there were Israeli cadets sitting on the ground being oriented and Israeli tour guides thumping out Palestinian rhythms on tablas. There was a large municipal billboard saying that this was the site of the First and Second Temples, that buildings on this site had been razed and rebuilt many times, and that it was the central hope of every Jew to build the Third Temple.

Israel uses Bible stories to destroy Palestinian lives.

In the southern corner of the plaza a caterpillar-like structure reared up on wooden scaffolding to attach itself to a high point on the Sanctuary wall. This was the entrance to Moroccan Gate. At its foot another checkpoint was admitting women in shorts and groups of men with settler slogans on their T-shirts. We stood in the line. Israeli soldiers went through our bags. A small silver cross someone was wearing had to be left on their counter because 'the Muslims don't like it'. Then we were allowed to climb into the ascending tunnel. Through chinks in the woodwork we could see the plaza below. From time to time we came upon stacks of riot shields. Eventually we stumbled out into a corner of the Sanctuary and into Israeli soldiers already harrying us – telling us to leave by the nearest gate, to walk by the walls, to hurry. But we struck out towards the centre, towards the broad steps, the welcoming arches, the canopied doorways of the Dome. When we were safely inside and away from settlers and soldiers my guests – I knew – would feel that expansion, that sense of space, of calm; the space would do its work, the mosaics, the lighting… But no, non-Muslims could not go into the Dome or the Southern Mosque or indeed any building. We were dressed modestly and had scarves over our hair but the Palestinian caretakers watched us suspiciously. Then one of them saw the tears spilling under my shades and was kind. Listen, he said, you've come through Moroccan Gate. That's the gate the settlers come through with the soldiers. Trouble comes through that gate; don't bring your guests through it.

In September 2000 when Ariel Sharon visited al-Aqsa with hundreds of Israeli troops and the second Intifada broke out, Israel was quick to interpret it to the world as Muslims objecting to non-Muslims coming into al-Aqsa. To protect Muslim sensibilities and non-Muslim safety, Israel would bar non-Muslims from entry. For the first time in its history, the Sanctuary was closed to non-Muslims. Three years later, Israel readmitted non-Muslims – but only through Moroccan Gate within Western Wall Plaza, not through any of the gates that open into the Old City. The vast majority of people admitted are Israeli settlers.

Settlers sometimes fight and sometimes kill and sometimes burn. And Israel cleans up after them. When Baruch Goldstein, a settler, went into the Ibrahimi Mosque in al-Khalil/Hebron on 25 February 1994 and killed twenty-nine Muslim men at prayer – then was himself killed by the congregation, Israel divided the mosque and made the larger half of it over to the settlers for Jewish prayers. A shrine for the 'martyr' Dr Goldstein was established near it, and Israel's military presence in the heart of the city and around the mosque was permanently intensified.

ONE NIGHT, A LONG, LONG TIME AGO, two years before the Hijra, the Angel Gabriel came to the Prophet Muhammad in Makkah. Muhammad had grown used to Gabriel visiting him with revelations from the Qur'an. But this time the angel brought him 'al-Buraq'. The year was 620 AD and Muhammad was grieving; his two champions, his beloved wife Khadija and his uncle Abu Taleb, had died within weeks of each other. His enemies, the enemies of the new faith he preached, were preparing to strike. Here, now, was Gabriel, come with the fabled winged steed to carry him to holy Jerusalem.

In a wasteland at the south-east edge of the city, Jesus, Moses and all the Abrahamic prophets were waiting to receive the last of their line. Muhammad tethered al-Buraq to a ruined wall and led his seniors in prayer. From a rock nearby a golden ladder appeared, and from there Muhammad ascended to the Seventh Heaven and the presence of God. When he came back to earth he took his leave of the prophets, mounted al-Buraq and returned to Makkah, his miraculous Night Journey completed, his spirit soothed, his vision energised: 'Exalted be He Who transported His servant by night from Makkah to the Furthest Place of Prayer'. The Qur'an gave the place its name: al-Masjid al-Aqsa.

The wall where Muhammad tethered his miraculous mount became known as 'al-Buraq Wall': ⁊a2it al-Buraq. b/r/q: to appear for an instant, bright and shining.

b/k/a: to weep.

After the fall of Granada in 1492 AD / 899 AH, and with the end of the world of al-Andalus, the hospitable Moroccan Quarter in Jerusalem became home to a great many Muslim and Jewish refugees from Christian Spain. With these new displaced arrivals there grew a practice of Jewish residents and visitors praying and mourning by al-Buraq Wall, and the wall took on the additional name of ⁊a2it al-Mabka: the Wall of Weeping.

Don't bring your guests this way. And Israel closes the other doors. How do I bring them in then? How do I bring them into the Sanctuary, allow them to feel all that it is? Al-Aqsa makes of Jerusalem a model of the world as it should be: industrious, competitive, worldly, but gently easing you towards a space that is tranquil, contemplative, communal and free of worldly concerns. In the city, though you cannot see the Sanctuary you know that it's there, never more than a few paces from you, its doors always open, its walls not borders to shut you out, but thresholds to mark your entry, to help your self shift as you pass through. University, cathedral, park, town hall, school, museum, library and playground. Free, accessible, inclusive; the centre of a world – now cut off from the world.

IN 1535 AD / 942 AH, FIFTEEN YEARS INTO HIS REIGN, the Ottoman Sultan Suleiman the Lawmaker undertook a massive restoration of the walls of Jerusalem and al-Aqsa. When he learned that his Jewish subjects in Jerusalem came to pray at al-Buraq Wall, and that they lamented there because they believed it to be the remains of their temple which Titus destroyed in 70 AD, Suleiman had the wall cleaned for them and his architects elevated it as part of the restoration. Two centuries later, another Ottoman sultan, Osman II, reaffirmed the status quo on all holy sites in Jerusalem: al-Buraq Wall and the space in front of it belonged to the Sidi Abu Madyan Islamic Waqf in perpetuity, but the Jewish right to pray there was binding in law.

In 1967 AD / 1386 AH Israel's bulldozers razed the Moroccan neighbourhood to the ground. They demolished the mosques of Sidi Abu Madyan and the offices, store-rooms and archives of the Trust Authority and on their ruins built Wailing Wall Plaza where only Jews could weep. b/k/a: to weep. We instead of you.

In 2010 we learned that it was possible to bring visitors into the Sanctuary properly if we arranged with the Waqf beforehand. At 9 a.m. we were at Lions' Gate and a representative of the Waqf was there to meet us. He had a list of our names and passport numbers and he had brought an armload of white cotton over-skirts and headscarves. The two Israeli soldiers stood and watched as the women authors pulled the skirts on over their trousers and arranged the scarves over their hair. Then, as we moved towards the gate, they told us we could not go in: the Muslims don't allow it. Again I was taken by surprise. But we've arranged it, with the Waqf, and their man is right here. Look! He's got our names. Our friend from the Waqf said yes, you're very welcome. He spoke to the soldiers. The soldiers said we could not go in. Lions' Gate was wide open in front of us. But we could not go in. It was Moroccan Gate or not at all, and through Moroccan Gate trouble came.

The settlers who walk into al-Aqsa today don't need to kill anyone. They just need to pray. Like the digging under the mosque, the construction on its southern flank, the plaza against its western wall, the act of praying in the Sanctuary is an act of appropriation. This, in Palestine, is i7lal. We instead of you.

SOPHRONIUS, BISHOP OF BYZANTINE JERUSALEM, besieged by the young Muslim army in the fifteenth year of the new Muslim world, sent word that the city would surrender peaceably, but only to Omar in person. And so, in 15 AH / 637 AD, Omar ibn al-Khattab, Commander of the Faithful, and the second Caliph after Muhammad, entered Jerusalem, on foot, to receive the gift of the city.

The Bishop met him and – perhaps to show why he'd not wanted the city attacked – took him to see the spectacular Church of the Holy Sepulchre. Omar admired the church, but declined Sophronius' invitation to pray there. With his young and vigorous armies encircling the city he signed al-3uhda al-Omariyyah, the pact that became the model for the treatment of cities vanquished in war: people had the right to leave the city or remain under the new rule. Everyone's safety, possessions, churches and crosses were secure. No tax would be collected until after the harvest. For the first time since the Roman period Jews were once again allowed to live and worship freely in Jerusalem.

At the ruined wall where the Prophet had tethered al-Buraq seventeen years earlier, Muhammad's friend and companion bent to clear a space and knelt in prayer. Al-Masjid al-Aqsa.

Between Western Wall Plaza and Jaffa Gate, the Temple Institute's shop has grown into a huge emporium. There's a viewing platform where you can look through a glass case with a model of the Third Temple in it and see the Temple obliterate the Dome of the Rock. A pick-up truck tours the streets with great boulders on its flatbed and a legend that says THE FOUNDATION STONES OF THE THIRD TEMPLE. The virtual world carries tidings of the breeding of crimson worms and the engineering of red heifers and the attainment of Stations on the road to Armageddon.

Circling, circling al-Aqsa. Wheeling and dipping and swooping around it. Destroying neighbourhoods, digging tunnels, closing

gates, killing people, street by street, house by house, moving in
with laws, with taxes, with administrative orders, with settlers,
with soldiers, with machine guns, with money, with barbed wire
and flags and pig-fat-coated bullets and security and soldiers and
guns and settlers.

Building the Third Temple, establishing Israeli hegemony 'from
the Nile to the Euphrates' and fast-laning to Armageddon may
be the goals of ideologically motivated settlers, but they would
remain a hole-in-the-wall dream without financial backing.
Settlers tempt persecuted, impoverished and increasingly abandoned Palestinians with vast prices for their homes and land,
wedge themselves into unwelcoming Palestinian communities
and build high-rises there, devote themselves to harassing and
terrorising Palestinians. It seems doubtful that the billionaires
financing them are paying for prime seats at the End of Days;
more likely they and the Israeli government are investing in the
stage just before it. Theme Park City of David has hardly anything
to show except tunnels and speculation. Theme Park Jerusalem,
though, will have a temple and priests in crimson robes and crimson curtains. A money-spinner.

r/b/t to tie. rabata nafsahu: to tie oneself to a place and a pledge.

Study-circles multiply in the gardens and on the terraces of the
Sanctuary. These are the murabitoun; people who have pledged
themselves to protect al-Aqsa. They are civilians, self-organising
and unarmed. Since Israel forbids men under the age of forty-five
to enter al-Aqsa, the murabitoun circles are made up of elderly
men, women and children. When Moroccan Gate is open they are
on high alert.

At Lions' Gate, standing between the soldiers with the guns
and the open gateway, our friend from the Waqf was helpless.
We turned and hurried through the Old City, past the great gates,
through the streets and through the Israeli checkpoint. We hurried
over the ruins of the Moroccan Quarter hidden under the granite
tiles of the plaza. In front of the metal detectors at the foot of the
caterpillar we queued, but the soldiers at Lions' Gate had called

the soldiers at Moroccan Gate. They ushered settlers in past us until visiting hours were over and the door was closed.

Every day Israel kills at least one Palestinian. Every day it arrests and detains and interrogates and demolishes. Every day at Damascus Gate you see Israeli soldiers push young Palestinian men up against the walls to search them. Every day the settlers and soldiers stroll through Moroccan Gate into the Sanctuary. Every day the language of the authorities shades further into settler Third Temple language.

Sometimes a young Palestinian wakes up in the morning and takes a knife from her mother's kitchen and goes out to mount a solitary, hopeless attack on Israeli soldiers. Sometimes Israeli soldiers kill a young Palestinian and toss a knife onto the ground next to him. The language of justice and decency is no longer relevant. The language of human rights is bitter. The language of red heifers and crimson worms and red heifers and cable cars and crimson worms and holy package tours is swelling. Here. Here in the heart of the world that will burst. Soon.

January 2017

Draw Your Own Conclusions

J.M. Coetzee

I was born and brought up in South Africa, so naturally people ask me what I see of South Africa in the present situation in Palestine. Using the word *apartheid* to describe the way things are here I've never found to be a productive step. Like using the word *genocide* to describe what happened in Turkey around 1915, using the word *apartheid* diverts one into an inflamed semantic wrangle which cuts short opportunities of analysis.

Apartheid was a system of enforced segregation based on race or ethnicity put in place by an exclusive, self-defined group in order to consolidate colonial conquest, in particular to cement its hold on the land and on natural resources. To speak of Jerusalem and the West Bank, we see a system of enforced segregation based on religion and ethnicity put in place by an exclusive self-defined group to consolidate a colonial conquest, in particular to maintain, and indeed extend, its hold on the land and its natural resources. Draw your own conclusions.

Ramallah, 2016

THREE ENCOUNTERS ON THE WEST BANK

Mercedes Kemp

I travelled to the West Bank in 2010 as a guest of PalFest, and then again in 2013, spending time in Nablus and its adjacent refugee camps. I am left with fragments of what I've seen with the eyes of the heart.

THREE LADIES FROM OLD ASKAR CAMP

affirm life.
affirm life.
we got to carry each other now.
you are either with life, or against it.
affirm life.

Suheir Hammad

In Old Askar Camp there is a small yard where flowers grow out of old tin cans: jasmine, bougainvillea and a small lemon tree. I am invited into the home of three ladies. The eldest, reclining on a divan, dressed in white, has been a refugee here for more than sixty years. The room is decorated with mementos and festooned with plastic oranges draped in greenery, as if to remind her of her home village Abu Kishk, the scent of blossom and warm sea breezes. She remembers the Nakba. Running through the citrus groves, stalked by death. Her children were all born here, in this hive of sorrows, but her daughters look after her with tenderness, and there is much laughter, gossip and affectionate banter. Old Askar looks after its own.

THE GIRL FROM JAFFA

> I come from there and I have memories
> Born as mortals are, I have a mother
> And a house with many windows.

Mahmoud Darwish

My friend Wadi takes me to his mother's home, where I have been invited to have lunch.

Old Askar Camp was built in 1950 on a limited parcel of land. Its population has grown to vastly exceed dwelling capacity. Every nook and cranny has been used up. There is much ingenuity and very canny use of space. But natural light is scarce. In Maleka's home its source is a narrow slit framed by breeze blocks in a corner of her tiny kitchen. The corner is occupied by a cage in which two lovebirds are kissing. I wonder at the generosity in allowing the birds this privileged position.

Maleka's hands chop, slice and stir, and as she works she tells me about the house in Jaffa, and her grandmother who, as she fed her children with rijla (purslane), which grew in the rocky crevices of the long road to exile, dreamed of crabs stuffed with red chilli, stingray soup doused with lemon, squid with golden rice, sea bass, sardines and everything that swam in the clear waters that bathe Jaffa, the bride of the sea!

She dishes up the rice and chicken and says, 'I wish that I could offer you such a banquet, but I have never seen the sea. So I offer what I have.'

The rituals of hospitality are accomplished with elegance and generosity. As I take my leave Maleka says, 'I am a simple woman, but my daughters will study and grow wise. We'll go back to our land, inshallah. And if not us, then our children.'

A BOY

And it's a wonderful thing to be a boy, to go roaming where grown-ups can't catch you.

George Orwell

I meet Mohammad at New Askar Camp.

He is a young man of perhaps eighteen, tall and athletic, a footballer. He is wearing the Palestinian selection strip with a number 19 on the back. He is surrounded by a group of younger boys, pulling at his shirt, laughing, chattering and raising dust. Here at New Askar they take care of their own too. Older boys and girls look after the younger, teach them skills and resilience.

I want to see more of the camp, the overspill from Old Askar, equally strapped for space but with even fewer resources. Mohammad and his mates offer to take me for a tour. We walk the narrow, jerry-built alleys. The boys greet neighbours sitting on doorsteps, kick the ball for children playing in the street.

High on a wall there is the faded photograph of a young boy. I can see that the same poster has been covered by a new, clean version of the same image every time an earlier one faded. Now the tattered remains are ruffled by the breeze, like a palimpsest of grief. All my companions stand and look at the poster. Mohammad speaks. 'It's Odai, my friend. He was killed by Israeli soldiers.'

I look at the dates on the poster. It was seven years ago.

'We were children when it happened.'

'We were twelve.'

'Odai and I, we were friends since we knew life.'

'We lived very near to each other. Both in the same street.'

'We played football in the street every day.'

'We were good. One day, when we were playing on our street, we heard the army coming. We ran through the streets. All the children in the camp ran towards the olive field on the hillside. I will show you.'

We walk through the alleys until we reach the edge of the camp. A few olive trees cling to the remains of a terraced hillside. A road below. On the other side, the telltale cubic forms of an illegal Israeli settlement.

'We ran through the streets and we could hear the tanks coming. They were always coming. We could hear the gunfire. We reached the hilltop.'

'We could see the army coming, shooting tear gas and real bullets at us.'

'We were throwing stones at the army.'

'We shouted, This is our land! You can't come here!'

'We were only children.'

'The army were coming, shooting at us.'

'We all ran back, all of us, but not Odai. He was alone, facing the army.'

'We were hiding behind the cactus. We shouted, Come back, Odai! Come and hide!'

'But he didn't.'

As the story unfolds, my companions enact the moment: hiding in rocky crevices and behind the cacti clumps. They show me the rocks eroded by many bullet holes. Their eyes are a little wild as they remember.

Mohammad is very still.

'And then Odai was shot.'

'We wanted to help him, but the army were still shooting.'

'We couldn't reach him.'

'When the army retreated, we ran towards Odai.'

'We asked some people to call an ambulance, but the ambulance didn't come.'

'I went to Odai. When I reached him, he breathed his last breath.'

'We carried his body through the field.'

Mohammad leads the way, tracing the steps of his wretched journey, this Via Dolorosa for a twelve-year-old boy.

'We reached the pharmacy. The pharmacist tried to help him, but he couldn't.'

'A neighbour brought his car and took him to the hospital in Nablus.'

'I went to his house. I had to tell his family he had been shot.'

'Afterwards, I was broken. I was angry.'

'I had two choices: to become a martyr or to live.'

'I chose football.'

'My life had changed. I had to learn to do everything without him, Odai.'

'My friends helped me.'

'My family helped me.'

'But most of all, playing football helped me.'

'I came to this field to play every day.'

'And every week I came to visit his grave, my friend Odai.'

At Odai's grave, in a small cemetery at the edge of the camp, an extraordinary transposal occurs. I am frozen to the spot, crying. Mohammad puts his arms around me and consoles me. 'I understand your grief, you are somebody's mother.'

'I became very good at football. I joined the Palestinian team.'

'I wanted to do this for two reasons.'

'One, for myself, and for my talent.'

'The other one, for Odai.'

We reach our journey's end. From a ramshackle back yard a young boy lifts his hand in a victory sign. Mohammad responds, smiling. They both shout.

'For a better future!'

Through the Looking-Glass
Adam Foulds

A few weeks ago I stood by the tomb of Abraham in Hebron hearing the recitation of the Amidah, the rhythm of those familiar words of prayer suddenly accompanied by those of a Jewish poet that came to my mind in that moment. I felt moved and connected in ways I had not foreseen. The last time I was in that part of the world I was in my gap year, an eighteen-year-old enjoying the life of a secular kibbutznik before heading on to Oxford. This time I had arrived at Hebron after a very different journey, one that took me both deeply into my Jewish culture and showed it to me from the other side of the mirror, so to speak, challenging many of my previous assumptions.

The beginning of the journey was calm enough. We flew into Jordan, arriving late for a preliminary night at the Hotel InterContinental, Amman, a frictionless environment where the twenty or so international writers of the touring literary festival met and introduced themselves. By chance I found myself with the two other Jewish members of the group. Our conversation quickly turned to what possible consequences might follow from that identity when we travelled into Palestine. Sensibly, rationally, we reassured one another, a moment that reminded me of the reassurances I had offered my parents back in north-east London. On both occasions I had been calming my own anxieties too. All the voices of my education and all the years of news footage – charred car bodies, masked gunmen, wailing crowds, photographers pushed back to allow stretchers to be rushed into ambulances – told me to be frightened. Nevertheless I'd been sure then that I wanted to seize the opportunity to go and see inside the situation for myself. It is so much at the heart of contemporary Jewish life as well as our geopolitical weather that I couldn't resist the offer of first-hand experience.

The following morning we crossed into Palestine at the Allenby Bridge, a border under Israeli jurisdiction. The experience felt far removed from my memories of entering via the grandly appointed front door of Ben Gurion Airport. As we were being briefed on the bus as to how to be accurate and economical when answering questions, we pulled up at the low militarised building to see a line of Palestinians, men, women and children, waiting to pass through, blown on by a large swivelling fan, patrolled by a soldier in jeans and T-shirt with impressively muscled arms and a machine gun. The atmosphere seemed tense, businesslike, stoical, with no one wanting any trouble, but also from inside the bus the whole thing looked strangely theatrical. Several times during the trip the quality of the psychological power exerted by the structures and procedures of checkpoints reminded me of immersive works of art, installations or promenade theatre pieces designed to have a strong emotional effect, to make manifest the conceptual relations of power, of individual and state. It is an odd thought, perhaps, one that attests to my struggle to integrate the reality of what I was seeing with the world as I had understood it up till then.

This first checkpoint experience lasted a while, six hours from start to finish. Several members of our group, three Palestinian Americans and a British Asian from Manchester, were held for questioning. The most experienced of them conjectured afterwards that they were being toyed with, pointlessly discomfited, on the basis that a background check does not take that long to perform. Still, we were not turned away there, as we feared might happen during that lengthy delay and as Noam Chomsky was a couple of weeks later. The worst that occurred was the theft from one of our group's luggage of a pair of shoes and some jewellery. Later it seemed a useful introductory experience, a half-day immersion in powerlessness at the hands of an unpredictable military bureaucracy. I remember sitting there with the word *wasting* dilating in my mind: wasting time, wasting away, a terrible waste, the waste places.

The first day or so in Palestine was marked for me, however, by a great happiness, a sense of liberation. We stayed in East Jerusalem. I'd last been in that city in my year off before university, when I had been working and studying Hebrew on a kibbutz half an hour away. I was eighteen then and fearful. That Palestinians were violent, that a trip into East Jerusalem could be fatal, were axiomatic among the people I met. I had no reason to doubt it. In my days off I drifted in West Jerusalem, visiting an English-language bookshop, sitting with my new copy of Nabokov's *Bend Sinister* in a cafe before returning to the kibbutz at dusk. Now I found myself in the east, a grown adult meeting many Palestinians, and felt in that environment no sense of threat whatsoever. The fear that I was carrying melted away; my body relaxed, my breathing slowed and deepened. The sensation was of lightness and elation; it was born from a revelation that's so obvious, so bound to be true, I'm almost ashamed to admit it: Palestinians are normal people – friendly, intelligent, rational people. Not only that, their warmth and openness, given their situation, was very striking. All the Palestinians we met were extraordinarily hospitable and pleased to see us. Movement is all but impossible for Palestinians, and the presence of outsiders seemed to bring oxygen to their enclosed world. Everyone apparently welcomed the stationary travel of our visit, and those who came to the literary events expressed pleasure at being able to spend an evening enjoying the passing illusion that they had a normal cultural life. To explain a little more: identity cards issued by the Israelis are colour-coded according to the individual's home town, which is not always accurately recorded. To travel from one to another is extremely difficult. Jerusalem and Bethlehem, for example, are six miles apart and as attached to one another as, say, Richmond and London. Unsurprisingly many families (and, formerly, working lives) are divided between the two places. A Palestinian from Bethlehem must now apply for a permit to visit East Jerusalem at least a month in advance. The permit can be refused without reason. It can be granted and then access denied without reason at the checkpoint. Of course this makes it very easy to miss a relative's visit or death or the birth of a child, and so on. More than a generation of West Bank Palestinians now exist who have never seen the sea. I learned this in Bethlehem, where the experience of being in Palestine started to intensify, to cause pain.

But first, to get there, the checkpoint. You approach a low building or complex of buildings (it is hard to tell at first) with squat towers and machine-gun nests masked with camouflage netting. Next you find yourself walking down a system of channels that suddenly turn at right angles into narrower channels not much wider than your shoulders. These are fenced with heavy horizontal scaffolding poles. At a certain point you find yourself under a low roof, completely enclosed and at a floor-to-ceiling turnstile made of the same scaffolding poles, rather like those in the New York subway. There are lights on the top of it, red and green. If the light is green you go through, although how many do so at one time varies so it is easy in a moment of entirely humourless slapstick to walk into a locked gate. Now you are in the centre of a checkpoint which contains an X-ray machine for your possessions, a reinforced airport-style metal-detector portal and a brightly lit office of toughened glass typically containing, it seemed, two bored, languid Israeli teenagers doing their national service. They ask to see ID and may have further questions. There is a disconcerting disconnection between their mouths in front of you on the other side of the glass and their voices, which blast at near-distortion volume from a number of speakers above your head. During this time you are between two sets of turnstiles, completely shut in. If your answers satisfy them, they release you through the second turnstile. The whole time you're passing through you can be seen and heard but, unlike with CCTV, you don't know where from because you can't see the cameras or microphones. The effect is to make you introject the observing authority: you are helpless and feel entirely exposed. We had little trouble getting through the checkpoints, although there are obvious challenges for anyone claustrophobic, frail, hearing- or sight-impaired, or elderly: you can be standing there for a very long time. Stories we heard from Palestinians reflected different experiences, more brutalising, humiliating and capricious. At Hawara, the most notorious of the checkpoints, a number of deaths have been recorded of people waiting to get through for medical treatment. For those Palestinians who work inside Israel the checkpoint experience (one which in its mildest form I wouldn't wish on anyone I loved) is a twice-daily occurrence. Sometimes, without warning, the checkpoints are closed, and they can't get to their jobs at all.

Having said that it was easier for us, the first time one of our party got stuck in a turnstile and spent ten minutes trying to remain calm before someone came to release her, and the one member of the group with an identifiably Jewish name was, on every occasion, questioned with noticeable aggression as to who she was and what she was doing there. Why that was the case remains unclear, although the obvious inference is that the authorities have a particular dislike of Jewish people seeing inside the West Bank. Certainly it is almost impossible for Israelis to get in unless they're currently serving in the army or are settlers.

And what was it we saw in Bethlehem? We saw the separation wall and, crucially, where it is. From that physical fact about the world you know that the security rationale for its existence cannot account for its placement. The nine-metre-high wall, well beyond the 1967 Green Line, is wrapped so tightly around Bethlehem, rising up just beyond the last house on the perimeter, that the little town has been severed from the landscape and has no room to expand. Natural population growth can be expected to produce conditions of intense overcrowding. From certain

vantage points you can look over the wall and see the exten-
sive olive groves that used to support many Bethlehemites, which
they now cannot reach to tend. There is an Israeli law that land
'abandoned' for seven years becomes the property of the state.
The inhabitants of Bethlehem wait powerlessly for the land they
have farmed continuously for centuries to be taken from them.
You wonder what it does to the children who are growing up
behind that wall, which exists, they are told, because they are so
dangerous, and who see the only real power in the town wielded
by visiting soldiers with machine guns. If the wall were for security alone it would follow the proposed border of the Palestinian
state. It would also be continuous. It isn't at present. If you walk
far and knowledgeably enough you can get around it. A number
of impoverished migrant workers do so to find work as manual
labourers within Israel.

The illegal settlements are the other great lesson of the occupied territories. There are a huge number of them, instantly recognisable by their bare, prefabricated ugliness and position, placed
and fortified on the tops of hills, disfiguring the landscape their
inhabitants claim to love with all the aesthetic indifference of true
religious fundamentalism. Or have I strayed into rhetoric there?
Do they claim to love the land? Does love come into it? Surely it's
enough for them that their god has instructed them to take possession of it with whatever force necessary. I find that the settlers'
Judaism is both very difficult and worryingly easy to understand.
It bears very little relation to the tolerant, intellectual, profoundly
moral Judaism I am proud to have grown up in, a tradition that
is acutely aware of its outsider status and therefore highly sensitive to the vulnerabilities of other communities. Settler Judaism is
something else altogether: messianic, fundamentalist, indifferent to
pain, soaked in violence. But it arises from tropes well within the
Jewish tradition. Its claim on the land is there in the Torah, a land
that, after all, is promised to the Israelites rather than being their
place of origin. The Tanakh tells a story of bloody warfare waged
by the Israelites to take possession of it. The perversity of settler
Judaism is to privilege this of all parts of the Jewish inheritance, to

pursue the one commandment to settle the land at the expense of the other 612.

If you haven't spotted a settlement looking down on you, you might guess it's there by the vandalism of multilingual road signs. The settlers erase the Arabic place names. Some of the settlements, those that form a ring around Nablus, for example, are so far inside the territory necessary (and promised) for a viable Palestinian state as to make Israeli talk of a two-state solution seem in bad faith. They clearly could not exist without the active support of the Israeli state and military. They have prospered with the collusion of successively more right-wing administrations. Since the much-publicised withdrawal of settlements from within Gaza, more than 20,000 new settlers have moved into the West Bank.

This is the great reward for making it through the checkpoints to see the place for yourself. In the wider world the arguments about what is going on there are so fierce and fiercely contested as to produce, it often seems, a kind of stalemate of competing narratives; you choose which one you believe, finally, according to temperament and tribal affiliation. Being there springs you from that trap. The physical configuration of wall and checkpoints and settlements tells the real story. Visiting Bethlehem, you see that the wall is a land grab. Visiting Nablus, you know that a possible Palestinian state is already vitiated by the presence of heavily armed religious fundamentalists who will kill rather than move. You know that areas of Palestinian habitation are so divided as to produce disconnected enclaves rather than the beginnings of a country. The result for me was an excruciating combination of sadness, anger and sense of betrayal. An Israeli voice came to mind, the imperturbable reasonableness of government spokesman Mark Regev, often heard on Radio 4's *Today* programme. It is a voice I'd empathised with and wanted to trust. Seeing the flatly contradictory facts on the ground, its even tone was revealed to me as the sound of a propaganda machine. I felt great anguish at the unnecessary suffering of the Palestinians and anger on my own behalf, but also on behalf of all the loving, reasonable, humane Jews I know and love in the diaspora who have been beguiled by understandable fear for Jewish survival and an admirable solidarity with the people of Israel into supporting the insupportable.

Hebron provided the trip's most shocking encounter with the insupportable fundamentalism that is ruining lives and our chances of peace. It was the place where I saw most vividly what the star of David, the Israeli flag – those symbols that to me have always meant home and familiarity – must look like to those on the other side of the power structures and cultural edifices they represent. The challenge afterwards, my challenge at the moment, is to integrate those perspectives and contradictory stories to form the whole that comes closest to encompassing the complex reality of the situation.

The city remains the largest population centre in the West Bank. It is divided into two sectors, H1 and H2, the new town and old city, under Palestinian and Israeli control respectively. The old city is the cultural heart of Hebron, an ancient market centre where Jews, Muslims and Christians lived and worked together for many centuries. It is now a ghost town. Its economy is dead, its busy arcades shuttered and silent apart from a final few shops that are hanging on. In all Hebron more than 700 shops have closed. The remaining Palestinians live with sixteen checkpoints and frequent curfews. Walking through the empty arcades felt a bit like being in a point-and-shoot video game – that same eerie stage-set feel, that latent violence. The Palestinians now live beside 400 or so settlers and 1,500 Israeli soldiers. The settlers are paid by various supporting organisations to be there, which means that they have nothing to do except pray and harass the local inhabitants. I can't speak for the former, but certainly the evidence was clear that they set about the latter with great energy. We walked down a narrow street directly above which settlers have built homes. A net is hung at first-floor height to catch the rubbish the settlers throw down on the Palestinians below, although obviously it can't prevent the dirty water, urine and occasional bottle of acid that is emptied over their heads. There is no flowing water in the old city; there is a system of wells and roof-top water tanks. Settlers vandalise the Palestinians' water tanks so that their water supply empties down through their ceilings and is gone until a new tank can be installed. Outside three Palestinian shops caught on the far side of a barrier between them and the very edge of the settlers' new conurbation, a van has been parked for many months playing loud settler anthems. It was playing them when we visited. I was told that they were doing it less than they used to. It had been playing them twenty-four hours a day for months.

Hebron is one place we saw the infamous division of different roads into those for settler usage and Palestinian usage that gives rise to talk of apartheid. Whether you agree with the use of that term or not, there is a technical sense in which it is very hard to disavow. Illegal settlers living in Palestinian territory do so under Israeli civil law. Palestinians in the same territory live under an accumulation of more than 1,500 military orders. Two populations in the same place under two different legal systems determined by their ethnicity. Clearly this fulfils the very definition of apartheid. From afar I had thought the deployment of that term crude and obfuscatory rhetoric. Now it seems an accurate description of the legal situation in the West Bank.

The reason Hebron is so important to settlers and Palestinians alike is that it contains the tombs of the patriarchs in the Ibrahimi Mosque. It is there that during my first visit to Israel in 1994 Dr Baruch Goldstein, now celebrated as a saint and martyr by the settlers, massacred twenty-nine worshippers at Friday prayers during Ramadan. Part of the Israeli response was to divide the mosque, turning 65 per cent of it into a synagogue. Muslim pilgrims pass through a checkpoint of turnstiles and metal detectors to get in.

As I wandered around the mosque I stopped beside Abraham's tomb. It was an awesome experience to be in that place at the very wellspring of the Jewish tradition, to stand by Abraham, the first Jew and father of all three heavenly faiths, all of their genius, beauty and unending violence. I noticed that there was one position from which you could look through and glimpse the synagogue. In a moment that encapsulated for me the strangeness of seeing the world through the prism of this journey, I lingered there, staring across, in my socks with my head uncovered and, as I've said, heard the Amidah being chanted. I felt intensely connected to those words, to that world I was now seeing from outside, but also deeply upset and disturbed by all I had seen it could mean. What came to mind was the Jewish poet Paul Celan, in particular a poem of his I have by heart. I started reciting it to myself. It contains the mysterious line 'How many dumb ones? Seventeen.' One critical conjecture is that seventeen falls just short of the formerly eighteen sections of the Amidah, the central prayer of Jewish liturgy still commonly referred to as the Eighteen. The poem, suffused for that moment with all I now knew of the erasure of the Palestinian landscape and the disappearance of a plausibly hopeful Palestinian future, seems to refer to the erasure of ancient Jewish culture in the Shoah, or Holocaust. The poem ends with a devastating effect: the same line is repeated three times with letters removed until only the vowels remain. Those, you realise, are the letters that are not written down in Hebrew; all that is left on the page finally is the invisible, the absent. From memory it goes like this:

> No more sand art, no sand books, no masters.
> Nothing on the dice.
> How many dumb ones? Seventeen.
> Your question, your answer.
> Your song, what does it know?
> Deep in snow.
> eepinow
> ee-i-o

Many years after that historical tragedy we are beset by questions of how the wider population could have tolerated the actions of its government or the minority of ideological extremists, how complicit they were, why they didn't say anything, how much they knew and how possible it was not to know. I am hugely grateful that such questions regarding the Palestinian situation have been settled for me. I have seen and I know. Now, like many thousands of other Jews in Israel and around the world, I protest.

July 2016

SLEEPING IN GAZA
Najwan Darwish

Fado, I'll sleep like people do
when shells are falling
and the sky is torn like living flesh.
I'll dream, then, like people do
when shells are falling:
I'll dream of betrayals.

I'll wake at noon and ask the radio
the questions people ask of it:
Is the shelling over?
How many were killed?

But my tragedy, Fado,
is that there are two types of people:
those who cast their suffering and sins
into the streets so they can sleep,
and those who collect the people's suffering and sins,
mould them into crosses, and parade them
through the streets of Babylon and Gaza and Beirut,
all the while crying:
Are there any more to come?
Are there any more to come?

Two years ago I walked through the streets
of Dahieh, in southern Beirut,
and dragged a cross
as large as the wrecked buildings.
But who today will lift a cross
from the back of a weary man in Jerusalem?

The earth is three nails
and mercy a hammer:
Strike, Lord.
Strike with the planes.

Are there any more to come?

Translated by Kareem James Abu-Zeid

ONCE UPON A JERUSALEM
Susan Abulhawa

After eight years of higher education in science and medicine, and nearly ten years in medical research, I left that career to become a storyteller, because someone stole my story and retold the truth of me as a lie. Because that lie was an eraser, making me disappear, rootless and irrelevant. Because I needed words for the anguish of it all. Then, in language and story, I found a lonely and mesmerising truth of a land and her people, my family, whose passions, transgressions and faith form the terrain of an unredeemed history. This is a story of Deir el-Hawa, my namesake, and a few of her children.

———

Deir el-Hawa was once a village atop a breezy mountain overlooking the Surar Valley west of Jerusalem, where the villagers could watch the sun rise daily over Jerusalem's golden Dome of the Rock. Tradition has it that Deir el-Hawa was established by someone from the entourage of Caliph Omar who captured Jerusalem in AD 638. Others claim Deir el-Hawa had been a Christian village since the first century. In Arabic 'deir' means monastery, so villages whose names begin with that word tend to be Christian villages, lending credence to the latter theory.

El-Hawa means the wind. So our original village was the 'Monastery of the Wind'.

Whether dating to the first or seventh century, Deir el-Hawa lost one of her sons in the seventeenth, around the year 1680. A man named Hasan was cast out by his family and forced to leave the village. No one is sure why, but stories abound. Some say he was a Christian who converted to Islam to marry a Muslim woman against his family's wishes. Others claim he murdered a man and expulsion from the village was his punishment. To be disinherited of home, land and family was perhaps a fate worse than death.

Whatever the reason, Hasan left Deir el-Hawa, but he did not go far. He settled in el-Tur, a village east of Jerusalem, on the Mount of Olives, where he could now watch the sun set behind, rather than rise over, Jerusalem's golden dome.

As he was disowned, Hasan could not divulge his last name in this new town, and would simply answer that he was from Deir el-Hawa. So, locals took to calling him Abu el-Hawa. Thus the surname Abulhawa was born from Hasan, my ancestor six generations ago in the East Jerusalem village of el-Tur.

The Abulhawas were not from the high-born, educated or merchant class. My forebears were fellaheen, people of the land, who lived close to the natural world, even though Jerusalem was a centre of culture, libraries, education and the grand homes of sophisticates. In Palestine my ancestors were farmers who cultivated and harvested wheat and barley over approximately 400 acres on the Mount of Olives. They raised sheep and goats, tended orchards and nurtured ancient olive groves. They plucked thyme, which grows wild on Palestine's stony hills, and passed the time on Fridays eating pomegranates, oranges and all else the land had to offer in different seasons.

Among Hasan's grandchildren was a man named Mohammad Khalil, my paternal great-grandfather (also my maternal great-uncle, because my parents were cousins), who briefly gained international fame in 1957 when he celebrated his 136th birthday. Associated Press digital archives online has ninety-eight seconds of silent footage of Mohammad Khalil with his birth certificate, issued by the Ottomans in the year 1821. He credited his long life to the daily consumption of olive oil, pressed from his own harvest, and to the company of women. He had five wives, outlived them all and fathered twenty-six children, among them my paternal grandfather, Atiyeh.

For the fellaheen, it was not unusual for first or second cousins to marry. In fact, it was preferred, because staying within the family ensured the protection of daughters. But both of my grandfathers, who were first cousins, married outside the family – to strangers, as they were called. Atiyeh fell in love with a city girl from a family that had lived for centuries within the walls of the Old City of Jerusalem. When Atiyeh went to ask for her hand in marriage, what he got was an offer to wed her older, unattractive sister, a teenager named Soraya who would become my paternal grandmother. Together they had six children, but Atiyeh never loved his wife. I spent a summer with Sitti Soraya when I was a child. By then our family had already been expelled from Palestine by Zionist invaders, and my widowed grandmother was living in Jordan in a small refugees' shack, consisting of one room and a small outhouse. She was short, like me, and moved very slowly. What I recall most from that summer were the mosquitoes that feasted on me and left enough red weal on my arms and legs to make people wonder if I had chickenpox. She and I watched whatever appeared on a small television, a grainy black and white screen with only one channel. She told me stories I have long forgotten, and we survived on a daily diet of olive oil, crushed thyme, strained yogurt, bread and fried eggs. The best part was her turtles, five prehistoric creatures that crawled around in the tiled space by her front door and constantly nibbled on lettuce. She loved those turtles, and so did I. Years later, I learned that people believed she used the turtles for magic spells and love potions, which was how she earned a living. Sitti Soraya died a refugee, alone in that small shack. The ancient stone home inside the Old City walls where she was born and where her family had lived for generations is claimed now by foreigners who insist that the Bible is a property deed to her home.

That summer with Sitti Soraya was all I ever knew of her. But my maternal grandmother Sarah would have a longer presence in my life. Teta Sarah was an imposing matriarch, with equal measures of sass, defiance, cunning, severity, gossip and love. She was an illiterate, badass hijabi. She was subversive. A Muslim Arab widow who refused to be put in her place and would trample the lives of men and women who dared try. She was a hajjeh who made the pilgrimage to Mecca several times, and she was a feminist who'd never heard of the concept. I feared her, and I loved her. And I was her favourite grandchild. She told me so.

I lived with Teta Sarah for much of my youth in Kuwait, and she's the one who sneaked me into Palestine, right under Israeli noses, with no passport or travel papers. There I lived for three years in a Jerusalem orphanage, where I got to know Palestine's hills. Jerusalem's daily calls to prayer mixed with church bells and embedded themselves in my skin. Until I was made to leave. According to the new foreign rulers of the land I was illegal. An 'infiltrator'.

But somehow, I never really left. Because Palestine is the landscape of my DNA. My lineage sings in her rivers. Her soil holds the bones and prayers of the family that came before me. She is the keeper of secrets and anguish whispered from the beds of my foremothers. Palestine is the body of all our stories, the place where we begin and return. Her olive trees, her ancient stone homes, her pomegranates and oranges, wild thyme, green valleys and sun-bleached hills are the stuff of our ballads and our books.

Like most Palestinians, we all became dispossessed, disinherited and exiled in one way or another. For a while I could return as a visitor, using my American passport, always enduring long hours of interrogation, searches, waiting and humiliation at entry and exit points. But it was worth it just to go back. In 2009 one of the interrogators advised me not to come back again because I probably wouldn't get in. 'Why would we let you into our country when you incite terrorism like this?' she said, pointing to a 2001 op-ed I wrote for the *Philadelphia Inquirer* on her screen. I wanted to correct her that I was coming to *my* country. That she was a foreign occupier. I wanted to cry or scream or throw something at her. But I only sat silently and waited.

The next year I was invited to participate in PalFest, the Palestine Festival of Literature. I thought being with a large group of international writers would make it easier to get through Israeli border control. Most Westerners, with Western names, were allowed through relatively quickly. I was held back with a smaller group, all with Western passports but with Arab or Muslim names, who were released one by one over a period of about six hours, leaving me alone on one side, as the others loaded their things into the bus, waiting for me. It was getting late, and the programme that evening would start soon. Ahdaf Soueif, founder of PalFest, sent through a message that she was going to send everyone off to the venue but would wait for me herself. At the last minute, as the bus was about to depart, I was granted permission to go through, seven and a half hours after we had all arrived at the border.

I was able to go back twice more after that. The third time I was turned away, my passport stamped 'Denied Entry' with two heavy red marks.

I watch now from afar, from those two heavy red marks, as foreigners with massive guns continue to claim the terrain of my ancestral home. An American-born man of Polish ancestry whose family changed its name from Mileikowsky to Netanyahu sits at the helm as prime minister. A former Russian bar bouncer named Avigdor Lieberman oversees the oppression of four million Palestinians trapped in isolated, heavily surveilled ghettos. Naftali Bennett, whose family came from San Francisco, is a high-ranking politician and minister of education committed to the destruction of Jerusalem's golden Dome of the Rock and al-Aqsa Mosque.

These foreigners, with absolutely no identifiable ancestry in the land, believe it is their right to remove us and take our place. To erase us and make our heritage their own. To destroy our monuments, cemeteries and history. To live in my grandmother's ancient home and pretend that the stories of those like Mohammad Khalil are their own.

Because God chose them.

Because God loves them more.

Permission to Enter
Jeremy Harding

In 1967, after the Six Day War, many Palestinians who'd been driven east over the Jordan River tried desperately to return to their homes by slipping back across. The bridges, including the Allenby Bridge, had been damaged, but the patched-up remains were serviceable. The Allenby Bridge crossing was closely guarded and used by the soldiers on Israel's newest frontier to put people out, rather than allow them in. Palestinian refugees trying to get home, as well as groups of fedayeen, preferred to ford the shallow river at dead of night, although fifty Israel Defence Forces ambush parties were stationed along the West Bank, ordered to fire on shadows in the water. By September more than a hundred people had been shot dead trying to return and a thousand had been deported back to Jordan.

On the Jordanian side of the river journalists were counting up to 80,000 refugees in tents, with more being driven in from the West Bank as Israeli soldiers fired over their heads to hurry them along. To avoid an international scandal, the Israeli government decided to stage the televised return of several thousand Palestinians. There was disagreement between the ministries about how to select the fortunate few. A Foreign Ministry official argued that the key point was demographic – children and women of childbearing age should be kept to a minimum – but according to the view that prevailed, the older refugees of 1948 were far more undesirable. Operation Refugee allowed for an intake of 20,000; in the event only 14,000 got in. 'And so,' Tom Segev writes in *1967*, his study of the Six Day War, 'Israel missed the great opportunity offered by the victory' to heal 'the malignant wound . . . left by the War of Independence.'

The original bridge, built of wood and iron, was completed in 1918 by the Royal Engineers (Allenby had conquered Palestine in 1917) and destroyed in 1946 by a few well-trained Palmach men laying explosives. The Night of the Bridges was a Haganah exercise designed to cut Palestine off from its neighbours and keep the British on the run. The bridge was repaired after the attack and survived for about twenty years, but after 1967 a new if similar structure was built. It's visible today in aerial photographs, standing idly to the side of the four-lane blacktop that spans the (much-depleted) river, courtesy of Nippon Koei consulting engineers and the Japanese government.

The crossing remains a place of uncertainty for Palestinians. Nowadays, in the vast set of hangars at Israeli border control, people puzzle over why they were allowed through in April, say, but not in May. Last month I entered Palestine from Jordan as a guest of PalFest. We got an intimation of these difficulties once we'd crossed the bridge and joined the thick press of people waiting to be dealt with by Israeli border security, the great majority Jordanian-based or West Bank Palestinians. Most of the festival guests with security-friendly names or neutral birthplaces got through in an hour or more. Others with dubious names (Gurnah, Mahjoub, Ghappour! Vassanji? Hammad!) were held up and questioned for three or four hours. 'What is the plot of your novel?' Robin Yassin-Kassab, the author of *The Road from Damascus*, was asked. Had it not been names, it might have been clothing or colour of eyes. In 2003, Ahdaf Soueif records in *Mezzaterra*, hundreds of students at Birzeit were prevented from entering the university until, in the end, a checkpoint officer decided that only the ones with gel in their hair would go through. 'Today,' he announced, 'gel will buy you an education.'

Like the refugees trying to get back from Jordan, the poet Mourid Barghouti became homeless in 1967. Unlike most of them, he was already out of the country, enrolled as a student in Cairo University and then, suddenly, unable to go home to Ramallah. In 1996 he was allowed to return. He was overwhelmed by the extent of the change and the scars of occupation, at a loss to find points of continuity between the Palestine he remembered and the one before his eyes. Occupation, he wrote, 'interferes in every aspect of life and of death; it interferes with longing and anger and desire and walking in the street. It interferes with going anywhere and coming back, with going to market, the emergency hospital, the beach, the bedroom, or a distant capital.' He had re-entered via the Allenby Bridge crossing. He was elated and nervous, a panicky list-maker, invoking the many names this transit point had acquired over the years – the Bridge of Return, the King Hussein Bridge, Al-Karama, Allenby. Yet for all its associations, he felt it in the end as the 'boundary between two histories, two faiths, two tragedies' in a landscape with few consolations: 'The scene is of rock. Chalk. Military. Desert. Painful as a toothache.' That's about how it feels today, if you add the buses backed up at Israeli barriers and the lines of people shuffling slowly through layers of Israeli security.

2009

PRIVATISING ALLENBY
Suad Amiry

'Dear Suad take the full board VIP, you pay $150 and you will NOT leave your car from Amman to Jericho . . . yalla (hurry up) come quickly. Love Islah.'

This was the SMS I received from a close friend encouraging me across the nightmarish Allenby Bridge on a hot July day. I had come from NYC to Amman and was on my way home to Ramallah. I must admit that learning about a new private initiative between Israel and Jordan (not yet Palestine) succeeded in reducing my anxiety about this trip. For crossing the Allenby Bridge, the sole designated entry/exit point for West Bank Palestinians, is one of the most exasperating experiences. If anything, Israel should be given a prize for putting in place and in practice one of the most Byzantine systems of control ever.

In normal places (certainly not in the Holy Land) crossing the fifteen-yard-long bridge, over a diverted hence dried-up non-existent Jordan River, should take two minutes maximum by car and five minutes on foot. However Israel's claimed mania for 'security' has ingeniously transformed the two-minute crossing into a four-hour journey in winter and an eight-hour trip during the hot summer months. The journey cannot but remind Muslims and Jews alike of the fourteen Stations along the Via Dolorosa in Jerusalem.

Having lost access to the pre-1967 Qalandia Airport, located in the vicinity of Ramallah, as well as being deprived access to

Tel Aviv Airport (since 2000, when Ariel Sharon gave orders that none of the four and a half million Palestinians living in the West Bank and Gaza Strip could use Tel Aviv Airport), all West Bank Palestinians like myself are obliged to cross the Allenby Bridge in order to use Amman Airport. Such a long detour not only means four extra days of travelling with two overnights in Amman, but it also augments the cost of crossing the border by $100–300 per person. And now, with the new VIP service, for those who want to bring the eight-hour trip down to one, the cost has come close to $600 per person, which is equivalent to a one-week excursion to Cyprus! This makes the crossing of the Allenby Bridge by far the most expensive border crossing on this planet. For one of the poorest of its populations.

Realising the lucrative nature of this private initiative, Israel has recently cancelled all travel privileges given to Palestinian businessmen in the past. It has also suspended the Israel–Palestine coordination that expedited the crossing for high-ranking Palestinian officials. The new arrangements mean that all MBC (magnetic business card) holders, high-ranking officials and desperate Palestinians like myself will pay $150 to cross the bridge in a bit of comfort and dignity.

Considering that 900 out of the 14,000 passengers who crossed the bridge daily during the month of July used the VIP service, one concludes that Palestinians like myself are contributing close to $50 million annually to the financing of our own occupation!

Having experienced the VIP service first-hand myself, I have to admit that it was by far the fastest crossing I ever had. Unlike for the thousands of the non-VIP passengers, gone for us – for now – were the long hours of waiting in a sweltering bus, waiting for the divine sign to proceed to the Second Station of the Via Dolorosa, the searching for one's suitcase thrown recklessly on the melting asphalt, the screaming and moaning of exhausted Palestinian children, the fussing of Arab porters trying to get a tip behind the backs of their Israeli bosses.

More significantly though, this was the most friendly – over-friendly, awkwardly friendly – encounter I have ever had with

Israelis, anywhere, in the long decades I've lived under occupation. It is hard to explain the unease and the discomfort my husband and I felt on being treated respectfully and humanely by Israelis.

A miraculous $150 changed the dynamics between Israel and Palestine. Where were the deafening shrieks of the Israeli soldiers as they boss around every Palestinian in sight in their distorted Arabic – *La wagha, la wagha* (Go back, go back), *Wakhad wakhad bi saf* (One by one in line), *Hajjeh hajjeh, uskut ta'al houn* (Old lady/old man, shut up and come here) – those pidgin commands, familiar not only from the bridge but from the 670 checkpoints punctuating the West Bank. Like everywhere else in Israel, spoken and written Arabic are massacred on the Allenby Bridge.

Having crossed the fourteen stations in less than an hour in an air-conditioned VIP car, I think of the 13,000 other passengers who have spent the entire day dragging themselves, their children and their elderly from one station to another. How I wished I could pay $150 for each one of them. Not only to end the humiliation and the never-ending saga of the bridge, but more importantly to transform the occupier–occupied dynamics between Israelis and Palestinians even if just for half an hour.

One last thought comes to mind: if the Israeli Border Authorities can take pride in handling sixteen million passengers a year at Tel Aviv Airport, why can't they handle one tenth of that number on the Allenby Bridge? I can only come to one conclusion.

ALLENBY BORDER CROSSING

Sabrina Mahfouz

Stop, take a minute, breathe
stop, take a step back, name
stop, tell them again
where you've been
waiting
how long you've been
waiting
waiting to hear your name
in the mouths that made it
not on the tastebuds of tongues
that baulk at its flavour.
Forgive me for giving my name a flavour
but sometimes a writer must give things
to words that don't work
because to give them nothing is worse.
Maybe not.
Perhaps it is worse to load them with something
that is sold in asymmetric lines
layered with all the stickiness of unstuck empires
and as we wait
we wait
stopped
stop
we consider this history
rewritten to find our landscape dominated
by white walls wishing to blind us
scrapyards of metal vans
that never carried us to familiar roads
stop take a minute, breathe.

QALANDIA
Gillian Slovo

Of the fragments of my memories of that fractured land, this one – of the poet in the turnstile – is the one that keeps coming back.

The poet was one of our group and he was in the West Bank for the first time, as most of us also were. We were trying to pass through the Qalandia checkpoint on our way from Ramallah to Jerusalem. By virtue of our non-Palestinian-ness, we could have stayed on our coach and been waved through to the other side, but PalFest wanted us to experience some of what Palestinians endure, and so we took hold of our suitcases and began to walk. It was mid-afternoon and hot. We walked down the enclosed narrow corridor, metal bars all around us, leading to the turnstile and soldiers. Apart from our group there were few people around. I was behind the poet as he led the way down the corridor. We moved slowly, partly because while the rest of us were pushing compact wheelies, his brown case was too big for the corridor and he had to work hard to jolt it forward.

I had time to notice how I kept brushing against the bars on either side and to wonder why a people whose past suffering was so much part of their present had built such a hard-edged chicken coop of a corridor for the use of human beings. I couldn't help imagining what it must be like when more people pushed down this corridor so they could move from one part of a piece of land that was supposed to be theirs to its adjacent other. I thought about the rules and regulations we'd been told about, which I was struggling to keep track of. A blue ID card, I reminded myself, was an East Jerusalem ID. A green ID was a West Bank ID. So far so good. But what happens if a blue ID marries a green ID? The green can't live in Jerusalem, and the blue could lose their right to live in Jerusalem if they move to the West Bank. What happens if the blue has a business and an old and sick mother in East Jerusalem but has to live in the West Bank because the blue loves a green? As I was trying to work my way through this ludicrous and labyrinthine logic keeping my hypothetical lovers with sick mothers and different IDs apart, it dawned on me that I could go no further because the poet was blocking my way.

He hadn't meant to. All he had done was the logical next step of getting to the end of the metallic funnel and stepping into the turnstile that clearly led to the other side. To do this, he had to lift his arms and hold his suitcase over his head, this being the only way both he and it could fit in. But once he got into the turnstile it failed to turn, so that he ended up trapped in the embrace of its spindles. He tried using his body to push forward like you do when you're in a turnstile and holding a case above your head. The turnstile would not budge. Standing impatiently behind him I couldn't understand what was going wrong – I was on the point of instructing him in the art of using a turnstile – when I realised that somewhere, out of sight, some soldier in a glass cubicle who was able to watch us on his monitor must have deliberately applied the brakes. Not because of the press of people because there wasn't one. Not because the poet and his oversize suitcase could, in any universe, have represented a threat. Because . . . who knows? Perhaps the soldier was looking for something to assuage the boredom of being made to sit there for hours on end. Perhaps he had gone to the toilet or was taking a slug of tea or even an illicit snooze, or perhaps he just felt like punishing someone who had the temerity to want to pass through. Whatever the reason, all we could do was wait as we backed up behind the poet.

When he twisted round, briefly, to look at our group, I caught a glimpse of his expression. What I saw was an already pale face bled white by humiliation: that somebody could halt you in your tracks for no apparent reason; that there could be no way you could tell them that you meant no harm or persuade them out of their misbehaviour; that you could end up caught in those unyielding arms hefting a cumbersome suitcase above your head, which you realised as the minutes ticked by and your arms grew tired, was far too big for purpose. When his eyes met mine, he looked away. He was a poet drained of words to describe what he was feeling. He stood, suitcase aloft, no longer trying to get out of there, until at long last a loudspeaker coughed and the turn-stile was released, spewing him out so suddenly that he staggered forward. While behind him I thought, what has just happened is not about security. The soldier had frozen the turnstile not because he needed to but because he could. What I had witnessed was the petty exercise of power.

I have thought about this moment many times since the end of our trip. I know Palestinians get shot at these checkpoints, that women end up giving birth while waiting to pass through, that breadwinners lose their jobs because of their arbitrary closure and that people travel, sometimes for hours, to get to the other side of their street. I know that in order to get to the hospital they badly need, patients are made to get out of one ambulance which has green – or was it blue? – licence plates, allowing it to drive on West Bank roads only, and stagger across into a different ambu-lance with blue – or was it green? – licence plates which mean that it can drive on other roads.

So I try and figure out why this comparatively petty pain I witnessed has stuck so hard. And I realise that what it reminded me of was my childhood in South Africa. At that daily sight of black men and women made to produce their green pass or their blue one, to prove their right to occupy the space in which they were. The expression on the poet's face that I glimpsed was an echo of so many other similar expressions I had noticed as a child. Those downcast eyes and the guilt in them: that they had done something wrong – were pushing a suitcase too big for purpose perhaps – and that is why they ended up being trapped. It is this that stayed with me.

When you are away from the West Bank it's possible to keep in touch with news of the big incursions. Of the children shot dead. Of so many lives lost. What is less easy to remember is the steady drip of humiliation that affects a people because of their race, their religion or their ID card. What becomes less immediate when you are far away from the turnstiles and the teenage soldiers with their guns and braces is remembering the rage that flows from being so regularly trapped and humiliated, and being powerless to do anything to make it stop.

After Ten Years
John Horner

Many years ago I attempted to write a book about the Lebanese civil war. It came to nothing, but the massacres in the Sabra and Shatila refugee camps really opened my eyes to the Palestinian plight. When I was asked to become a trustee of Engaged Events – and its offspring PalFest – it was something I had to do. But, in spite of my earlier researches, which taught me a lot about the horrors of the Israeli occupation, nothing could have prepared me for the inhumanity and brutalism I came to witness when I visited the West Bank.

After nearly ten years and many visits to Palestine, it is the anecdotal evidence that haunts me, not the statistics and political rhetoric.

In Hebron I met a young boy who worked in the town. He lived on the wrong side of Shuhada Street, which Palestinians are forbidden to cross (just a simple road), and he pointed to his house up the hill on the other side. It used to take him fifteen minutes to walk home, now it takes over two hours, each way.

I met him again, two years later. His problem was solved, he said: they had bulldozed his home and replaced it with the Israeli watchtower he now pointed out.

I was with Jillian Edelstein, a renowned photographer and one of our PalFest visitors. We had met an old man and his wife and were on the roof of their home, in the Aida refugee camp, in Bethlehem. He pointed to the monstrous wall that surrounds them and showed us the land that has been cut off. Palestinians aren't allowed on it and, after seven years, it will be confiscated as the current owners are effectively absentee landlords. The hideous, soulless Israeli settlement sprawls slowly down the hill soon to encapsulate and steal it.

The same man, in his eighties, pointed to the shell holes in his wall. Bullets fired as target practice. He took us to his basement and showed us his now defunct weaving machines. He'd moved them here twelve years ago having been given one week to do so. The Israelis were closing a section of the camp – a terrorist threat they had pronounced. He used to employ seventeen people, but overnight the Israelis issued an embargo on his produce – towels and flannels. The factory closed and the threads are still there in a ghostly fashion, where the looms suddenly stopped, with dust gathering. A tomb he said, like the place in which he lived. Was he angry, did he hate Balfour and his declaration, the British, or Binyamin Netanyahu? No, not angry nor full of hate – but for one man: Tony Blair, the hypocritical Middle East Peace Envoy. Peace, the man asked, what peace?

I went to a market in Nablus and found an old lady selling bric-a-brac. I picked up a couple of large, rusted old keys. 'You may keep them,' a young English-speaking boy translated. 'They were from my family home. I will never return, I have no family left here.' I still have those keys and I often wonder where her stolen home lies, probably replaced by a settlement.

I met a barber and his apprentice son in Jerusalem. He usually washes his customers' hair. Not today, in fact not for several days. The Israelis take limitless supplies of water for the settlements where the grass is sprinkled daily, a verdant green. He has tanks on the roof to preserve the water, but the supply is only provided a maximum of three days a week. You can always tell a Palestinian home by the water tanks on the roofs. Israelis don't need them. The settlers consume an average 350 litres a day, the Palestinians just 60 litres.

Then there is Gaza.

The West Bank is about the 'enemy within'. Turn 360 degrees and you will see the omnipresence of Israel in Palestine. A watchtower, the dreaded wall, a barbed-wire fence, a settlement, soldiers, tanks, hideous little flags and whatever other affront they impose. Gaza is the 'enemy without'; unseen. It's the biggest concentration camp in the world, where no one has any freedom of movement in or out of the country and unemployment approaches 50 per cent.

There were the fishermen we met, whose catch for the day was two small crates of tiny sardines. Because the big fish have all gone – overfished in the small, Israeli-imposed, three-mile restriction zone. Fishermen tell me that gunboats decide if they have crossed the invisible border in the sea. They then arbitrarily circle the fishermen, swamping their boats and ruining their catch. Some men are washed overboard and have to be dragged back onto the boats. The soldiers board the boats in search of non-existent weapons. Occasionally, they fire their guns just to show who's boss. Often boats are deliberately sunk, under some false pretext, and livelihoods lost.

We went to a school to run a workshop with a group of young boys (segregated by Hamas dogma from the girls), and they were asked to express their feelings in writing. One, a lad of about fourteen, wrote a poem about waiting, waiting for what? Electricity, of which the Strip has virtually none, the generators targeted and bombed by the Israelis. Why electricity? we wondered. Because it was his metaphor for light and, therein, for freedom.

We visited the tunnels, no secret because they were huge, twenty feet across. But irrespective of the need for them, the Israelis stop the import of sanitary towels and sanitary pads. Why? Because, as one young schoolgirl told us, they like to humiliate women and deprive them of their dignity. An entire lorry-load appeared, no cement, no weapons, just the necessities of everyday life of which the people are robbed. The tunnels are now closed and the deprivation continues.

The sewage. The water is blocked, turned off, and the electricity shut down, deliberately. The sewage cannot be treated. Then suddenly the sluice gates open, and the raw sewage floods into the fields, destroying everything before it and spreading disease. It's impossible to imagine that some government department actually works out deliberately how to do these dreadful things to other human beings.

I had to leave early one year and took a taxi from Ramallah to the Allenby crossing. It usually closes at midday. Why? This day was a bank holiday and my driver made excellent time as we raced towards the Dead Sea, the Arabic place names graffiti'd out of the signs, leaving just Israeli and English. Then suddenly we encountered a snake of hundreds of cars, Palestinians trying to cross into Jordan to see their loved ones or visit the sick. Some even attempting to get themselves to hospital. The driver raced past everyone and, near the front of the queue, bundled me into a car of very confused Palestinians. It was the only way I would cross the border in time.

As we approached, we were blockaded and a side road opened for maybe twenty minutes to let through just two Israeli coaches. And so it went on. Ours was nearly the last vehicle allowed through.

There are so many stories that they begin to appear unbelievable. They should be. When I return home after just one week I am emotionally drained. When I try to describe the situation and what I have seen and heard, I cry. The Palestinians do not cry. This is their life, and they lead it with courage, dignity and hope.

One day, waiting at the Qalandia checkpoint, I watched a little bird hopping either side of a barbed-wire fence, eventually to fly off to its own freedom. What a thought.

DIARY

Brigid Keenan

I was twenty in 1960 when Otto Preminger's blockbuster film *Exodus* hit the cinema screens and a whole generation (of Westerners) swooned over Paul Newman and his struggle for the state of Israel in the face of dastardly British and Palestinian machinations. A year later I became a fashion writer and, still star-struck, admired Vidal Sassoon as much for fighting for Israel in the 1948 war as for his revolutionary hair cutting. Then, in 1962, I was invited to the first Israeli Fashion Fair. I met Ariel Sharon (young and handsome then), watched catwalk shows in Tel Aviv, went to the parties and never thought for a moment that perhaps I wasn't seeing the whole picture or hearing the whole story. I don't recall Palestine or Palestinians being mentioned at all.

With the 1967 war and the Israeli occupation, doubts began to surface, and then I married a man who spoke Arabic, knew the Middle East and had Palestinian friends. And I began to learn about what was really happening in Israel/Palestine.

By the time we were posted to Syria in the 1990s, where the huge Palestinian refugee camp at Yarmuk housed people I came to know, there was absolutely no doubt about which side I was on.

In 2001 various of us who felt passionately about this issue came together for a fundraising event at the Royal Geographical Society in London. We had distinguished speakers: William Dalrymple and Colin Thubron, whom I knew, and Ahdaf Soueif, an Egyptian/British writer whose novel *The Map of Love* had not long before been shortlisted for the Booker Prize. I had never met her, but she and I chatted in the ladies' room while nervously combing our hair before we went on stage and eventually became good friends. Once we were both invited to a literature festival in Jordan; we discussed whether we would accept or not (in fact, the festival never happened). 'The only festival I'd really like to go to', said Ahdaf, 'would be one in Palestine.'

Time went by, and I was invited to a literature festival in Paris. It was small-scale, fun and beautifully arranged – partly by a young woman called Eleanor O'Keefe (who subsequently invented the 5x15 literary events). I was impressed, and when I saw her at a party in London a few weeks later rushed up to tell her how much I had enjoyed Paris. But weirdly and mysteriously the words that came out of my mouth were: 'Eleanor, why don't we start a literature festival in Palestine?' We were both struck with astonishment at what I had said and hurriedly left the party to telephone Ahdaf.

And that is why, two years later, a motley crew of writers, poets and helpers from around the world gathered at a hotel in Amman, Jordan, and clambered on to the coach that would take us to the Allenby crossing for our very first Palestine Festival of Literature. We took with us messages of support from Patrons John Berger and Chinua Achebe (filmed by my nephew Perry Ogden) and from Mahmoud Darwish. We were missing playwright David Hare, whose wife had been mugged in London, but we'd gained Esther Freud, who had cancelled when her daughter got chickenpox but changed her mind and decided to come. And we'd added a last-minute rendezvous to our schedule – a meeting in Ramallah with Raja Shehadeh, whose book *Palestinian Walks* had just won the Orwell Prize.

Not knowing what to expect, I took with me my pillow, a cafetière and a pack of real coffee, a bottle of gin and my notebook – from which I quote here.

JERUSALEM, 7 MAY 2008

The first thing I noticed on the coach to the Allenby Bridge this morning was that Esther Freud was reading *Dip Bag* . . . a good omen I think. (My book *Diplomatic Baggage* had just been published.)

Everyone was chatty and friendly. There is an American woman with us who heard that Roddy Doyle (one of our group) is a Chelsea fan, and thought that meant Chelsea Clinton, which caused some secret hilarity.

Laughter ceased at the Allenby crossing. All the people in our party with Arab names were stopped – in spite of holding US or British passports – and escorted away for questioning. The Israelis said they were checking with the British Council to make sure they were all writers, but tonight we discovered they hadn't been in touch with the BC at all, it was just a show of power. It was four hours before our friends were released.

The drive to Jerusalem was a total shock: I had been imagining 'settlements' as small beleaguered outposts on the tops of some hills – but in fact they are *huge* towns with high-rise buildings that cover every single hilltop, all running into each other to make one vast urban sprawl dominating the country. Why don't we all know this? It seems like an incredibly well-guarded secret – I wish everyone could come here and see what is going on. As for the idea of demolishing any of them – dream on. No one is going to be able to dismantle any of these illegal towns. Maybe the most alien thing about them is their greenery: the trees of the Holy Land are umbrella pines, cypress and olive, but the settlers go in for plantations of Christmas trees so they have not only taken over the land, but the landscape as well.

I was already feeling nervous because I was to be part of our opening event in Jerusalem tonight, along with Esther Freud and Willie Dalrymple and moderated by Hanan Ashrawi. But after our experience at the Allenby crossing and seeing the settlements, I got into a real panic because I thought my contribution would be too lightweight and flippant. I needn't have worried: a Palestinian lady came up to Esther and me after the talk and said that it was the first time she had laughed in three years.

RAMALLAH, 8 MAY 2008

This morning we came face to face with the hideous grey cement wall (higher and uglier than we'd imagined) that we'd seen in the distance, snaking its sinister way round the landscape, and we went through our first checkpoint at Qalandia en route to Ramallah – and here's another thing: I'd always imagined the checkpoints to be sheds manned by a couple of Israeli soldiers, but they are more like airport terminal buildings. Soldiers you can't see yell at you through megaphones; you queue to go through tightly revolving barred gates, drag your suitcase across concrete for miles, and everything is fear, ugliness, hostility, hate. The only light relief was Banksy's paintings on the wall at the checkpoint; he immediately became a hero to us all.

BETHLEHEM, 9 MAY 2008

Back to the Qalandia checkpoint this morning (en route to Hebron and then Bethlehem). We were made to queue up and go through *twice*, once by ourselves and the second time with all our heavy luggage from the bus. I don't know why we had to do this, but you very quickly learn not to ask questions because things will get worse if you do. As we were queuing to go through the gate for the second time, a Palestinian couple with a toddler hobbled slowly towards us: they'd obviously been turned back at the checkpoint. The husband was young but clearly very ill – there was a tube with blood in it coming out from his clothes, and his wife was practically carrying him. Her face was shiny with tears and the toddler was clinging to her legs as she walked.

I can't get the image of the couple out of my head.

Later. A new image has lodged in my mind. As we drove through the outskirts of Jerusalem we saw, sauntering along the pavement, a young hippy in T-shirt and jeans with shoulder-length blond hair and a semi-automatic rifle on a strap slung over his shoulder. 'Who is that?' we asked our driver. 'Why is he carrying a gun?' This is when we learned that all settlers are allowed to carry guns wherever they go.

Hebron has been a terrible shock to all of us. This city, which used to be the busiest on the West Bank, where 160,000 Palestinians lived and where once there was a huge market serving the surrounding area, is like a ghost town. There are 500 Israeli settlers here, in the centre of town, and they have 2,000 soldiers to guard them. The market has been closed, the shops are closed, the roads are mostly closed to Palestinians, and on rooftops you can see Israeli soldiers with their guns pointing down at you. We walked along one of the few streets that Palestinians are allowed to use, but even here they have to keep behind a barrier at the side, while macho Israeli settlers jog down the centre of the road carrying guns.

One of the settlements in Hebron is above a narrow street in the old part of town still used by Palestinians. They have had to put wire netting over the top of the street to catch the missiles that the settlers throw down on them: you can see the big things caught in the net: bricks, bottles, rubbish – but of course it doesn't prevent poo or pee – or acid – coming through. We walked through, warily, on our way to the Mosque of Abraham, which was accessible to everyone until in 1994 an armed settler walked into it and shot dead twenty-nine Muslims at prayer, and injured over a hundred. Now it is divided in two, with a synagogue in one half. We joined Muslims going to pray in the mosque: we had to pass through *three* Israeli checkpoints in the space of a hundred yards before we could enter.

None of us had experienced anything like Hebron before, and we grew more and more appalled as the day went on.

BETHLEHEM, 10 MAY 2008

This morning we were taken on a bus tour to see the wall that nearly encircles Bethlehem now. We were as shocked as we had been in Hebron. Bethlehem is on a hill with carefully tended olive groves on terraces down the sides. The route of the wall is not at the bottom of the hill – no, it presses against the last houses in the town, it is the view at the end of the street, its watchtowers loom over the houses. When it is complete it will cut the land off from its owners, and here is the catch: there is an Israeli law which says that if land lies untended for seven years it can be confiscated by the Israeli government. Everyone knows in advance their land will be taken because, when the wall is finished, no one will be able to get through it. We passed an old monastery where for centuries monks have been making communion wine from their vineyards for the churches of Bethlehem; when the wall is finished it will lie on the Israeli side, what will happen to them?

JERUSALEM, 11 MAY 2008

We had a few free hours today so Hanan al-Shaykh and Esther and I visited the Church of the Holy Sepulchre with one of our Palestinian volunteer guides, Hamada Attalah, who is a theatrical costume designer. As we went into the church I said to Hamada, 'I feel so moved that I am going to pray by the body of Jesus.' He gave me a funny look, and said, 'What do you mean? Of course the body isn't here!' I had just forgotten the whole central tenet of my Catholic faith, which is the Resurrection . . .

I left them to go and prepare the speech I had to give tonight. Esther and Hanan took what they thought was a short cut back to the hotel across some wasteland and stumbled straight into an Israeli military post. The soldiers who surrounded them said they were lucky not to have been shot on sight.

Tottenham Hotspur beat Chelsea in the English Premier League yesterday – Roddy Doyle told us that he was woken in the middle of the night by a call from a distraught friend in Ireland yelling, 'Chelsea lost – for God's sake get to the Wailing Wall.'

This evening was our last event. There were speeches of thanks and then the writers read out passages from their favourite books. I read from the love story *Ali and Nino*. Then we all went to dinner in a nearby restaurant and danced. Arabs are genetically programmed to be able to shimmy their hips; Brits are definitely not – I was so conscious of looking like a cartoon of an English person doing Arabic dancing that I gave up. To think that only a few days ago we were all at the Allenby Bridge full of fear and trepidation and worrying about all the things that could go wrong, and *none* have – but our hearts are heavy with the scenes of oppression we have witnessed.

AMMAN, 12 MAY 2008

When I was packing in Jerusalem this morning I realised that though I'd used my pillow every night, I had never had time to make coffee with the cafetière or even drink my gin, so I gave them to a Palestinian friend.

ENDINGS . . .

A camaraderie grows in the bus as the days go by: it starts at the Allenby Bridge crossing when every year our guests see the authors with Arab names being taken away for questioning despite their American or British nationalities. Then, with every ugly checkpoint, every true and terrible story we hear, with every bullying settler or soldier, every Israeli act of callousness or cruelty or just blatant rudeness, we witnesses in the bus get closer to each other. And it's not all grim – we bond over jokes and silly incidents and shared falafel sandwiches and Arab sweets until in the end we can't bear to part from each other. To have been on PalFest together forges friendships – I feel a lasting kinship with anyone who has ever sat on our bus.

INDIA AND ISRAEL: AN IDEOLOGICAL CONVERGENCE

Pankaj Mishra

Literary festivals, for most writers, are a release from prolonged and solitary labour. The few obligations of authors – solo talks or panel discussions – are lightened by the thrill of being recognised, even lauded; and any enforced sociability with prickly compatriots is sweetened by free alcohol and adoring groupies. PalFest, which I accompanied in its very first incarnation, may be the world's only literary festival that broadens the mind and deepens the heart.

I certainly cannot overestimate its revelatory quality. I grew up among fervent Zionists, who were either ignorant or disdainful of Palestinians. One of the first books that I read in English was *Ninety Minutes at Entebbe*, the account of a daring Israeli raid in Uganda to free hostages captured by Palestinian militants; and one of my earliest heroes was the Israeli general Moshe Dayan. I was introduced to both in the 1970s by my grandfather, an upper-caste Hindu nationalist. He recounted keenly how Dayan had outmanoeuvred numerically superior Arab armies in 1967; how he had snatched the Golan Heights from Syria at the last minute.

India did not have diplomatic relations with Israel until the 1990s. My grandfather was among many high-caste Hindus who idolised Israel because it possessed, like European nations, a proud and clear self-image; it had an ideology, Zionism, that inculcated love of the nation in each of its citizens. Most importantly, Israel was a superb example of how to deal with Muslims in the only language they understood: that of force and more force. India, in comparison, was a pitiably incoherent and timid nation-state; its leaders, such as Gandhi, had chosen to appease a traitorous Muslim population.

This is what I also believed as a curious child. I remember that when news of Dayan's secret visit to India in 1978 as Israel's foreign minister leaked, and pictures of him appeared in the Indian newspapers, I was transfixed by his black eyepatch and mischievous grin.

As I grew older, I became aware of the plight of Israel's victims. There were Palestinians in small Indian cities, mostly students at engineering and medical colleges, and their dispossession was often discussed in the left-wing circles I fell into at university. But even then Palestine signified to me a tragically unresolved dispute, in the same way that Kashmir did, between parties that had somehow failed to see reason.

In 2000 I went on a reporting trip to Kashmir, where tens of thousands of people had died in an anti-Indian insurgency and counter-insurgency raging since 1989. Hindu nationalists have long vended an image of Indian Muslims as fifth columnists breeding demographic and other vast anti-national conspiracies in their urban ghettos. In fact, Muslims are the most depressed and vulnerable community in India, worse off than even low-caste Hindus in the realms of education, health and employment, frequently exposed to bigoted and trigger-happy policemen. Their condition has deteriorated in recent decades. After dying disproportionately in many Hindu–Muslim riots, more than 2,000 Muslims were killed and many more displaced in a pogrom in 2002 in the western Indian state of Gujarat, then ruled by a hard-line Hindu nationalist called Narendra Modi. But, as I discovered in 2000, India, in the eyes of Kashmiri Muslims, had never been less than a Hindu majoritarian state despite its claims to secularism and democracy.

Seven years later, the trip to the West Bank with PalFest brought me face to face with the brutality, squalor and absurdity of the occupation. Far from being embroiled in a mere boundary 'dispute' with its neighbours, Israel, it became clear, is the world's last active colonialist project of European origin, sustained by high-tech armoury and the fervour and guilt of many powerful white people in the West. I also realised, like many visitors to the region, how much Israel's claim to represent the victims of the Holocaust serves to hide the cruelties it inflicts on its captives in the West Bank and Gaza. For me, however, PalFest also unveiled another way of looking at India: together with Israel, another 'secular' and 'democratic' country.

It has made it easier for me to understand the extraordinary ideological convergence, so much hoped for by my grandfather and others and now accomplished, between countries that had started out as formally democratic and economically left wing. Their cosmopolitan founding fathers – Nehru, Gandhi, Ben-Gurion, Weizmann – and egalitarian ideals helped give the new nation-states, both created within months of each other, their glow of heroic virtue. It mattered little during their early years that both countries were born of imperialist skulduggery and nationalist opportunism, of clumsy partition, war and frenzied ethnic cleansing, or that, in the case of Israel, the inferior status of Arabs was formalised in citizenship rules.

As it happened, a mere decade – between 1977 and 1989 – separated their political transformations, when hard-line right-wing groups long deemed marginal – Likud, the BJP – began to change the political culture of the two countries. Unrest in occupied territories (the Intifadas of 1987 and 2000, and Pakistan-aided insurgency in Kashmir from 1989) helped give the post-colonial nationalisms of India and Israel a hard millenarian edge. In the 1990s both countries embarked on a deeper economic and ideological makeover, rejecting ideals of inclusive growth and egalitarianism in favour of neo-liberal notions about private wealth creation.

That process is now complete. Narendra Modi is now India's most powerful prime minister in decades while tens of thousands of his Muslim victims in Gujarat still languish in refugee camps, too afraid to return to their homes. A portrait of the Hindu nationalist icon V.D. Savarkar, one of the conspirators in Gandhi's assassination in 1948, now hangs in the Indian parliament. When Netanyahu won re-election in 2015, Modi tweeted his congratulations to his 'friend' in Hebrew (Israel is now one of India's biggest arms suppliers). The two prime ministers, both allied with big business, flourish in the ideological and emotional climate of globalisation, in which, backed by popular consent, violence and cruelty enjoy a new legitimacy.

Kashmir has for years been subject to a draconian Armed Forces Special Powers Act, which grants security forces broad-ranging powers to arrest, shoot to kill, and occupy or destroy property. The summer of 2016 witnessed, in addition to the routine killing of scores of protestors, a sinister escalation: mass blindings, including of children, by pellet cartridges that explode to scatter hundreds of metal pieces across a wide area. Right-wing demagogues in both India and Israel seek to forge a new national identity – a new people, no less – by stigmatising particular religious and secular groups. And, as though emboldened by them, security forces in Kashmir this summer attacked hospitals and doctors in a display of impunity that was worthy of the Israel Defence Force.

Indeed, fanatical Hindu organisations that assault Muslim males marrying Hindu women seem to mimic Lehava (Flame), an association of religious extremists in Israel which tries to break up weddings between Muslims and Jews. A lynch-mob hysteria in significant parts of the public sphere – traditional as well as social media – fully backs the atrocities of security forces in Kashmir and Palestine. More importantly, bigotry is now amplified in both countries from people placed on the commanding heights of government.

A senior minister in Narendra Modi's cabinet last year described Indian Muslims and Christians in India as 'bastards'. Staffing educational and cultural institutions with zealots, both

governments seem obsessed with moral and patriotic indoc-
trination, reverence for national symbols and icons (mostly
far right), and the uniqueness of (a largely invented) national
history. The supremacism of these ethno-nationalists goes with
a loathing of dissenters who seem to be undermining collective unity and purpose. Indeed, the most striking aspect of the
upsurge of fanaticism in India and Israel is mob fury, sanc-
tioned by their ruling classes and stoked by the media, against
anyone who expresses the slightest sympathy with the plight of
their victims.

Lost in a moral wilderness, India and Israel make one
ponder, even more than the unviable and fragmenting states
of the Middle East, the paths not taken, the missed turning
points, in the history of the post-colonial world. But it is hard
not to suspect that figures like Modi or Avigdor Lieberman are
the clearest consummation of the European-style nationalism
that my grandfather so admired. Murdered by a Hindu fanatic
who accused him of being soft on Muslims, Gandhi was an
early victim to its deadly logic. It is now manifest in the brutal
occupations of both India and Israel – nation-states that are, as
PalFest first revealed to me, committed to not resolving their
foundational disputes.

IN THE COMPANY OF WRITERS

Kamila Shamsie

Entering the West Bank with PalFest in 2014 was the second occasion on which I had come to Palestine in the company of writers. The first time had been in the 1990s, when I was a student in America, and my friend, teacher and guide to and through the intersection of politics and aesthetics was the Kashmiri poet Agha Shahid Ali. It was Shahid who gave me a copy of the journal *Poetry East* which he had guest-edited in 1989, and to which he wrote an introductory essay entitled 'Dismantling Some Silences'. In this introduction he quotes Gregory Oraela writing about the assassination of the Palestinian poet Kamal Nasser. He 'was sitting at his desk at home on 10 April 1973 when a commando unit of Israelis burst into the room, killing him and two others. One Israeli shot him in the mouth because he was a poet: a legend among Palestinians . . .'

I opened that copy of *Poetry East* yesterday for the first time since my university days, when it was among the handful of books that I kept on my desk as I wrote, and which served in various moods as talisman or yardstick or reprimand. When I read those words about Nasser I had to put the book down, stand up and physically walk away from it for a while. Or rather, walk around it, able neither to leave nor return to it. I may well have responded exactly so when I first read those sentences, but I wouldn't, in the mid-90s, have thought to do what I did yesterday: go online to find what else I could discover about Kamal

Nasser's assassination. And so I wouldn't have known then that the commando unit was led by Ehud Barak, or that Kamal Nasser – poet and PLO spokesman – was shot in the mouth and also in his right hand, the writing hand.

What to do with such images in your head except seek out other images that give utterance to grief and injustice? And so I turned the pages of *Poetry East* to find the lines further in which played an even greater role than the story of Nasser's assassination in first taking me to Palestine by making it a place I learnt to imagine, though it would be twenty years before I would visit it: the lines, pages and pages of them, written by Mahmoud Darwish.

> We did not come to this country from a country
> we came from pomegranates, from the glue of memory
> from the fragments of an idea

and

> You will say: no. And you will rip apart the words and the
> slow-moving river. You will curse this bad time, and you will
> vanish into the shade. No – to the theatre of words. No – to
> the limits of this dream. No – to the impossible.

Translated by Lena Jayyusi and W.S. Merwin

And so much more beside.

It was not just the poems, but the company they kept which drew me to them. In that journal the Darwish poems end and Faiz Ahmed Faiz's poems (translated by Shahid) begin; it is as if a baton is passed between those two great poets of exile and broken dreams, both writing with that expansiveness of expression that can be found in Arabic and in Urdu. Although I had grown up in Pakistan and knew of Faiz's reputation (and knew also my mother's tears the day he died), I didn't know his poetry, which was too anti-authoritarian for the school lessons, which were the only way in which Urdu poetry came to me in those days in the strangely cut-off anglophone world in which I grew up. It was Shahid who told me, in America, that it was unacceptable for a Pakistani to be unversed in Faiz. Handing me his translations of Faiz's work, which also had the Urdu text alongside the English versions, he said, 'Take this and don't come back until you've read it.' I fell headlong in love with Faiz – with his poetry, his humanity, his internationalism. And Faiz, I knew, had spent some years in Beirut while exiled from Pakistan. Many of his closest companions were exiled Palestinians, so later, when he was asked what Palestine meant to him, he replied, 'After all these years that I spent with the Palestinians, I became one of them.' Faiz and Darwish knew each other in Beirut – as friends, though not without their differences. But most significantly, to me, Faiz wrote about Palestine, explicitly so in several poems.

There were days on PalFest, stunned by the ferocity of hatred written into law and enforced by those who are little more than children, when I would stop to look around at the fellowship in which I found myself and wonder, but what can writers do? And a little while later I would find myself in a verse by Faiz, the only place of solace in the universe.

> though tyrants may command that lamps be smashed
> in rooms where lovers are destined to meet
> they cannot snuff out the moon

> *Translated by Agha Shahid Ali*

Sometimes, it would be Shahid's poems I'd turn to – those great, heartbreaking poems about Kashmir which placed him in the pantheon of poets such as Darwish and Faiz.

> In this dark rain, be faithful, Phantom heart,
> this is your pain. Feel it. You must feel it.

Well, Shahid, I felt it. Even though it wasn't my pain, not directly. What might still be done with that pain, and what it might mean to be faithful to it, has yet to fully reveal itself. But for today, I can do this much. I can take the best known of Faiz's Palestine poems and render it into English, so that some of those who didn't know it in Urdu might know it now.

LULLABY TO A PALESTINIAN CHILD

Don't cry, child
Your mother has only just
cried herself to sleep
Your father has only just
taken leave of grief

Don't cry, child
Your brother
chasing dreams as if butterflies
has wandered into a faraway land
Your sister's bridal palanquin
has entered a foreign land

Don't cry child
In your courtyard
they have bathed the sun's corpse
they have buried the moon

Don't cry child
For if you cry
parents, siblings, moon and sun
will make you shed more tears
But if you smile, perhaps one day
they'll cast off their sorrows

they'll turn to you
and play.

The Gaza Suite: Jabaliya

Suheir Hammad

a woman wears a bell carries a light calls searches
through madness of deir yessin calls for rafah for bread
orange peel under nails blue glass under feet gathers
children in zeitoun sitting with dead mothers she unearths
tunnels and buries sun onto trauma a score and a day rings
a bell she is dizzy more than yesterday less than
tomorrow a zig zag back dawaiyma back humming suba

back shatilla back ramleh back jenin back il khalil back il quds
all of it all underground in ancestral chests she rings
a bell promising something she can't see faith is that
faith is this all over the land under the belly
of wind she perfumed the love of a burning sea

concentrating refugee camp
crescent targeted red

a girl's charred cold face dog eaten body
angels rounded into lock down shelled injured shock
weapons for advancing armies clearing forests sprayed
onto a city
o sage tree human skin contact explosion these are our
children

she chimes through nablus back yaffa backs shot under
spotlight phosphorous murdered libelled public relations

public
relation

a bell fired in jericho rings through blasted windows a woman
carries bones in bags under eyes disbelieving becoming
numb dumbed by numbers front and back gaza onto gaza
for gaza am sorry gaza am sorry she sings for the whole
powerless world her notes pitch perfect the bell a death toll

Letters from Gaza

Atef Abu Saif

When I was at school one of our English-language classes was writing a letter to your friend abroad inviting him to visit you in your hometown. With our bad English we were taking a long time finding words and forming sentences to make the invitation generous and the place exciting. We were paying attention to this class in particular; we knew that this letter always came up in final exams.

When I grew up I would find out that this invitation would never be written. Now I am forty-three years old and I have lots of friends all over the world and I have never invited a friend to visit.

In the letter we would write descriptions of how beautiful Gaza was. We would refer to the beach, the huge orange orchards, the souks and the historic sights – Christian and Muslim. We thought they were attractive; the forty-five kilometres of sandy beach where – so close to the sand they almost hugged its visitors – grew vineyards, orchards of figs, olives and orange trees.

When I studied in Europe I always suffered from this inability to invite people – especially during vacation times. You can visit a friend but a friend cannot visit you. When everybody was talking about vacation plans I had to keep quiet. I never spoke about how beautiful the place was – every place is beautiful in one way or another. I never made any effort to convince others to come and see me in my hometown. The impossible visit would never take place, visitors would never arrive and they would never enjoy the welcoming hug and hospitality. Journalists, human rights activists, international delegations, a few politicians might arrive, especially in times of escalation and tension, but your guests will never arrive. When you grow up in Gaza you know that that invitation is only a question in your high-school exam, just a language exercise, something you train to do but never practise.

And when everybody left for home I stayed in the student dorms contemplating the hundred obstacles I would face if I decided to cross the road to Gaza. This started when I did my BA at Birzeit University in the West Bank and all us students from the Gaza Strip would stay on in the empty student hostel during all the Eids and all the vacations when all the other students went home to different West Bank cities to be with their families. I remember when I entered Birzeit in 1991 I needed only one permit – a blue one – to cross from Gaza to the West Bank. By the time I finished my studies there I needed a permit to leave Gaza and another to enter the West Bank and another to stay in the West Bank. There was also a permit that allowed you to leave despite the blockade, a card that stated your identity as a student and a magnetic card with your security information. Mostly you had to have all those on you at all times. And you had to show them to the Israeli soldiers on demand. No complaints.

Are the Palestinians victims of geography? Is it their fault that their homeland happened to be the most holy place on earth! The idea of God and religion was created after the Palestinians had made this piece of the earth their homeland. Prophets were sent after the people had built their Canaanite cities and cultivated their farms. Geography is an enemy. Its very logic runs against the course of nature. History as well is not much different. But when it comes to history, it depends where you're reading history from and according to whose narration. But Palestinians like their geography, their landscape and their history. They love to name their children after their cities. I did for example. My only daughter is named after Yafa, the city where my family lived for centuries before being forced to leave to make way for the state of Israel. For my grandma, Aisha, no city is like Jaffa; no sea is like its sea, no fragrance is scented like the breeze there. Her lamentations for Jaffa no writer can capture. Living in Gaza, her soul remained in Jaffa. The refugee camp she lived in, and where I still live, never became a hometown for her. In her memory and mind she used to make up another present that rested on the continuity of the past. And then, when many people were forced to leave Gaza in 1967 after the Israeli occupation of the Strip, she said she'd rather die than leave. At least Gaza was part of the big country called Palestine where her beloved Jaffa was. Thus I was actually lucky to be born in a geography that limits my ability to move. Because you have to be more than lucky, you have to be given a hand from heaven to be able to leave and come back, to see other places and return. A student of mine lives exactly on the border fence with Egypt. When she opens her window she sees the streets of the Egyptian border town of Rafah: people walking and cars moving. Her only dream is to cross that border, a dream she's now finished university without fulfilling.

Gaza is a hot place for news only. It is a bakery for delicious exciting breaking news. People come here to make stories about wars. Nobody comes just to visit. Dignitaries and public figures come to find out about Gaza. Sartre came to Gaza. My dad saw him in the street.

I always felt I was living inside the television, permanently standing in front of the news anchors. And I always wanted to escape this feeling. But even when I manage to leave Gaza – especially when I was studying in England and Italy – I don't succeed in escaping; always worrying for my family and thinking of the death that seeks them. We were born during war and we die during war. What we live are moments stolen from the devouring mouth of death. These are the moments that can be written about. The moments that Aisha, my grandmother, lamented and wanted to revisit. The moments we want always to share with our beloved.

Now, nearly twenty-five years after the imagined invitation letters I wrote to 'friends from Europe inviting them to visit me in Gaza', I still write letters to people who do not come – who cannot come, who are not permitted to come – visit. But Gaza is always there in the news and in any presentation about 'the Middle East Conflict'. One day it should escape the news. One day it should be able to think of its dream away from the noise of war. One day her people should live normally and their imagined invitees must come.

Gaza, from Cairo

Selma Dabbagh

Like most foreigners I travelled into Gaza with a mission and as part of a delegation. The year I went, 2012, PalFest was composed mainly of Egyptian writers, bloggers, musicians and film-makers who had been constructing and energising their own revolution at home. We were known as the 'Egyptian Delegation', and as an English-Palestinian writer I was in a minority of one. I didn't know it then, but my energetic, optimistic gang of fellow travellers were then probably at their peak as a group. Since 2012 some, most notably the blogger Alaa Abdel Fattah, have been imprisoned in Egypt on the basis of spurious allegations.

Permission had not been granted by the Egyptian authorities for their nationals to travel until two days before we left. There was mention of tunnels without any details (steps and mud? possible collapse and attack?). A media campaign was postponed by a day because of violence outside the Ministry of Defence in Cairo, but then 'Yay!' is tweeted and facebooked from Cairo and Gaza; we get the go-ahead and are off. Slowly off: seven hours to the border and four sitting at it. In the hateful space that the Rafah border crossing is, an oud player from the band Eskandarella started strumming softly from one of the moulded plastic seats next to the waiting, smoking, pacing crowd that we have become. The holding station is momentarily transformed as if a magical circuitry now networks throughout the space, communicating something deep and connecting that we feel for a transient moment, until the oud player is asked to stop.

And then to leave.

He does not have the right papers.

We're lurched into Gaza by a swinging coach and greeted with a WELCOME TO PALESTINE sign. We all cheer – it's a sign that has been fought for, a forbidden word now writ high – although we're not so dim that we can't absorb the tragic disappointment masked by this proclamation.

Darkness falls in a deep, soft way that makes the sky and full moon appear like a felt collage. An abandoned missile-struck building grinning toothlessly out to sea reassures us that we're in the right place before we drive up along the coast of the most populated strip of land in the world. The sea breeze billows in cubes of glowing fabric that are greenhouses shaped like modern-ist oriental tents. It feels as though we've sneaked into a secret garden, a forbidden city. For a long time on that slow, meditative, evening drive, I thought that we were driving through an unin-habited part of Gaza.

It took daylight to show me how wrong I was.

It wasn't uninhabited at all. The population had, quite simply, been blacked out; the plug had been pulled on them. Driving down the same road the next day, the busy villages, refugee camps and towns became visible. Without the sun, Gaza is a place with hardly any light. The Israeli air, land and sea blockade, and their bombing of the main power plant in 2006, have made fuel and electricity scarce. A couple of hours from the grid is the norm. Those who can afford to, back up their supply with generators, which in turn need fuel to run.

Almost all the petrol stations are roped off, waiting. It only takes one person to generate a rumour that a delivery is on the way for a petrol station to become blocked up with queues of cars, tractors, motorbikes and pedestrians that stretch for miles and can last all day. 'From the time I came to the Festival until I left at night, they were there waiting – a long, long line,' said one student volunteer from Deir el-Balah refugee camp. 'I could not even see my town as I approached it, since everything was so dark. Only when the car's headlights shone on it, did I realise we were at my house.'

Without electricity, that first night's sky had the depth desert skies have. Seeing the full moon above the sea and a broad tree with outstretched boughs standing over the haphazard mounds and glinting tomb plaques of an unwalled graveyard, I was overcome with wonder. It was a night that flattered and deceived. The same graveyard, by day was a desolate place. The tree was scraggy and under-watered, the land dusty with blue plastic bags worrying at the bumps that told of hurried, unanticipated deaths too frequent to deal with properly.

I was on the hotel's fifth-floor balcony overlooking the sea before anyone else got up. As I breakfasted a group of boys cartwheeled along the beach, the clumsy ones trying to follow the vertical pirouettes of their mentor. This is the same beach where two years later, in 2014, four boys will be killed by an Israeli missile in front of foreign correspondents – also eating breakfast. The Israeli Military Advocate General later deemed the action to be entirely legal.

By the side of a building that houses aid workers busy with laptops, briefcases and water bottles, a group of men come to work. They step out of cars, wearing suits, gripping plastic carrier bags by the neck, and then gather at a table under a makeshift pagoda in the unused garden of an old hotel. They stand to greet each other. They have pieces of A4 paper that they pass from one to the other and then they sit. I wonder if theirs is the future of the cartwheelers.

We fill our days with talking and observing. 'Watch! Photograph! Observe!' a green-eyed man with a dust-clad face shouts at us, as he rides past on an open-backed truck with others similarly pasted with sweat and grime, while we walk along by bullet-hole-ridden buildings in Rafah. 'Witness our Tragedy!'

I turn heads by walking around the Islamic University with mine uncovered, accompanied by a bearded English literature professor (a man of extraordinary manual dexterity; I have

113

watched him scoop individual grains of rice off the table with a ring-pull) who points out the construction of new laboratories. The previous ones were bombed during the Israeli assault of 2008–9.

I ask about the strike on the university. 'They did it more than once. Every time they flew over us they dropped a bomb. Four times it happened. Maybe five, six.'

'Anyone killed?'

'Two, maybe three?'

There is an exhibition in the university hall of photographs from the 2008–9 Israeli attacks: a picture of white phosphorus being dropped, the smoke streaking down like giant pipe-cleaner spider legs, straddling the buildings. 'Do you know white phosphorus?' asks my guide, a young student from Gaza City. In my mind's eye I see images from newsreels of children screaming down streets with it stuck burning on their skin. 'Yes,' I say, 'I do,' although this feels feeble as I probably don't know it, nor do I ever want to know it, nor should anyone ever have to know it in the way that this young population does. As I nod solemnly all the girls around me giggle.

Probably about my hair.

The students in Gaza are as students in an ideal world should be: ballsy and bright. 'Why should Palestinian writers have to write about politics? How do you write from a child's perspective? Does revolutionary writing go stale? What do you think about our campaign for the hunger strike in the prisons? Do you support the boycott of Israel? Why are people so ignorant about Gaza? What are you doing about it? What can we do about it?' In the main lecture hall a banner for a conference on reconciliation between Hamas and Fatah is strung up. At Al-Aqsa University the lights go off every ten minutes and the students laugh like it's a big joke, 'Ha! It's done it again!' Poetry is read by the light of a mobile phone.

We have a battle of mobile phones on our closing night. Plain-clothes security – said not to be Hamas by Hamas and to be Hamas by everyone else – grab a phone from a girl in the audience and yell at us that if we film security we will be shut down. We shout. A cry comes from the poet Tariq Hamdan that seems larger than him and breaks my heart: 'You do this for Palestine?' and security film us in revenge with their mobile phones. We try to continue but get shut down anyway and are then apologised to profusely by the government.

The unexpected nature and swiftness of the night's trajectory, from the calm of the concert to petty harassment, to a potentially extremely dangerous situation, leaves me shaken. But everyone else is obviously hardier than I, and the girls, who have no time for watching dust settle, start discussing blogging competitions with me as soon as we get back to the hotel. We continue with oud playing and poetry reading on the top floor. 'Let's be constructive,' they say as we try to find out where the girl whose phone was snatched has gone. She comes back later (phone returned) to hang out and listen with the rest of us.

Security waits downstairs.

Gaza, from the Diaspora – Part One

Jehan Bseiso

I

Even from space Gaza is on fire, is
children sheltering in UNRWA schools (hit), is
entire families huddled in hospitals (hit), is
you sitting perfectly still in the dark, hoping this one
will miss you.

II

From Amman, from Beirut, in Chicago.
We, online, yes.
But no 140 characters this.
1,000 killed, 4,000 injured, thousands displaced no place.

III

Twitter feeds and Facebook timelines and
10 Reasons Why You Should Boycott Israel Now, and
5 Ways Children Die in Gaza Today, or
How to Lose 18 Members of Your Family in One Minute
(@Bibi54 stop saying the rockets are in the damn hospitals, in
    the schoolrooms, under the beds of four-year-olds).
Maybe it helps that 8 Celebrities Expressed Their Outrage.
Tweeted and deleted.
(@CNN@Foxnews bas rewriting history, bas lies on TV)
@Jon Stewart, thank you for educating the silent majority
    with satire.

IV

Day 17: What happened? What is still happening?
In Jabaliya, the dead console the dying;
Anisa, with one child in her arms, and another in her belly
    (dead).
In the hospital they put the pregnant women alone because
    they're carrying hope
because they don't want them to see what can happen to
    children.
Oh white phosphorous (and unconfirmed reports of illegal
    dense inert metal explosives).

V
I can confirm this:
international law is clearly for internationals only.
By now, a seven-year-old in Gaza has survived three wars
    already, and you're still talking about talks, and sending
    John Kerry to the Middle East, and thanking Egypt for
    facilitating nothing.
There's more blood than water today in Gaza.

Darkening the Dramaturgy

Omar El-Khairy

My father said: Speak the language that pays for your bread
My grandmother said: Speak the language that keeps its
distance
from what has taken place in words
My brother said: Speak the language that gives life to the
machine
My mother said: Speak the language worth the price of
betraying me

Athena Farrokhzad, *White Blight*

'Palestinians can be cunts too,' I fired back. It was the early hours of the morning, and I'd just received another email from the director with this one stubborn, recurring note on the latest draft of my play. 'You sure this is how you want to represent Palestinians on a London stage?' The implication was clear. The burden of representation was a dramaturgical weight that could now be strategically deployed to tie down artists. For, in most cases, it is no longer self-imposed – laced with the anger and expectation of past national liberation projects – but rather politely lenied on them by white, well-meaning liberal tastemakers. Despite a new generation of Palestinian artists – working both at home and within the diaspora – openly rejecting a renewed politics of performing respectability, there remains a burden – an expectancy, even – on certain artists to not only represent their particular communities, as imagined by institutions, funding bodies and commissioners, but equally to shed a particular light – either revelatory, focusing on certain repressive socio-cultural practices, or celebratory, reorienting the noble savage for our modern times.

It is important to stress that, us artists, caught up in this twisted logic of the culture industries, have been equally complicit in its propagation. There are those fighting for a new language, a new aesthetic, that neither occludes past struggles and their yet-unrealised dreams nor submits to the culture talk of our creative industries. However, there are others who choose to play along – either in the hope of changing such reductive perspectives or for the simple, short-term rewards that come with reaffirming certain undisturbed narratives. For, although usually left unspoken, we are all aware of what play, novel or art piece would garner the necessary attention to afford us a public(ised) career. Such rewards, however, always come at a cost – in this case, a self-defined, long-term career being the primary causality. A recurring motif with such artists – usually once the flashing lights have shifted on to the next bright young thing – is the expression of frustration at being pigeonholed (usually by their compromised, breakthrough work) and their subsequent inability to move beyond the words and images that have brought them such success.

It is for these reasons that I was reluctant to write about Palestine so early on, as I was finding my footing as a playwright. *Sour Lips*, my first play, although set during the 2011 Syrian uprisings, was very much an exploration of Western fetishism around what was to be become the Arab Spring. It was a period in which everyone was clamouring for work about the revolts spreading across the region. I was becoming increasingly uncomfortable with artists, those entrusted with the necessary cultural capital – both from within the region and in the West – serving as cultural translators for Western audiences, usually to put them at ease with all the turmoil. So, I wrote a fake verbatim play about Tom MacMaster, the man behind the 'Gay Girl in Damascus' hoax. Many were rightly angered by a middle-aged white man appropriating the identity – albeit fictitious – of a young Syrian woman. There is no denying the obvious violence of such an act. Nor can one ignore the real lives his blog unintentionally put at risk. However, what interested me more was both MacMaster's fantasy of what a liberated generation in a new Middle East would look like and his astute appreciation of how best to attract the gaze of the culture industries – for seemingly good intentions. His ability to manipulate the Western imaginary of the Arab world, in particular its manifest desires for the region, was an act of surprising subversion. For, his creation, Amina Arraf, was beautiful, (American) educated, sans hijab – having taken it off at some point, of course – religiously ambivalent, leftist and a lesbian. MacMaster began blogging at a time when Syria was in a state of near media blackout, especially since the breakout of revolts in March. Amina, however, spoke directly to liberal English-speaking readers – becoming an overnight media sensation, bamboozling both the *Guardian* and the BBC. And despite his subsequent vilification, MacMaster ultimately showed up the paternalistic inner logic that links Western cultural institutions of all political persuasions.

At a time when we are witnessing a resurgence of identity politics – and with it a return to the comforting clamour for authenticity – our cultural landscape feels especially fraught. It is a particularly precarious moment – one in which Lionel Shriver, donning a sombrero, can arrogantly dismiss cultural attachment, believing it is fair game for everyone. While others – unwavering Beyoncé fans, most notably – forcefully exalt the reification of subaltern cultures, leaving little room for any ambivalence, play or critique. Given the relentless drive to dehumanise Arabs and Muslims – unwittingly elided in most imaginaries – in our news reports, television dramas and Hollywood blockbusters, I fully appreciate the instinct to both defend our territory and counter such depictions with more positive representations. However, both camps in this reignited debate on cultural appropriation are retreating into dangerous territory – the same territory, ultimately. They have both managed to manufacture a false – mutually self-serving – dichotomy in which culture is reduced to the realm of authenticity and ownership.

So, although *The Keepers of Infinite Space* was marketed as a play documenting the history of incarceration of Palestinians in the Israeli prison system, for me it will always be an inter-generational family drama – Chekhovian in its approach to class, land and heroism. The family at the heart of this story are neither imbued with the romance of the freedom fighter nor the pity inflicted upon the refugee. They are the proud bourgeoisie – headed by a comprador patriarch, helping develop Rawabi, the first planned city (or neo-liberal wet dream) built by Palestinians in the West Bank. I had little interest in romanticising the already over-signified figure of the Palestinian. Although the code of not airing our dirty laundry in public still resonates within certain quarters of the Palestinian community, particularly in the dias-pora, where an untarnished memory of the homeland must always be kept intact, I sought out ambivalence instead. I chose to shun the arrogant presumption that I – and my play – stood in for Palestine – thus creating space for critique to work along-side solidarity. I – and seemingly everyone else in London – love Mahmoud Darwish, but he was not an inspiration for the play. His poems are neither recited by any of the characters nor set to the sounds of Marcel Khalife as mood music. I am reminded of the dilemma faced by the protagonist in Percival Everett's blister-ing novel *Erasure*. Thelonious 'Monk' Ellison's writing career has bottomed out – with one reviewer wondering what his reworking of Aeschylus' *The Persians* has to do with the African-American experience. He seethes on the sides of the American literary estab-lishment as he watches the meteoric success of *We's Lives in Da Ghetto*, a first novel by a woman who once visited 'some relatives in Harlem for a couple of days'. In his rage and despair, Monk rattles off a novel intended to serve as an indictment. However, *My Pafology* – written under the pseudonym Stagg R. Leigh – soon becomes a smash hit. It is this very bind – moral, political and artistic in nature – that many Arab artists working in the West find themselves having to negotiate.

The transnational flows of Arab culture (and capital) are there to be celebrated, but sometimes we take for granted the privileged position afforded to those who manage to position themselves between places – Jerusalem and New York, Ramallah and London. For the most part, these networks are left unchallenged. It is not simply a question of one's ability to travel freely in an increasingly administered world of militarised borders, but how such a positionality essentially leaves Western culture undisturbed. It fails to appreciate how Western cultures – in the past, but also in the present – are being shaped by young Arabs born and raised in them. These transnational elites may speak of the unruly nature of culture – collapsing racial or national markers – but ultimately, they fall back on traditional ideas of 'home(land)'. Such an outlook, however, fails to recognise the messiness of cultural formations taking hold outside the region – of what British Arab culture actually looks like, for example. And with respect, it is not shaped by cooking classes or calligraphy workshops organised in particular London enclaves by centres of mutual understanding. For us, it resides in Prince Nassem Hamed's 'Thriller' ring entrance and oversized Adidas leopard-print shorts or with Mighty Moe, the Palestinian member of the Heartless Crew – the iconic London garage motley crew.

It is this outernational spirit that runs through the spine of PalFest. Although the festival never presumes to replicate the Palestinian experience for the international literary figures it invites to traverse historical Palestine. Neither does it shy away from taking writers – star-studded or not – out of the safe enclaves of hotel lobbies and embassy gardens. The organisers' radical gesture is to continually unsettle canons, geographies and uncontested cultures. Waiting has become a central feature of contemporary Palestinian life. And I will always cherish a seemingly inconspicuous exchange with a writer I greatly admire. It was early on in the festival. I was a young buck surrounded by acclaimed writers – and as a Palestinian, I was still questioning whether or not my place on the trip was going to waste. But there I was, sat beside China Miéville on the coach, waiting at a checkpoint on the outskirts of Jerusalem, talking Emile Habibi and science fiction. However, it was not until our conversation shifted to our mutual admiration for *PhoneShop*, the classic British sitcom set in a mobile-phone shop in Sutton, that I fully appreciated the rare conviviality, radical alterity and simple humanism that this remarkable festival affords all those fortunate enough to be invited to take part and share in.

THIS POEM WILL NOT END APARTHEID
Remi Kanazi

this poem
will not end apartheid

my words, no matter how beautiful
clever or carefully strung together
will not end the occupation
allow the return of refugees
or create equality
within Israeli society

the status quo is a fantasy
telling us it's ok
to sit on our hands
call political art propaganda
rather than calling those
who politicise our lives
propagandists

every American
should ask this question
why are mortars and missiles
devastating open-air prisons
with money that should be paying
for our medical expenses?

to the academics
            and pseudo leftists
I appreciate your books
on Israeli massacres
but you refuse to take
bullets out of Israeli guns
with your stances

the problem is not just the occupation
or putting a better face on Zionism
because 750,000 Palestinians
            were displaced

before those settlements
        were constructed
half of them before
Israel was created

we don't need another book
explaining the situation
we need a lesson plan
to stop the next bomb
from dropping

silence is complicity
over-intellectualisation tells us
to theorise on the power of art
while farmers are kicked off land
children are stoned
        on the way to school
people are caged in
        beaten and split
        from loved ones
blasted and broken
        in blockaded dungeons
bought and paid for
        with our tax dollars
we are part of the problem
that is not theoretical

        it is time
        to boycott *all*
        Israeli products
        and go to the root
        of the conflict

every 729
cultural institution
and dialogue farce
from Sabra to Ahava

Max Brenner to Aroma
Lev Leviev to SodaStream
switching drink preferences
stacks up little to 67 years
of continued dispossession

finally
to the artists
building bridges
between apartheid
and normalisation
you serve an agenda
that rebrands colonialism
as enlightened liberalism
concerts, ballets, and raves
in Israel's Sun City
a haven and party stop
for pinkwashers
who callously ignore
Palestinian LGBTQ groups
working against all systems
of oppression

Palestinian civil society has spoken
don't cross this picket line
or cash in a paycheck
signed apartheid

cancel that gig
put down Stolen Beauty
and join the rest of us
on the right side of history

An Image

Geoff Dyer

What makes this picture stand out from the thousands of others showing the effects of Israel's assault on Gaza? It was taken by Finbarr O'Reilly on 24 July 2014, in a hospital, after the shelling of a UN-run school where sixteen people were killed. Other images were more heart-rending, showed more appalling scenes of injury and death or provided more comprehensive views of the scale and intensity of destruction. But I kept coming back to this one – partly *because* I couldn't work out why I kept coming back to it.

The answer came as soon as I stopped searching for it: Don McCullin. Specifically his picture of a Vietnamese man crouching with his back to a wall, holding a blood-soaked girl injured in the wake of a US attack in Hue in 1968. The resemblance between the pictures is extraordinary – and, on reflection, completely unextraordinary: when a civilian population is bombed scenes like this are inevitable.

John Berger refers to the McCullin picture in his well-known essay 'Photographs of Agony' (1972). Berger claimed that the publication of images like McCullin's could be taken either as a sign that people 'want to be shown the truth' or that growing familiarity with images of suffering was leading newspapers to compete 'in terms of ever more violent sensationalism'.

Rejecting both of these options, Berger concluded that such pictures place events – which are the product of politics – outside the realm of the political, where they become, instead, 'evidence of the human condition'. They accuse 'nobody and everybody'.

It's a thesis that still merits consideration more than forty years after the essay was written. Shortly after O'Reilly's picture was published Israel announced that it was 'investigating' the accusation that it was responsible for the school shelling. This was to be expected. No government will readily admit that it bombed a school if this is in any way deniable – or even postponable. The calculation is that by the time responsibility is conceded the degree of blame or temperature of outrage – and the attendant political consequences – will have somewhat diminished.

So in spite of the way that images can be disseminated ahead of state censorship, the situation today – with enhanced awareness both of the power of photography as an instrument of war and of how to neutralise that power – can induce a resignation deeper than that described by Berger. I became conscious of the result or paradox of impotent solidarity while watching *5 Broken Cameras* about a Palestinian who filmed his village's resistance to occupation and to the ever-encroaching settlements. It is a record of endless defeat and setbacks. How, I kept wondering, do Palestinians avoid sinking into despair? The answer might be found in another essay by Berger, about the Italian writer Giacomo Leopardi, where he invites us to suppose

> that we are not living in a world in which it is possible to construct something approaching heaven-on-earth, but, on the contrary, are living in a world whose nature is far closer to that of hell; what difference would this make to any single one of our political or moral choices? We would be obliged to accept the same obligations and participate in the same struggle as we are already engaged in; perhaps even our sense of solidarity with the exploited and suffering would be more single-minded. All that would have changed would be the enormity of our hopes and finally the bitterness of our disappointments.

There is one crucial difference between the Gaza picture and McCullin's: whereas the eyes of the Vietnamese child are turned imploringly towards us, neither the Palestinian man nor the girl pay us any mind. Could it be that, in spite of everything – in a situation that seems hopeless, when Palestinians are dependent on the political intervention of others – we are left looking to *them*, to the powerless, for hope?

POETRY AND PROTEST
Maath Musleh

The Palestinian political scene has changed drastically since the launch of the first Palestine Festival of Literature ten years ago, in 2008, just one year into the Hamas–Fatah civil war.

The launching of PalFest coincided with a shift in the political dynamics of the West Bank and Gaza Strip. Seven months after the first edition, the Israeli army launched Operation Cast Lead, a brutal attack on the besieged Gaza Strip which left more than 1,400 Palestinians dead, 30 per cent of whom were children. This began a new phase in the Palestinian struggle. Even though there had been inter-Palestinian conflicts in the past, 2007 could be seen as an unprecedented era of Palestinian division. Voices within the Palestinian Authority in the West Bank came out in support of the Israeli military operation in the hope that this would result in the reinstatement of Fatah control of the Gaza Strip. These voices were echoed by several neighbouring Arab regimes. There is evidence that points towards these regimes even providing logistical support to the Israeli army.

New political facts were instated on the ground, a new Palestinian political dynamic was created. Palestinian groups were no longer fighting in unison. Palestinian citizens no longer had a voice. A new era in the relationship between the Arab countries and the Palestinians began. As a new generation of Palestinians emerged from the rubble of the Aqsa Intifada and the devastation of Cast Lead, Palestinian tactics in the battle against Zionist hegemony were called into question.

Many turned to alternative methods of resistance and so began the rising influence of the Boycott, Divestment and Sanctions (BDS) Movement worldwide. There was born the hope that public pressure could be brought to bear on Israel, that Israel could then be forced to abide by the dozens of UN resolutions it had ignored for the past seven decades. This approach was not spared the cynicism of those who believed that – at a time when the state of Israel receives $3 billion of American military support per annum – boycott strategies were ineffective.

Organisers of PalFest believed that the first-hand experience of cultural figures brought in every year can make a difference. One cannot ignore the influence of these figures and how they contribute to undermining the propaganda that Zionism relies on.

I have been part of the PalFest team since 2013, joining the tour around historic Palestine as poets and writers got the chance to experience the cruel realities of the old city in Hebron. I have seen their shock at the unimaginable apartheid wall eating the land, and I have watched them speak to devastated citizens losing their homes and livelihoods to settlement expansion and the deepening control of Palestine. The jolt was no less when they saw the suffering of the Palestinians living in the areas occupied in 1948.

These cultural figures have written and spoken out about what they experienced and saw. Many came to understand that describing the state of Israel as an apartheid regime was not inaccurate. Some were left speechless as they came to encounter settlers face to face in Hebron, the settlers' arguments bringing to mind the racist discourse of the KKK or apartheid gurus of South Africa. The experience clearly touched most of the participants in PalFest – twinned as it was with such a clear appetite for culture at each evening's events.

Although I could see the importance and influence of the festival, I also listened to the scepticism of my Palestinian peers. Many viewed the festival as a pointless cultural activity that in some aspects undermined the boycott. The scepticism still echoes in some discussions despite the fact that PalFest is a signatory to BDS, and that large numbers of participants have gone on to become active proponents of the boycott. Some activists believe that the very act of entering Palestine through the Allenby Bridge is no different from visits through Ben Gurion Airport. Getting an entry visa from the Israeli authorities is seen as an act of acceptance and submission. One question kept coming up: why can they enter Palestine and move freely around while we are deprived of that right?

These discussions and arguments were part of larger debates emerging over the visits of several Arab artists and literary and political figures to Jerusalem, Haifa, Nazareth and other cities in the past decade. Many viewed these visits as crucial to building bridges between Palestinians – especially those living in areas occupied in 1948 – and the Arab world. They saw them as a way to break the siege imposed on Palestinians by the Israeli regime. But for many activists this is not enough; there are only 'minimal' advantages to such visits, which are then exploited by the Israeli government as good PR, bolstering the deceit that Jerusalem – for example – is an open city where people of all faiths are free to move and reside.

I was out with friends from Tulkarem the other day, friends who feel that they are locked up in a big prison in the West Bank. They are apolitical, just regular citizens aspiring to live as normal a life as possible. The protests against the visits of artists to Palestine came up. A young woman burst out, 'Should we just be sad all the time? We need some joy in our lives.' She had come to lose faith in any overall strategy. She does not feel that she has any role or word in the future of Palestine.

And this is the unfortunate reality. The Zionist regime has systematically worked to break the will of the people. We, as people, have also lost empathy towards one another. Everyone speaks from their own podium. The loss of a unified and effective strategy means that urban professionals can be dismissive of stone-throwing and daily protests while someone from a village that regularly protests is critical of those living more stable city lives. We are losing the fabric of our society.

Do we put a hold on culture, on joy? Or on protests and confrontations? No. Events like PalFest keep us going. They add much-needed colour to our lives. We need to have them, just as we need the confrontations without which we would slide into oblivion faster than we would think. The reality is that PalFest and boycott movements and confrontations don't play as lone strikers and do not seek to monopolise the struggle. There need to be midfield players, defenders holding the back lines – everyone has to find their role in the collective effort if we're to have results. We need a holistic strategy that will get us back in the game as a harmonious team.

COLD VIOLENCE
Teju Cole

Not all violence is hot. There's cold violence too, which takes its
time and finally gets its way. Children going to school and coming
home are exposed to it. Fathers and mothers listen to politicians
on television calling for their extermination. Grandmothers have
no expectation that even their aged bodies are safe: any young
man may lay a hand on them with no consequence. The police
could arrive at night and drag a family out into the street. Putting
a people into deep uncertainty about the fundamentals of life,
over years and decades, is a form of cold violence. Through an
accumulation of laws rather than by military means, a particular
misery is intensified and entrenched. This slow violence, this cold
violence, no less than the other kind, ought to be looked at and
understood.

Near the slopes of Mount Scopus in East Jerusalem is the
neighbourhood of Sheikh Jarrah. Most of the people who live
here are Palestinian Arabs, and the area itself has an ancient
history that features both Jews and Arabs. The Palestinians of
East Jerusalem are in a special legal category under modern
Israeli law. Most of them are not Israeli citizens, nor are they
classified the same way as people in Gaza or the West Bank; they
are permanent residents. There are old Palestinian families here,
but in a neighbourhood like Sheikh Jarrah many of the people are
refugees who were settled here after the Nakba (Catastrophe) of
1948. They left their original homes behind, fleeing places such

as Haifa and Sarafand al-Amar, and they came to Sheikh Jarrah, which then became their home. Many of them were given houses constructed on a previously uninhabited parcel of land by the Jordanian government and by the UN Relief and Works Agency. East Jerusalem came under Israeli control in 1967, and since then, but at an increasing tempo in recent years, these families are being rendered homeless a second or third time.

There are many things about Palestine that are not easily seen from a distance. The beauty of the land, for instance, is not at all obvious. Scripture and travellers' reports describe a harsh terrain of stone and rocks, a place in which it is difficult to find water or to shelter from the sun. Why would anyone want this land? But then you visit and you understand the attenuated intensity of what you see. You get the sense that there are no wasted gestures, that this is an economical landscape, and that there is great beauty in this economy. The sky is full of clouds that are like flecks of white paint. The olive trees, the leaves of which have silvered undersides, are like an apparition. And even the stones and rocks speak of history, of deep time and of the consolation that comes with all old places. This is a land of tombs, mountains and mysterious valleys. All this one can only really see at close range.

Another thing one sees, obscured by distance but vivid up close, is that the Israeli oppression of Palestinian people is not necessarily – or at least not always – as crude as Western media can make it seem. It is in fact extremely refined, and involves a dizzying assemblage of laws and by-laws, contracts, ancient documents, force, amendments, customs, religion, conventions and sudden irrational moves, all mixed together and imposed with the greatest care.

The impression this insistence on legality confers, from the Israeli side, is of an infinitely patient due process that will eventually pacify the enemy and guarantee security. The reality, from the Palestinian side, is of a suffocating viciousness. The fate of Palestinian Arabs since the Nakba has been to be scattered and oppressed by different means: in the West Bank, in Gaza, inside the 1948 borders, in Jerusalem, in refugee camps abroad, in Jordan, in the distant diaspora. In all these places Palestinians experience restrictions on their freedom and on their movement. To be Palestinian is to be hemmed in. Some of this is done by brute military force from the Israel Defense Forces – killing for which no later accounting is possible – or on an individual basis in the secret chambers of the Shin Bet. But a lot of it is done according to Israeli law, argued in and approved by Israeli courts, and technically legal, even when the laws in question are bad laws and in clear contravention of international standards and conventions.

The reality is that, as a Palestinian Arab, in order to defend yourself against the persecution you face, not only do you have to be an expert in Israeli law, you also have to be a Jewish Israeli and have the force of the Israeli state as your guarantor. You have to be what you are not, what it is not possible for you to be, in order not to be slowly strangled by the laws arrayed against you. In Israel there is no pretence that the opposing parties in these cases are equal before the law; or, rather, such a pretence exists, but no one on either side takes it seriously. This has certainly been the reality for the Palestinian families living in Sheikh Jarrah, whose homes, built mostly in 1956, inhabited by three or four genera- tions of people, are being taken from them by legal means.

As in other neighbourhoods in East Jerusalem – Har Homa, the Old City, Mount Scopus, Jaffa Gate – there is a policy at work in Sheikh Jarrah. This policy is twofold. The first is the system- atic removal of Palestinian Arabs, either by banishing individuals on the basis of paperwork, or by taking over or destroying their homes by court order. Thousands of people have had their resi- dency revoked on a variety of flimsy pretexts: time spent living abroad, time spent living elsewhere in occupied Palestine, and so on. The permanent residency of a Palestinian in East Jerusalem is anything but permanent, and once it is revoked is almost impos- sible to recover.

The second aspect of the policy is the systematic increase of the Jewish populations of these neighbourhoods. This latter goal is driven both by national and municipal legislation (under the official rubric of 'demographic balance') and is sponsored in part by wealthy Zionist activists, who unlike some of their defenders in the Western world are proud to embrace the word *Zionist*. However, it is not the wealthy Zionists who move into these homes or claim these lands; it is ideologically and religiously extreme Israeli Jews, some of whom are poor Jewish immigrants to the state of Israel. And when they move in – when they raise the Israeli flag over a house that, until yesterday, was someone else's ancestral home, or when they begin new constructions on the rubble of other people's homes – they act as anyone would who was above the law: callously, unfeelingly, unconcerned about the humiliation of their neighbours. This twofold policy, of pushing out Palestinian Arabs and filling the land with Israeli Jews, is recognised by all the parties involved. And for such a policy the term *ethnic cleansing* is not too strong; it is in fact the only accurate description.

Each Palestinian family that is evicted in Sheikh Jarrah is evicted for different reasons. But the fundamental principle at work is usually similar: an activist Jewish organisation makes a claim that the land on which the house was built was in Jewish hands before 1948. There is sometimes paperwork that supports this claim (there is a lot of citation of nineteenth-century Ottoman land law), and sometimes the paperwork is forged, but the court will hear and, through eccentric interpretations of these old laws, often agree to the claim. The violence this legality contains is precisely that no Israeli court will hear a corresponding claim from a Palestinian family. What Israeli law supports, de facto, is the right of return for Jews into East Jerusalem. What it cannot countenance is the right of return of Palestinians into the innumerable towns, villages and neighbourhoods all over Palestine from which war, violence and law have expelled them.

History moves at great speed, as does politics, and Zionists understand this. The pressure to continue the ethnic cleansing of East Jerusalem is already met with pressure from the other side to stop this clear violation of international norms. So Zionist lawyers and lawmakers move with corresponding speed, making new laws, pushing through new interpretations, all in order to ethnically cleanse the land of Palestinian presence. And though Palestinians make their own case and though many young Jews, beginning to wake up to the crimes of their nation, have marched in support of the families evicted or under threat in Sheikh Jarrah, the law and its innovative interpretations evolve at a speed that makes self-defence all but impossible.

This cannot go on. The example of Sheikh Jarrah, the cold violence of it, is echoed all over Palestine. Side by side with this cold violence is, of course, the hot violence that dominates the news: Israel's periodic wars on Gaza, its blockades of places such as Nablus, the random unanswerable acts of murder in places such as Hebron. In no sane future of humanity should the deaths of hundreds of children continue to be accounted collateral damage, as Israel did in the summer of 2014.

In the world's assessment of the situation in Palestine, in coming to understand why the Palestinian situation is urgent, the viciousness of law must be taken as seriously as the cruelties of war. As in other instances in which world opinion forced a large-scale systemic oppression to come to an end, we must begin by calling things by their proper names. Israel uses an extremely complex legal and bureaucratic apparatus to dispossess Palestinians of their land, hoping perhaps to forestall accusations of a brutal land grab. No one is fooled by this. Nor is anyone fooled by the accusation, common to many of Israel's defenders, that any criticism of Israeli policies amounts to anti-Semitism. The historical suffering of Jewish people is real, but it is no less real than, and does not in any way justify, the present oppression of Palestinians by Israeli Jews.

A neighbourhood like Sheikh Jarrah is an X-ray of Israel at the present moment: a limited view showing a single set of features, but significant to the entire body politic. The case that is being made, and that must continue to be made to all people of conscience, is that Israel's occupation of Palestine is criminal. Nothing can justify either anti-Semitism or the racist persecution of Arabs, and the current use of the law in Israel is a part of the grave ongoing offence to the human dignity of both Palestinians and Jews.

THE CITY OF DAVID
Ghada Karmi

Silwan is a village that lies on the outskirts of East Jerusalem immediately to the south of the Old City walls. Until the war of 1967 it had been a quiet, rural place, unremarkable and much like any other in its vicinity. But when the victorious Israelis took over East Jerusalem in that war, Silwan's fortunes took a dramatic turn. It became the pivot and focus of an impassioned Israeli archaeological hunt for the biblical past. Religious Jewish settlers had associated it with the biblical King David, and from then on it was doomed. Israelis viewed archaeology as less a scholarly pursuit for its own sake than a battleground in which to promote Jewish history as they saw it, at the expense of any other kind. The imperative was to find proof of an ancient Jewish presence in Palestine's modern land that would show the world how justified, indeed how natural, was the modern Jewish desire to reconnect with those imagined Israelite ancestors the Bible spoke of in such realistic and concrete terms. If the evidence could be found, it would give their presence in Palestine a legitimacy they still felt they lacked.

Unluckily for Silwan, Hebrew legend identified it with the original site of Jerusalem at the time of King David. It was accordingly dubbed the City of David – Ir David in Hebrew. A particular focus of this Jewish settlement was the Bustan area at the northern end of the village, allegedly the site of the biblical Garden of the King, where supposedly David and Solomon walked. Israeli religious organisations, headed by the especially fanatical Elad, offered generous funding, thought to be from American sources, and spurred forward the archaeological excavations designed to validate the biblical claims to Silwan. The Israeli Department of Antiquities and the Jerusalem municipality gave these groups free rein with the aim of clearing Palestinian housing from village land up to the southern wall of the Old City to make room for a massive National Biblical Park for Jewish visitors and tourists. At the time of my visit a demolition order had been issued for eighty-eight Palestinian houses standing in the area designated for the national park. Their owners, desperate to have the order withdrawn, had managed to delay the decision for the time being. But it remained an imminent threat hovering over them like an executioner's sword. Israeli soldiers harassed them constantly with night raids and hold-ups at impromptu military checkpoints and, along with the settlers, kept up an unrelenting campaign of intimidation and attack.

Silwan is a hilly place with a deep central valley, its traditional white flat-roofed houses built picturesquely into the hillsides. Looking at them from above one could see in and amongst them the settler houses flying the blue and white Israeli flag, incongru-ous enclaves pointedly fenced off from their neighbours. To the right was a huge gash in the ground like a giant bomb crater. This was the major archaeological excavation site, where the search for biblical authenticity was conducted. It was massive, stretch-ing over an area of more than one acre and sinking to a depth of twenty metres; to my mind, the ground exposed by the excava-tion looked violated, as if it had been forced to yield up its entrails for inspection. The heat of the day having subsided, I could see several men at the bottom of the shaft working with chisels and hammers. Thick plastic sheeting roofed over parts of the site, and steps went down into it. My companion and I climbed down, led by an elderly Palestinian who offered us coffee. He greeted a thickset, fair-haired European-looking man, an Israeli archae-ologist I presumed, overseeing the Palestinian workers chiselling into the walls. Not a single Palestinian archaeologist was in sight, but I did not mention it and the Israeli obviously took me for a sympathetic visitor. I asked him what they were excavating.

'We're doing some important work on the Jewish heritage here,' he explained. His manner was pleasant and friendly, and he seemed to assume that I shared his views. 'You see these stone structures,' he said, blithely pointing to the largest which, according to what I had read, dated from the Roman period, 'they're almost certainly from the biblical age.' He must have known better, but chose to conceal it. 'We're connecting this dig with the tunnels under the southern end of the Temple Mount.' Israeli archaeologists had excavated a network of deep tunnels, which they found under the Haram al-Sharif (the Noble Sanctuary) in the area of the western wall and extending to the Via Dolorosa, against strong international protestations that such digs could undermine the foundations of the eighth-century Islamic buildings and the fourth-century Church of the Holy Sepulchre above; if not halted, they could ultimately lead to their collapse, they warned. A year or so earlier an UNRWA school in Silwan had partially fallen down because of the damage to its foundations caused by the digging. But nothing could be allowed to stop the archaeological search for the Jewish past.

As the excavations continued, any layers of history that came after the biblical age were demolished in the process of reaching back to it. Hellenistic, Roman, Byzantine and Islamic remains were cut through and forever lost to archaeology. The remnants of an eighth- to ninth-century Abbasid building were dismantled in this manner, and the tunnels uncovered by the excavations under the Old City walls passed beneath Roman, Crusader and Mamluk historical layers that no longer existed as a result. I pointed this out to the archaeologist. He shrugged. 'I don't know about that, but the search for truth must go on,' he said firmly. I pressed him further, making much the same point. But he remained confident of his position and serenely indifferent to what I had to say.

It was the same with the Israeli guide in the City of David tourist centre above ground, which had been built in the open area opposite to the excavation site and close to Silwan's ancient cistern, a source of water the villagers had used for centuries, but now renamed Jeremiah's Cistern. The guide, who was eager to tell us about the biblical marvels that had been unearthed, pointed to a structure labelled BATHSHEBA'S BATH. Did he really believe it was Bathsheba's bath? I asked. He nodded vigorously and indicated the tourist shop behind him with a broad sweep of his arm, as if the historical proof lay there; it contained a rich collection of biblical pamphlets, books on ancient Israel and posters of how the biblical park would look, once completed. 'This is where it all began,' he proclaimed proudly, 'from King David, all down the ages, and on to us today! Isn't it wonderful? When the digging is finished and the tunnels are all connected up, visitors will be able to go down and walk underground all the way from here to the Mount of Olives and to Mount Zion.' From his enthusiastic description, it seemed that an entire underground city was in the making to create the 'biblical experience', as he called it, and I had no doubt that, when completed, it would feel more real to the Jewish faithful who flocked there than the concrete Islamic structures on top. And perhaps that was the aim of the project.

Near to the Israeli tourist centre and standing bravely on its own was a small Arab shop, selling what it advertised as antiquities from the archaeological site. The shopkeeper showed me Roman coins with the emperor's head on one side, and claimed they were genuine. To my untrained eye they looked authentic enough; some had been mounted on gold frames to make tasteful articles of jewellery which he tried to sell me. There were cracked glass jars and broken pottery, all allegedly from the excavation site too, though how they had come into his possession was not clear. I felt sorry for him in his dusty, empty shop, and I doubted he did much business there.

What did the local people who watched their village being torn up and reshaped according to this historical Jewish fantasy think about it all? I wondered. From what I could see they had got used to it and went resignedly about their business, their main anxiety that the houses they lived in should escape demolition. Before leaving Silwan, I was taken to see a place in which just such a calamity had occurred, a rubble-strewn patch of ground where the house that had previously stood was bulldozed by the army. Groups of international volunteers sympathetic to Palestinian suffering were working to clear the area prior to helping the owner rebuild his house, although there was the constant danger that the authorities would demolish it again, as had happened repeatedly after many such brave endeavours. The owners of houses thus destroyed were usually required to pay the authorities for the costs of demolition.

Sometimes, driving along a beautiful road like the one going north from Ramallah as the sun was setting on the horizon, I would gaze at the long shadows of ancient trees slanting down onto the quiet hillsides and imagine how it must have been before anyone was here, before modern Israel and its soldiers and bulldozers arrived, before its settlers, religious zealots and military checkpoints disrupted that gentle harmony. In these imaginings I knew I was not alone; I had a rival in every religious Jew who saw the same landscape and fancied it came straight out of the Hebrew Bible, just as the Christian travellers who came to what they called the Holy Land thought themselves to be walking 'in the footsteps of Jesus'. It was Palestine's great misfortune that it fed so many fantasies and answered to so many emotional needs. For centuries people had pinned their dreams and delusions on its land, seen it as their salvation, and tried to make it exclusively their own. If only it had been an ordinary place, without a special history or a sacred geography, without religion or scripture, then perhaps we, its people, might have been left in peace.

The Writer's Job
William Sutcliffe

There can be no knowledge without emotion. We may
be aware of the truth, yet until we have felt its force, it is
not ours.

Arnold Bennett

In my study, within arm's reach, is a well-thumbed notebook,
every page covered with spidery, almost illegible handwriting. I
filled it during PalFest 2010, jotting down as many observations,
quotes and ideas as I had time to set down. But since the subject
of this essay is memory, I shall leave it where it sits. I want to
examine not what I experienced during that fortnight, six years in
the past, but what stays with me now, and why some experiences
can be shrugged off while others pinion themselves to your heart.

As anyone who has ever helped a child with homework
will attest: we remember what we understand, we forget what
confuses us. I knew immediately that PalFest had given me a revelatory, epiphanic understanding of a complex situation, but I only
grasped why it had affected me so deeply several years later, when
I stumbled across the above quotation from Arnold Bennett. My
thoughts had been far from the topic of Palestine at the time I
sat down to read, but those two sentences immediately sent me
back to spring 2010, to the West Bank. A profound 'YES!' surged
through me. This was a perfect description of the impact PalFest

had made on me. I instantly wrote it down and tried to commit the words to memory, savouring the sensation of a half-thought, half-grasped idea popping into focus, sharpened into acuity by another writer's wisdom.

This illustrates just one of the unique aspects of PalFest. Other literary festivals may be enjoyable or interesting but are unlikely to leave a lasting impact. After PalFest you can be sitting in a comfortable British living room, years after the event, reading about a Victorian writer, and a single line of prose will shoot you back in time and space to the visceral never-forgotten experience that only seconds earlier seemed a distant memory.

The word *unforgettable* has become a cliché we attach to any event that seems stirring or powerful, but much of what we describe as unforgettable is soon forgotten. Experiences that genuinely stick do so not simply because they have excited or moved us, but by touching something even deeper. The moments in life that sow the deepest roots are those which transform our understanding of the world or of ourselves. PalFest did both those things to me.

I thought I had a good understanding of the West Bank wall before flying out to Amman to join the PalFest 2010 group. The first draft of my novel *The Wall*, which at that point in time I intended to be loosely based on the barrier in the West Bank, was already well under way. I had researched the subject in depth, reading several books on the history of that vast structure, which has a different name for every opinion you have of it, from 'separation barrier' to 'apartheid wall'. I knew the statistics. I could reel off quickly that it was 525 kilometres long; that 85 per cent of it was inside Palestinian territory; that the concrete sections were 8 metres high, twice the height of the Berlin Wall; that it had cost $2.6 billion to build; that 35,000 Palestinians were trapped between the barrier and the Green Line. I had researched it in the way that novelists research things, which I thought gave me a decent understanding. I was pleased to be going, knowing this would give me access to deeper visual and atmospheric detail with which to describe a wall of this kind, but I had not accounted for what Donald Rumsfeld famously called 'unknown unknowns'. (It has always seemed strange to me that he was mocked for this statement, which may in fact have been the only intelligent thing he ever said. The pursuit of known unknowns, during which you stumble across unknown unknowns, is the very essence of research.)

Arnold Bennett's formulation crystallises precisely the 'unknown unknown' which was to strike me with such force that those ten days in Palestine would remain embedded permanently within me. In the simplest terms, I was to discover the difference between intellectual understanding and emotional understanding. I was to learn that when the latter crashes over you, the former splinters like a beach hut in a tsunami.

For a novelist in the middle of a researched novel to have his understanding of his subject shattered is no small thing, but the destruction of everything I thought I knew about my novel-in-progress was nothing compared to grasping for the first time a simple but devastatingly stark truth about the nature of oppression.

Nothing I had read about the injustices and cruelties of partitioned Hebron prepared me for the physical, emotional and intellectual impact of walking down the shuttered and abandoned high street of the old town under the gaze of Israeli soldiers and crowing settlers. No statistic gave me even a fraction of the understanding I took from standing in the narrow gap between eight metres of concrete and a dark, overshadowed Bethlehem home. No account of passing through a checkpoint compared to the experience of physically doing it myself. No words on any page or screen could come close to finding myself in a cafe chatting to a man describing what happened to him in an Israeli cell when he was arrested aged sixteen for stone-throwing. And when everyone you meet greets you with warmth and hospitality, before, if elicited, relating some other comparable tale of injustice, brutality and humiliation, the cumulative effect is overwhelming.

By the end, I knew my first draft of *The Wall* was destined for the dustbin, and I knew this was only a small part of the effect PalFest was to have on me. As a British citizen who could return to the comforts and privileges of a free society after what was only a short visit, I knew that my new-found comprehension of what it means to live under military occupation was sketchy and superficial compared to the reality of living an entire life under those conditions. I also knew it was infinitely deeper than everything I had gleaned from books and journalism. As Bennett puts it, 'there can be no knowledge without emotion'. You cannot truly know anything until you also feel it. PalFest gave me that emotional understanding, an understanding that has made a permanent imprint on my mental landscape.

One of the many spurious defences of Israel is that at any given time some other country (currently Syria, in 2010 it was Sri Lanka) is 'worse', and that if you are attacking Israel, instead of this other more egregiously unjust country, you must have picked Israel due to anti-Semitism.

My personal defence against this nonsensical but often-repeated argument, where being Jewish fails to prove the point, is that I feel impelled to think and talk and write about Israel because, in among all the other brutal injustices on our planet, this is one that I understand. Moreover, I can measure my limited comprehension of every other injustice by recognising how even the best journalism taught me only a fraction of what I needed to know to truly grasp the nature of the occupation.

To be invited to PalFest is a great blessing, one from which it took me many years to recover. PalFest was a humbling and viscerally memorable experience because in opening up new realms of knowledge and understanding to me, it also taught me how little we can really comprehend in one lifetime. It may well be that nothing is worth knowing quite so much as the knowledge of how little we can know. As a novelist, having the connection between emotion and understanding seared into my imagination was like an unplanned mid-career apprenticeship. I had to rethink everything. And that, after all, is the writer's job.

August 2016

GAZA, FROM THE DIASPORA – PART TWO

Jehan Bseiso

I
Today in Jabaliya, Khan Younis, in Rafah and Shujaiya,
we are still burying the dead we find, but the living ask:
wayn nrouh?
(where to now)
shu nsawwi?
(what to do now)
samidoun, which means we last.

II
Habeebi, today you reminded me we are under the same sky.
But nowhere refuge. Only refugees.
Skip breakfast with militias in Benghazi, have lunch in Homs
    under the rubble.
Leave your house in Mosul.
Leave your house in Mosul.
Leave your house in Mosul.
Three times in one week.
Take your body to Beirut, your heart still beating in Aleppo.
Take your body to Amman, your heart still beating in Gaza.
Escape.
Take the death boats from Egypt and Libya to Italy, leave
    your children on the shore.

III
Arab Offspring forecast is cloudy
with prospects of unseasonal paradigm shift.
I don't know politics but something about this brand of terror
    tastes like Burger King.
Take back your jihadis for hire.
Take back your F16s, your drones, your bombs from the sky
    in Iraq, in Libya, in Yemen.

IV
Dear Diaspora,
Maybe you have a good job.
You're happy.

You work with Pepsi.
You work at Memac and Ogilvy.
You don't know if they will close the Novartis head office in
    Beirut tomorrow because
another bomb went off.
You don't take cabs in Cairo anyway.
You don't want to move to Dubai like everybody.

V
Dear Diaspora,
boycott.
Don't sponsor occupation with your Jordanian dinars,
    dirhams, dollars and pounds sterling.

VI
Habeebi, I thought you lost my number, turns out you lost
    your legs
on the way to the hospital from Khan Younis to Jabaliya
    to Rafah.
The border is closed, but my heart tunnels.

EQUALITY, SUPREMACY AND SECURITY
Ed Pavlić

Since returning from the West Bank I've been tuned into the news, the news that stays news, and the news that isn't news at all. The top story in the *New York Times* one Wednesday in 2015 begins 'Israel and Hamas escalated their military confrontation on Tuesday . . .' Inches away, the World Cup story allows, 'The final score was Germany 7, Brazil 1. It felt like Germany 70, Brazil 1.' The juxtaposition of balance on the one hand and the exaggeration of how unbalanced the World Cup rout felt on the other is too close to ignore. It's worth tracing its contours in our media, in our minds and in our lives.

I know. It's the oldest of old hats to note the distended shapes American journalism creates to preserve the Israel-first false impression of some symmetry or parity between interests and powers in the contested territory split, shared and struggled over by people known as Palestinians and Israelis. Even the names are disputed. Many Palestinians would refute the idea of Israelis and simply say Jews. Many Israelis have contended that, in fact, there is no Palestinian people. It's territory – rhetorical, ethical, religious, ethnic and geographic – so complexly, at times hideously contested that many people in the West, certainly in the US, simply look away. As a person who, since childhood, has lived a life athwart American racial codes and territories, I've always kept an eye on Israel/Palestine for the focused, if challenging, clarity it can offer one's perspective on American experience.

That might sound strange. But it's true. In a recent tour with the Palestine Festival of Literature, in fact I found much clarified.

This clarity is not complete, of course. It's based on my own observations as well as conversations with people such as Ray Dolphin from the United Nations Office for the Coordination of Humanitarian Affairs (UNOCHA), Dr Tawfiq Nasser, director of the Augusta Victoria Hospital in East Jerusalem, and Omar Barghouti, founding member of the Palestinian Campaign for the Academic and Cultural Boycott of Israel (BDS). While touring the region, I was also reading, widely and variously and, at times, all night long (jet lag), James Baldwin's letters (one from Israel) published in *Harper's* in 1963, Etel Adnan's incomparable two-volume *To look at the sea is to find what one is* (2014), Sarah Schulman's great memoir of (Jewish-American) political re-awakening *Israel/Palestine and the Queer International* (2012), the report *East Jerusalem: Key Humanitarian Concerns* (2011) and the *Humanitarian Atlas* (2012) put out by the UNOCHA, and the *Legal Unit Annual Report* (2013) from the Hebron Rehabilitation Committee. The HRC recorded over 600 violations of Palestinian human rights during the calendar year 2013. They're very thorough. The report contains month-by-month charts in which each violation has its entry. Incidents are tabulated by category: against people, against property, by settlers, by Israeli soldiers. This daily array of violence presents, for one, a background I've yet to see appear in the American media reporting the abduction and murder near Hebron (in Arabic al-Khalil) of three Jewish teenagers in June 2015.

There's active and latent anger and violence everywhere in the region. But, according to these sources, even in so-called Palestinian territory (occupied by and often under the control of Israeli military personnel), there's absolutely no parity in the legal, military and social contests between Israeli power and Palestinian struggle. One is a contemporary bureaucratic state whose legal system vigorously operates to sustain and increase its hold on geographic territory and is possessed of a cornucopia of surveillance and weapons systems to back it up. The other is a disparate array of factionalised, anti-colonial resistance that uses smuggled and home-built weapons when not employing such high-tech systems as slingshots and cutlasses or simply throwing stones. Simply put, there's no contest here.

Looking around, say, at the closed-off, shut-down and vacant business district in Hebron, Shuhada Street, or at the scorched guard tower and murals of martyred and imprisoned Palestinian leaders at the Qalandia checkpoint in East Jerusalem, Baby Suggs' comment from Toni Morrison's *Beloved* rang in my ears: 'Lay down your sword. This ain't a battle; it's a rout.' Staring at children at play in the Hebron streets under the shadow of iron bars and barbed wire and under the watch of Israeli guards with machine guns, or, just down the street from there, staring at armed soldiers, near-children themselves, deep in so-called Palestinian territory at yet another checkpoint, this one stencilled with a mural: FREE ISRAEL, I heard June Jordan's visions in 'Requiem for the Champ' of Brownsville, Brooklyn in the 1980s: 'This is what it means to fight and really win or really lose. War means you hurt somebody, or something, until there's nothing soft or sensible left.'

Let's stipulate that the Palestinian Authority does its best. But the reality is that the PA is, at best, superintendent to Israel's occupation. The people know it; many resent it. At bottom they work for the landlord. They're in dialogue with Baby Suggs. Hamas, meanwhile, newly beset again now by el-Sisi's rule in Egypt and contested within Gaza by even more militant factions, seems to be playing out the gambit June Jordan observed in the blasted-out Brooklyn blocks of the 1980s. At the core of the Palestinian struggle, however, is the fundamental – not to say universal – urge that the Israeli/Jewish people – from their point of view, the oppressor – will not lead normal lives while Palestinians live in cages of restrictions made of law, concrete and razor wire, and very often watched over by men with machine guns.

That Palestinian aim, in fact, isn't foreign to an American sensibility, not at all; it's incoherently twisted deep in the core of what America is supposed to afford people ('freedom') while at the same time it's there at the crux of what the United States has inflicted on subordinate, mostly non-white, populations of people, within and beyond its borders since before it existed and until today.

This is the basis of the disturbing power of clarity the situation in Palestine/Israel confronts an American viewer with. When and if, that is, one is allowed a glimpse. This is why the American media operate in the way they do, and it's at the heart of why most Americans look away. In order to admit the most basic, blatant facts in the one situation – and exactly to the degree one finds a home in the American 'mainstream' (itself an incoherently contested mythology), or 'dream' – people would need to give up or radically adjust primary illusions about the country in which they live: 'individual achievement', 'equality of opportunity', 'an open society', etc. In short, clarity about Palestine destroys the mainframe illusions of American whiteness, no matter the colour of the person who aspires to it. No wonder Palestinians identify to the extent that they do, and they do, with the African-American freedom struggle and with the history of American Indian quarantine and displacement in the US.

Back from Palestine, I found myself re-engaged with the psychological gymnastics of contemporary life wherein media images of LeBron James' free agency and Neymar's fractured vertebra butt up against gruesome political and social intensities – massacres in Coastal Kenya, eighty-two shootings and fourteen dead in Chicago over 4 July and, of course, renewed warfare in the West Bank and Gaza – as well as duties such as teaching my five-year-old to ride a bike in the parking lot across the street. The struggle is to keep some semblance of perspective and proportion.

So it was on Wednesday morning that I found myself reading aloud to my wife Stacey from front-page stories in the *New York Times* as she got ready for work. One story frankly depicts Germany's rout of Brazil, 7–1, from Tuesday 8 July plain enough. Another though, just inches apart on the page, frames conflict between forces in Gaza and Israel as a 'military' contest of some plausible parity. ISRAEL AND HAMAS TRADE ATTACKS AS TENSION RISES reads the headline over a photo of a sizeable explosion in an urban era. The silent suggestion in the headline being that the photo could be from either an Israeli or Hamas attack. Is that really possible? Is it plausible? Do Palestinians have a 'military' at all? One report in the article ominously held that one Hamas-launched rocket made it almost seventy miles into Israeli territory. No mention was made of exactly what kind of navigation/aiming system those rockets use and what kind of explosives are attached. The previous evening, CNN's Erin Burnett interviewed Israel's Ambassador to the US, who described the near-total precision of Israeli strategic capabilities. His description served at once as assurance about limited 'collateral damage' and also as a bold declaration of unassailable Israeli power. The ambassador's interview stood alone as CNN's report on the increasing violence that evening. The scorekeeping continued. In the war.

After the jump to page 8 in the *Times*, about the 'military confrontation', we're told, 'Israeli military said . . . that more than 150 rockets had been fired at Israel.' Meanwhile, the military reports that 'Israel hit some 150 targets' in Gaza. So, at a glance, it's a tie?

No scorecard was offered for how many targets, if any, in Israel were actually hit. One guesses that, had there been hits, we'd know. Later in the story, confirming the ambassador's comments as to Israeli accuracy or not, we're told that targets hit in Gaza included, 'five senior Hamas officials, ten smuggling tunnels, 90 concealed rocket launchers, and 18 weapons storage and manufacturing sites'. That's 123. No mention of the other 27 hits in Gaza. No mention of how many firings were required to hit 123 targets. Elsewhere in the article the tie score diverges – 'Palestinian officials said that at least 23 people were killed in Gaza on Tuesday' – while Israel reports 'two people were wounded in rocket attacks on Monday' though it doesn't say exactly how these injuries occurred or note their severity. If you're willing to actually follow the news out of the region in American media, these are the kinds of feigned attempts at balance that portray an evenly matched 'military' struggle on the one hand and, on the other, assure that one side has the unassailable upper hand and, of course, the unquestioned right to secure its territory.

So it is that equality, supremacy and security all go together. Just don't try it at home, these are trained professionals at work. Even so, exactly the same thing is happening at home, which is the whole point. Middle- and upper-class Americans are assured that everyone's equal in the eyes of the system; meanwhile they insist that their privileges and comforts (supremacy) are secure and that their right to safety is ensured.

When it comes to sports we're free to feel the elasticity of the facts in pursuit of deeper truths – 7 to 1 felt like 70 to 1, we say, adding that 'it wasn't as close as the score suggests'. Such elasticity is delightful. No wonder why ESPN is what it's become. Inches away, however, a story about an occupying power (one in violation of scores of international laws and accepted rules controlling political occupations) is told in ways that pre-empt and even invert a reader's freedom to extend the facts into coherent feelings in order to understand the world. That elasticity is dangerous.

When it comes to Israel and Palestine, for Americans it doesn't matter if the careful phrases contradict the most basic facts or if numerical equivalences depict 'military' parity in one paragraph and describe unassailable supremacy in the next all the while affirming a people's (one can't but think, 'all people's'?) unquestionable right to security. No one's looking that closely. They can't. Close examination of Israel's relationship to the Palestinians under their control, its quest for simultaneous supremacy, security and the semblance of democracy or equality, would reveal more than Americans are willing to admit about our own towns, schools, states and the filmy mythology that coats – whether with security or numbness no one investigates too far – our experiences of our own and each other's lives.

A Gift for PalFest

Alice Walker

On my website alicewalkersgarden.com, where this poem appears, there is a picture of a small child's smashed and bloody shoe. Beneath the poem there are photographs of children who were murdered by Israeli soldiers, one of them in a church. Also there is a picture of Chief Joseph, the Native American holy man and wisdom carrier of his people who were massacred by the US military and forced from their homes and lands so that immigrants from they knew not where could 'settle' the beloved valleys and hills where they had lived for hundreds of years. There is also a photograph of Emmett Till, a black boy brutally murdered when he was fourteen years old by grown white men who then threw his mutilated body into a river. The killing of children is especially heinous, hard to bear, difficult to fathom. It is occurring now in rates so astonishing as to make all of us wonder who so-called 'humans' actually are.

One thing is certain: the one who murders a child may be called many things, including 'patriot', but he or she will never be called beautiful.

THEY WILL ALWAYS BE MORE BEAUTIFUL THAN YOU

They will always be
More beautiful
Than you
The people you are killing.
You think it is hatred
That you feel
But it is really envy.
You imagine if you destroy them

We will forget

How tall they stood
How level
Their gaze
How straight their backs.
How even the littlest ones
Stood their little ground.

Meanwhile
You stand
Hunched as a cobbler
In your absurd
Killer's Gear
Yelling
Like a crazy person,
Your face contorted
Dripping sweat
From what would be
With or without
Your lethal weapons
A bullying brow
And feral chin.

Killing everyone
but especially children,
For sport.

Looking cool
In your own mind;
As you crunch bones
Beneath your boot
That are still
Forming.

Conquering.

II

Don't forget the entertainment value

Of your daily work
For the folks back home.
Who witness from the hillsides
In their lounge chairs.

What beautiful fun!

We are not like
Those people being broken
Over there
They tell each other. And for this moment
They are right.
They are not.

But what does this mean
For broken humanity?

Selfie this.

Silence Is a Language
Jeremy Harding

A bunch of (mainly) British writers, guests of PalFest, have been asked to run workshops for the students at Birzeit University. I'm paired up with Robin Yassin-Kassab. Our workshop title is 'The role of writing in creating new political realities'. OK. Something about change then. Yassin-Kassab is a novelist; he knows what it is to ring the changes. I'm a journalist; I know how to change an inkjet cartridge. We both agree that polemic tends to lock 'old' political realities in place, so why not turn this into an experiment about making a point without banging a drum?

The majority of our students, between twenty or thirty people, are enrolled in the English Department. (The political science students have opted for other workshops, among them a packed session on Guantánamo.) All except one are women. Many are wearing hijab. Soon it emerges that most speak good English. We introduce ourselves and Robin says a few words about stories, lyrics, film scripts, rap and YouTube. About speed of transmission, low costs, ubiquity of access. About the way that anyone can have a hearing; all they need to do is to get the content right.

The students divide into groups and prepare a piece about the situation in Gaza since Operation Cast Lead (2008–9): a text, a song, a scenario, a poem, a dialogue, an outline for a story, anything. No opinion about the assault, or open condemnation of it, is allowed. I've already steeled myself for the question 'You mean like the BBC?' and the terse laughter that's sure to follow, but it turns out the students are too polite for that, and before we know it one of the groups has sailed out of the lecture theatre to rehearse in the corridor. Another asks if they can perform a mime. This is about language, I say. 'We believe that silence is a language,' a young woman replies.

Another group has come up with an ambitious draft for an epic movie: they've already packed scores of refugees from around the world onto a bus – this could soon need David Lean or Richard Attenborough. It's a global perspective – no polemic! – that casts the plight of the Palestinians as part of a bigger story. 'Uzbekis too!' says a young woman in a fawn head-scarf, determined not to use the P-word. They're jolting along a mountain pass somewhere in northern Anatolia, and we're looking at our watches. They've got five more minutes.

When time's called, each of the seven groups presents its work to the others. The mime group is intriguing. Three students are on stage. A rucksack is hurled onto the ground in front of them. They study it, withdraw, approach again with care; they look as if they're about to sing to it but instead all three kneel and start to write on it, gingerly at first, and then with more confidence; they're scrawling frenetically when the rucksack detonates.

The actors explain this mystery by saying that the rucksack should be seen as something originating in Israel that's come the way of Palestinians: it could be a 'peace' initiative, say, or a description of their own identity and history that they don't recognise. However seriously they try to take it, respond to it or make a mark of their own on it, it's sure to go off in their faces. The other groups, who've enjoyed the minimalism of the piece, don't seem to need the explanation: it's for Robin and me.

These raw presentations were worked up in roughly fifteen minutes; some contained the kind of detail you'd only expect to come with the finishing touches. What if we'd had more time? But time in the West Bank is eaten up by the Byzantine demands of the occupation, which interfere with everything, including sitting final exams – any moment now. The rucksack, I notice, as the owner shrugs it onto her back, is full to capacity.

2009

The sound system has gone into attack mode. Every time one of my students reaches towards the middle of the table for the biscuits, there is a peal of thunder from the speaker in the ceiling, followed by the sound of supersize rats in a warehouse full of tinfoil. The conversation comes to a halt for a moment, but the students are oblivious: this is a video conference. I'm in a building in Ramallah and they're fifty miles away in Gaza, with the biscuits in front of them and Israel in between. The sessions have been put together by the Palestine Writing Workshop, a project supported by PalFest. The workshops happen once or twice a year. I'm here to take part in editing and non-fiction sessions. (Non-fiction means journalism, and a bit of memoir: we look at a few models and build from there.) Most of the students are in their twenties; some are doing similar workshops in Arabic, when they're available; others use the workshops to sharpen their English. This is the second year we've tried a video link to Gaza. This year, thanks to the British Council's facilities, it's no longer as though we're shouting into two tin cans joined by a long piece of string.

A session about images: Y, a journalist, has sent a picture of a blue sky, streaked with cirrus cloud and inscribed with a white arabesque that corkscrews from right to left. From the print I've made of the jpeg it might just be a painting. The image, it transpires, is a photograph and Y wrote about it in February: the photo and her text appeared on the website of *Target*, an alternative outlet for film-makers and journalists covering the Middle East. In Gaza, she writes, 'people keep talking of a new war . . . About two weeks ago, I saw what looked to me like a confused Israeli pilot flying around in his F16, drawing circles in the sky. People immediately took it as

171

a threat and a signal that war was coming. They even made up memories . . . and were convinced that on 27 December 2008, an Israeli jet, possibly even the same one, drew the same circles in the sky, and that was when war started . . . Well, congratulations Israel for winning the psychological war on Gaza.' This is the second reference, in the time we've spent together on this link, to the confinement and killing of Palestinians in Gaza. The first was from A, who wrote a stoical piece about Operation Cast Lead, quoting a remark by his little brother that the best thing about these terrible days was the splurge of meat-eating. Once the grid was down, all provisions, frozen or refrigerated, had to be eaten before they rotted.

Last year, when Birzeit put up the workshop link to Gaza and several participants aired their memories of the Israeli offensive, the fury was full on. There's a sense of narrative distance now. It's not that things have 'moved on' for this year's participants; more that there's been a kind of packing down. The ground feels firmer and the writing is freer to roam across it without falling into a bomb crater. The workshop term for this is 'consolidation': it's what people do when they're staying put, biding their time.

2011

DRAWING PALFEST

Muiz

A picture may be worth a thousand words, but there is no comparative metric to experiencing something first hand.

At sixteen years old my identity had already been the subject of debate on a global scale in a post-9/11 world, so much so that I would purchase every major newspaper title each morning on my way to school, in part for information but more so to explore the variability a single story would manifest in the headlines or reportage. It was my introduction not only to the power of language but, more importantly, the image.

This propelled me to explore ways of introducing Palestine to a wider audience within my final art exam piece. It would be judged not by my professor of seven years, but by an external examiner whom I would never meet. The piece was a twist on Michelangelo's iconic pietà, with the ivory-white marble replaced with a black cloth draped over a Christendom-like arch, which was then wreathed around the clay-sculpted head and hands of a faceless mother. In her hands lay the limp body of a chicken-wire child, bandaged completely in a pure white shroud made of gauze. The photo of an Israeli soldier, whose outstretched hand nearly eclipsed the photographer's lens, was printed onto an exhibition stand and placed in front of the artwork, to both distance the viewer from the piece and block a clear view of it.

By recontextualising an icon of Western art and culture with a narrative often typified by 'other' and orientalised language and imagery, I managed to bridge an emotional connection to the situation in Palestine with those who had never heard of it, so much so that the entire faculty of my school came to see it. My initial concern with this attention was calmed by reassuring handshakes for producing something that had sparked a debate among them. A more extreme reaction to my work was by another art student, whose work was exhibited on a wall directly opposite to mine, who, while I was in the room, decided to deface his own abstract art piece by graffitiing a giant yellow star of David over it.

I was awarded the highest grade possible, 100 per cent, and for me this became not only a first-hand experience of validating the power of the image but, more crucially, the importance of maintaining a level of integrity and conviction in your authorship, no matter the perceived odds against you.

THE PERSONAL IS POLITICAL

Five years later someone retweeted about @PalFest successfully delivering a shipment of books into Gaza through the British Council. This instantly piqued my interest, as most proclamations of shipments to Palestine that I'd encountered were related to food or charity, and as such were fleeting.

I tracked down PalFest's email address and offered to supply more academic books via my university for any future shipments. They assured me that none were needed, but having noticed my email signature told me they needed a designer. The following year, after custom-designing and art-directing their marketing materials, I embarked with PalFest on my first trip to occupied Palestine.

My first artwork for the PalFest campaign used deconstructed typography of the full festival name in both English and Arabic as a way to announce our existence to both the country and the world. The letters were created using fragmented geometric shapes, each word a different tonal colour from the national flag. I was fascinated by the interpretations people drew from the work, especially by the differences between those of the international and diaspora writers and those of our Palestinian audience. This further asserted the power of the image – that something as deceptively simple as coloured shapes could trigger such significant variability of relatable thought and therefore resonate beyond its base use as an advertisement.

I also established lifelong relationships in this time – from the local student tour guide who assumed I was a stray student from the university and demanded to know what I was doing alone on the festival tour bus, to my delaying a tour of Nablus because the two volunteer guides had assumed they'd been replaced when they saw me talking about the city with our writers while we waited.

Those six days were a life-changing experience that both built and broke me. It is the country where I fell in love. It was and always will be home.

ALL ART IS POLITICAL

All art is political because those who create art are governed by it, as is every space that that art may occupy once it is created. So in a country where your birth, existence and even your death is a political act, I understood that PalFest and – more importantly – our audience in Palestine would not benefit from nor appreciate further politicisation of their private spaces by my design work. They are all too aware of the visceral realities of the colonisation and cancerous occupation of Palestine and its unrelenting suffocation of every aspect of their every day.

Graphic design, or visual communication, is not only the process of effectively articulating a message to an intended audience, but understanding the impact of how it is delivered and its legacy.

The Palestinians in Palestine need not be lionised, nor do they need to be pitied or preached at. They are people, just like us; it is their dignity and creativity in the face of the brutal threat of oblivion that makes them exceptional and inspirational. They too need respite to reconnect their hearts and minds to beauty, happiness and laughter.

Nowhere was this better reflected in our design work than when I created the campaign for PalFest's Gaza debut. The work featured the city's name rendered in a traditionally cursive, elegant Arabic calligraphic script, which erupted with olive-laden branches. The pride and emotional subtext of the piece proved so popular that we had to print twice as many posters because they were being taken down by passers-by as keepsakes within hours of being put up around the city.

By reflecting and reinforcing what was inspiring about our audience in Gaza, we refused to imprison and traumatise their imagination and self-image the way Israel has their bodies. When existence is resistance, then every facet of Palestine, from the cuisine, the language, the fashion, the ceramics to the architecture, can and have become politicised. What purpose, then, is a design that would continue to scratch at the open wound of a siege and decades of massacres when aimed at a community experiencing and surviving them?

We've continued to subvert expectations in our work just as the Palestinians subvert the expectations of their colonisers, reflecting our hosts' playfulness and ingenuity in our campaign visuals and poster artwork. I'm honoured our work continues to be so well received by our family and friends there each year, and hope that we will celebrate and honour them in a free Palestine.

Diary

Deborah Moggach

Literary festivals are where writers go to whinge. Not to the audience, if they've got any sense – why should the paying public feel sorry for people who don't have to commute to work every day or deal with a ghastly boss?

But get writers together backstage and they're off. They moan about their agents and their editors and not seeing their books in bookshops and not getting on *Start the Week* and only getting one review in the *Daily Express* – of all newspapers. They moan about literary festivals themselves. About travelling all day to be greeted by an audience of three and a dog, about not getting a fee and being snubbed by a more famous author who's snaffled the last glass of wine, and of being put up in a B & B with nylon sheets and tinned tomatoes for breakfast.

How writers moan! Not realising how deeply privileged we are compared to most of humanity. For we are so very lucky – not just as authors, but as human beings. How comfortable and free our lives are, and how much we take for granted! And nothing could throw this into greater relief than travelling to Palestine, where the lives of writers are astonishingly hard. But then so are the lives of everybody else.

I went there with PalFest back in 2009. It was its second year of celebrating, in Edward Said's words, 'the power of culture over the culture of power'. The fifteen other writers included Michael Palin, Claire Messud, Jamal Mahjoub, Abdulrazak Gurnah, the late Henning Mankell and the dazzling poet/performer Suheir Hammad.

We travelled in from Jordan. After being held for five hours at the checkpoint we arrived in East Jerusalem for our first event, at the Palestinian National Theatre. The audience was just sitting down when armed police barged in and ordered us all out. Despite our protests that we were hardly a dangerous bunch ('Oh I don't know,' whispered Palin. 'Far too many people were crossing their legs.') we found ourselves outside on the street, where the French came to our rescue and offered us an alternative venue. So we picked up the plates of food and walked through the streets to the French Cultural Centre garden, where we started the whole thing all over again, with eight police cars parked in the street outside. Dangerous things, poetry readings.

So began our Kafkaesque journey into the West Bank, a journey punctuated by checkpoints where teenage Israeli soldiers smoked in our faces and disembodied Israeli voices ordered us through holding pens like cattle in an abattoir, where the high, hideous concrete wall sliced through communities, cutting off farmers from their land and children from their schools, a barrier which was graffiti'd with paintings of trees and the pitiful CAN I HAVE MY BALL BACK? For a newcomer, the brutality was hard to comprehend, for however much you read about something, nothing prepares you for the reality.

The next evening, in Ramallah, we listened to Suad Amiry. She's an architect but has written a hilarious best-seller called *Sharon and My Mother-in-law,* about the absurdities of everyday life in the occupied territories. She talked most eloquently about the disconnections of time and geography in a place where the journey to Nablus, which should take an hour, can take all day. She told us how time is measured by curfews and checkpoints, themselves so arbitrary that people are constantly disorientated and can rely on nothing. Where roads are constantly blocked, disappeared and reinvented. Where everything conspires to obliterate certainties and instil a low thrum of fear and humiliation. Where you can never, ever, simply get on with your life.

(If you want to see this thrilling woman in action, log on to her TED talk.) The only way to cope, she says, is through laughter; it's the only thing left.

We were blown away by meeting her, and she was the first of many. As the days passed we travelled around in our bus, stopping at various towns, where we met students, did workshops and readings, listened to poets and musicians, talked for hours and ate delicious food. Everywhere we were given the warmest of welcomes and were astonished by the courage, humour and resilience of those we met. 'We don't have the luxury of despair,' one man told me.

One memorable afternoon Raja Shehadeh, whose book *Palestinian Walks* is an elegy to a lost landscape, took us for a walk through the Ramallah hills, now designated Zone C, which meant we all could be arrested. It's the most beautiful biblical landscape, filled with wild flowers and the occasional tortoise, which wisely carries its own tank on its back. There was a surreal moment when Michael Palin told me about being crucified in *The Life of Brian*. They all had little bicycle seats to sit on when on their crosses. The real thing happened, of course, only a few miles away.

This ancient landscape is now blighted by illegal Israeli settlements: huge concrete blocks of flats sitting on the tops of the hills, dominating the countryside and built so the occupants have no sight or connection with the local people living below. The roads to them are forbidden to Palestinians. In the past, we were told, there was more interaction between Israelis and Palestinians, but now they are so separated that it has become easier for the occupied population to be demonised – faceless people can so quickly become the enemy.

Not only are the Palestinians cut off from the future; they're cut off from the past. In the Aida refugee camp in Bethlehem, a few days later, a youth-club worker told us how he had managed to take some children out of the occupied territories and behind the Green Line into Israel, to visit the lost family villages they had never seen, which their parents had never seen, and how they filled plastic bottles with fresh spring water to take back to their grandparents, who hadn't set foot in their homes for sixty years.

Our last visit was to Hebron, an ancient and beautiful town where Israeli settlers have actually moved into the centre, taking over the upper floors of the buildings above the bazaar, which over the past few years has slowly been throttled by intimidation and lack of access. There were 101 checkpoints in the city, and many places are now unreachable due to roadblocks. Outside the mosque only two Palestinian shops remained. In one the old man burst into tears when talking to us. 'I shall never leave,' he said, while the Settler Centre opposite blared out nationalist Zionist songs, drowning out the call to prayer from the mosque. An old and enduring way of life is slowly being exterminated by this ethnic cleansing.

The only people who could walk freely were the settlers, who had four security guards to every person and strolled around with large dogs. One of them was filming us. When asked why, he replied, 'I'm filming for God.' When we asked, 'What sort of God would permit this?' he replied, 'God wants me to photograph you so you can go to hell.'

When we returned to East Jerusalem for our final event we found the theatre closed again, and we had to decamp to the British Council garden. After only seven days this seemed perfectly normal.

I can hardly describe the horrors of what is going on. It reduced many of us to tears, and of course the situation has deteriorated since then. As we left I thought of my favourite *New Yorker* cartoon. Two men are walking away from the crucifixion. One says to the other, 'Why don't we just put this behind us and move on?'

2009

UNTIL IT ISN'T
Remi Kanazi

death becomes exciting
tolls, pictures, videos
tweeting carnage
instagramming collapse
hearts racing to break

24-hour entertainment
every glimpse, splinter
and particle of pain
jammed into torsos
and cheekbones

loved ones
want to sit
for a minute
and cry quietly

no words, no poetry
before Internet and
dialled-up emotions
before black and
white ideologies

before a person
        I called friend
        defended massacres
before the victims
        were laid to rest
before chemical weapons
        ravaged insides
before refugee
        meant grandmother

suffering 2.0
keyboard clicks
like bombs so effortlessly
                dropping

all damage collateral

never personal
voyeurs hop on and off
like carnival rides

death becomes
            exciting
until it isn't
until boredom sets in
and desensitisation begins
until the next ride emerges
            somewhere else
            more captivating

SIGHT

Ru Freeman

It takes seven hours to cross a few hundred yards into occupied Palestine. We are the last ones left in the empty waiting room tiled so smooth it turns my mind to dance. Someone finds music on his iPhone and I stand up, defying the odds.

In Ramallah we sit under a slivered new moon, a venue so open it holds everybody and no late arrival disturbs. Our readers speak of Guantánamo and Palestine. A child peers down over a high wall, holding his father's safe-keeping hand, listening.

There is an American-city edge to the bar we sit in, late. Arrack, licoriced, slightly sweet, intoxication growing within, undetected, like the place itself. 'Fever' plays on the sound system, chosen by a man who designs T-shirts. I buy one for twenty dollars, black, its red declaration: I AM A CITIZEN OF THE EARTH, THOUGH I HAVE NO COUNTRY.

A Palestinian friend says, 'Ramallah has three bars, but we Bethlehemites can pretend we aren't occupied.' Enigma: Bethlehem lies broken into pieces like candied brittle. We have learned to navigate shards.

Time is made of elasticity and imagination. Will I ever forget dancing to 'Rock Around the Clock' in the waiting room of the

Allenby Bridge crossing, risking everything for an act of defiance? That, instead of speaking of hunger and fear, we spoke of how my seventy-year-old partner did not want to dance without proper heels in front of the handsome older man in our group?

O Palestine. How quickly we learned to wrest joy out of denial. How swift, this transformation from righteous indignation to acknowledging the euphoria of the allowable moment.

———

In Qalandia, between steel bars, funnelled like consumer products off to the next destination for packaging and bar codes, we suppress everything except our laughter at the discombobulated voice floating down from the manacled watchtower: 'No pictures! I saw one picture!' I hand out mints on the other side and celebrate us, we who have taken more than two hundred pictures in that crossing.

Armed soldiers idle outside the oldest library in Jerusalem, where the Khalidi family patriarch speaks proudly of his ancestors. He omits nothing.

Inside the Church of the Holy Sepulchre we place palms over the stone where Jesus is said to have been embalmed. Around us, doors, crosses, an extravagance of windows above beckoning stone paths.

At night the streets fall silent. An eerie lustre pervades this sacred place. The pink and yellow walls rise, containing.

———

In the old city of al-Khalil/Hebron the occupation is relentlessly evident. New plaques on renamed streets announce fictions that permit desecration. Checkpoints are as ordinary as red lights. We examine this new normal: to require a permit for any journey;

186

to have your home demolished and then be forced to pay the demolisher to remove the debris; to rebuild, then, in anticipation of demolition, take a hammer to your own roof and salvage the possible; to circumnavigate a wall for seven miles to make a half-mile trip; to have filth thrown on your head as you walk down romantic cobbled streets that in any European town would be where bright cafes spring up.

Safe passage means quiescence. So you take pictures: of vine leaves in bunches, pickled vegetables; children jostling to see themselves on your camera; the curved road of shuttered shops with their pretty green and blue doors – now sealed with chains, wrought-iron balconies in disrepair; four American teenagers on a 'birthright' trip, sipping Coke and laughing on the porch that once belonged to a Palestinian, while soldiers patrol, and settlers with machine guns drive too fast or pace the silent roads.

The call to prayer rises over the heads of soldiers and barricades, cuts through checkpoints, fills every trench and barrel, slips through the bars of rusty gates and coils of barbed wire that are supposed to block and exclude, wraps around the rubble and ruins of pale pink rock, collects each shard of glass in its embrace.

You think of God.

Al-Khalil/Hebron. Fifteen hundred soldiers guard four hundred illegal settlers. Watchtowers point in four directions above Palestinian homes, the muzzles of cocked rifles. Water barrels on Palestinians' roofs riddled from the gunfire of settlers. Ahead, a road carves through the home of a Palestinian family. 'We did not destroy it,' the soldiers say. 'See, it is still intact.'

Everywhere the twenty-five-foot-high wall stretches, hooded in sharp angles over roads, bridges, tunnels. I imagine setting fire at one end. Like an incendiary Andy Goldsworthy installation of land art, I want to watch its 650 kilometres implode in orderly flames. The left ash would settle into the earth releasing us to grieve.

The stage in Haifa is set up like an open-air political podium, bare and stark. A rostrum and mike. Beyond it an amphitheatre. A table on the side with food and drink. A young woman sings ballads in Arabic, which are always about love, longing, home and freedom. I listen in translation: 'The stabs of daggers are better than the rule of the treacherous.'

Despite missing pages, a replacement translator and lights so blinding I cannot see the words before me, I read of recognisable things: family and revolution. We make the best of whatever remains.

There is a comic madness to the term *present absentee*, coined to define 335,204 Palestinians who live in what is called Israel but not in their original homes, which have been confiscated. If numbers are measured by Israeli textbooks – whose maps omit Gaza and the West Bank – that number would be five million. Palestinians return the favour: they pretend not to see the settlers and soldiers, denying the oppressor his validity.

There are ghosts who walk among ghosts here, and we are visitors wading through the thicknesses of fiercely held history.

Like this: the Hilton Hotel rises above Palestinian graves in the Abd al-Nabi Cemetery in Jaffa, and the Wadi Hunayn Mosque in Ramla is now a synagogue. Israel's Museum of Tolerance is being built over Palestine's Mamilla Cemetery. Those claiming there were no people on a barren land preserve the home of the Abu Kaheel family in Sheikh Muwannis; it is the club house now for the faculty at Tel Aviv University.

On the bus someone recalls meeting Arafat and how much regard she had for an unsophisticated man who, despite his failures, gave his life to Palestine.

———

The mountains en route to Nablus are deformed by settlements that fall and fall and fall into verdant valleys. Palestinians exist in the crevices left to them and yet, around the most basic shelters, flowers and plants are cultivated. Colour wrested from thin air.

At the souk in the old city we buy za'tar, star anise, saffron, olive soap. In a thin perfumery I stop. The owner and I smell essences and talk of books, life, his young child. His private collection of bottles, tiny and expensive, he refuses to sell, but before I leave he applies a dot of his favourite, a white musk, on my wrist. It lasts all day and through the night.

Every shop is like this, a portal into a world where nothing hostile awaits. Every turn reveals slopes climbing into other realms in these intimate centres of town that recall communal life. Cars creep down stairways built shallow, resilient enough to carry more than they were meant to.

A man gifts me a keffiyeh for my father. He makes me photograph his name and address. 'Remember me,' he says.

Our evening programme is in a space decorated with small Palestinian flags and traffic lights. Birds interrupt the first reader, and at one point we stop for the adhan. Around us fat felines wander, but on the way back through streets surfeit with secrets I see a skinny cat leaping over a high roof, sure-footed against the skies.

———

In Nablus the wheels of cars break the quiet as though they are fleeing, tyres squealing.

Late, I look for cardboard to protect the maps I've been carrying on and off our bus, visual proof of a brutal occupation whose specificities may escape my memory and voice. A.J., the hostel receptionist, finds construction paper, twine. During the second Intifada A.J., trapped in Ramallah, forfeited his education to work in film and media until the company could no longer pay after a year of Israel seizing tax revenues belonging to Palestinians. Movies from ISIS have begun to be released, and we talk about the cost involved in producing such things. They are similar to Israeli propaganda films, he tells me. Has anybody followed the money?

Social media changed perceptions of America, he says. 'The hashtags showed American advocacy for Palestine, people marching. Things will change.'

Outside, gunshots. He translates the rhythms: a family member returned from jail . . . mourning the dead.

On Facebook a friend request from a boy in Gaza: 'Welcome to my country. You will be changed forever.'

———

Palestine is desiccated by settlements.

The first outpost is the Orange mobile tower on a hillside. Mobile homes follow, often spaced across some distance. The government deems roads necessary to connect these homes. Then that the roads must be protected from Palestinians. In these incremental ways land is annexed.

Al-Walaja is being split to connect Gilo – the oldest, largest settlement in the area – to West Jerusalem. Israel's wall will confiscate the last green space left in Bethlehem District and prevent farmers from accessing their land.

The Israeli government is intent on forcing Palestinians into the service sector; the settlers' sprawl effectively carries out government policy. Forced unemployment in the West Bank means 100,000 Palestinians withstand the misery of checkpoints every day, starting as early as 2 a.m. to labour in Israel.

The word *settlement* evokes temporariness. The permanence of these structures devastates.

––––––

The Catholic university in Bethlehem observes the call to prayer on Friday. In its gardens memorials to students killed by the Israelis.

Our readings cover the Nakba, American life, the Egyptian revolution, Palestine, Grenada, Guyana, London. The discussion after is electric.

At a falafel joint in Bethlehem I talk with students who travel from Dheisheh refugee camp. Our conversation is easy: clothes, boyfriends, families, what led each to choose to wear the hijab, their preferred breakfast – hummus made by their mothers – their future, the possibility of attending Bard University in Jerusalem, how to take a better selfie.

Later, a taxi driver defies the law and races us to the church of the newly canonised nun – the first Palestinian – at the Carmelite convent. We are six, perched on laps, sometimes breaking into hysterical laughter along with the driver, giddiness born of getting away with bad behaviour, other times solemn as we pass memorial after memorial to the war dead.

Around the corner from the church I buy a piece of luggage. When I go to pay, the young shop-owner stops me from mistakenly offering the price in Jordanian dinars, the sixth most valuable currency in the world, ranked far higher than the Israeli shekels we must use inside Palestine. He offers to change it for me, and disappears with all my money. I feel a sense of panic, but someone offers me coffee and laughs at my concern: *you don't have to worry*, he says, *Palestinians don't steal*. The boy returns quickly, bearing my change.

The Church of the Nativity, being renovated by the Palestinian Authority, contains the spot where Jesus is said to have been born. I kneel and pray for the believers in my life.

Aida, the largest of 59 camps, contains people from 41 of the 543 villages depopulated by Israel in 1948, 61 per cent below the age of 24. Graffiti on the apartheid wall exemplifies the Palestinian concept of sumoud – steadfastness, perseverance. One says: FERGUSON, PALESTINE. A half back-bend is required to see the top. The beauty of the movement juxtaposes with the unassailable atrocity of this wall, its existence stains the life and spirit I celebrate in dance. I weep.

Unlike the elegance of old Palestinian architecture, camps are rudimentary. There beauty was visible, though the occupation wove through with the virulence of weeds, choking life out of orchards, homes, people. Here survival dictates everything. What were originally tents became sheds became rubble became brick became homes.

From the roof of the Alrowwad Cultural Centre we see the wall jag around three sides of a single home that has resisted demolition, imprisoning it in a sharp U that reminds me of Hebrew script. Inside the centre a nineteen-year-old boy dances like his very life could take flight. A fourteen-year-old girl sings 'We Shall Overcome' and my heart clenches. I hear the anthem 'Mawtini'. 'Will I see you in your eminence? Reaching to the stars. My homeland, my homeland.' Her voice around the Arabic is suffused with longing.

The al-Aqsa Mosque stands in the most disfigured and militarised holy ground in the world, the approach barred by a checkpoint barbellate with ordnance. To reach the mosque, Palestinians must first pass settlers coming to celebrate mizvahs amid raucous singing and drums, the guards joining them in dance, guns and fists in the air. After that more security and through a long caged tunnel lined with riot gear. There is no escape.

Inside, Palestinian women take turns to sit in a circle and read audibly from the Qur'an. A group of settlers comes threateningly close and the women raise their voices: 'God is great!' Palestinian guards tell the settlers they must leave. The threat of tragedy and political disaster is the norm; all that the Palestinians can do is attempt to avoid it.

It is beautiful here. Pale walls built in time long past, the skill apparent in the details, the sheer scale. It is hard not to compare monument to monstrosity, that other wall that grinds itself into the earth.

A Palestinian man sweeps the long narrow floors of the checkpoint.

The climb through Ramallah's hills leads through furrowed fields, grooved like the outside of walnuts. The trees are small, the spacing between each enough to allow travel, the leaves silvery in the light. Along each path there are shrubs: nettles, pungent farrow, the blood of Jesus (a dark pink flower that is the last to die), thyme, sage, other herbs. We climb on unsteady rocks all the way to a qasr used by the farmers during the harvests. It is made of the creamy peach rock that I associate with this country. Stairs ascend to the open roof from the cool interior with its uneven floor. I imagine weathered men and women working here, their children running wild, unwatched for a day.

The light falls yellow-gold as we leave, gilding the thin grasses.

———

Our closing event is at the Sakakini Cultural Centre in Ramallah. There is a chill in the air, and we shiver as we sit in the gardens. The last reading begins with lines from Darwish. At dinner I walk a bartender through making me a drink I've come to know, rum enfolded in sambuca and Yellow Chartreuse. They call it Palestine Libre.

The End of Apartheid
Henning Mankell

About a week ago I visited Israel and Palestine. I was part of a delegation of authors with representatives from different parts of the world. We came to participate in the Palestine Festival of Literature. The opening ceremony was supposed to take place at the Palestinian National Theatre in Jerusalem. We had just gathered when heavily armed Israeli military and policemen walked in and announced that they were going to stop the ceremony. When we asked why, they answered, You are a security risk.

To claim that we at that moment posed a viable terroristic threat to Israel is absolute nonsense. But at the same time they were right. We pose a threat when we come to Israel and speak our minds about the Israeli oppression of the Palestinian population. It can be compared to the threat that I and thousands of others once were to the apartheid system in South Africa. Words are dangerous.

That was also what I said when those who organised the conference had managed to move the whole opening ceremony to the French Cultural Centre: What we are now experiencing is a repetition of the despicable apartheid system that once treated Africans and coloured as second-class citizens in their own country. But let us not forget: that apartheid system no longer exists. That system was overthrown by human force at the beginning of the 1990s. There is a straight line between Soweto, Sharpeville and what recently happened in Gaza.

During the days that followed we visited Hebron, Bethlehem, Jenin and Ramallah. One day we were walking in the mountains along with the Palestinian author Raja Shehadeh, who showed us how Israeli settlements are spreading, confiscating Palestinian land, destroying roads and building new ones which only settlers are allowed to use. At the different checkpoints harassments were commonplace. For my wife Eva and I it was of course easier to get through. Those in the delegation with Syrian passports or of Palestinian origin were more exposed. Take out the bag from the bus, unpack it, put it back in again, take it out once more . . .

In the West Bank aggravation is a matter of degrees. Worst of all was Hebron. In the middle of a town with a population of 40,000 Palestinians, 400 Jewish settlers have confiscated parts of the town centre. The settlers are brutal and they do not hesitate to attack their Palestinian neighbours. Why not urinate on them from highly situated windows? We saw photographs of settler women, along with their children, kicking and punching Palestinian women. The Israeli soldiers watching did nothing to stop it. That is the reason why there are people in Hebron who, in the name of solidarity, volunteer to walk Palestinian children to school and back. Fifteen hundred Israeli soldiers are guarding these four hundred settlers, day and night. Each settler is being constantly watched over by a team of bodyguards of four to five people.

In addition, the settlers have the right to carry weapons. When we were visiting one of the most awful checkpoints inside Hebron this one settler, extremely aggressive, was filming us. At the sight of anything Palestinian – it could be the smallest thing, a bracelet, a pin – he ran straight to the soldiers and gave a report.

Naturally, nothing of what we experienced can ever be compared to the situation of the Palestinian people. We met them in cabs and on the street, at readings, at universities and theatres. We talked to them and listened to their stories.

Is it strange that some of them in pure desperation, when they cannot see any other way out, decide to become suicide bombers? Not really. Maybe it is strange that there are not more of them. The wall that is currently dividing the country will prevent future attacks, in the short term. But the wall is an obvious demonstration of the desperation of the Israeli military power. In the end, it will face the same destiny as the wall that once divided Berlin.

What I saw during my trip was obvious: the state of Israel in its current form has no future. Moreover, those who advocate a two-state solution have not got it right.

In 1948, the year of my birth, the state of Israel proclaimed its independence on occupied land. There are no reasons whatsoever to call that a legitimate intervention according to international law. What happened was that Israel simply occupied Palestinian land. And the amount of land under possession is constantly growing, with the war in 1967 and with the increasing number of settlements today. Once in a while, a settlement is torn down. But it is just for show. Soon enough it pops up somewhere else. A two-state solution will not be the end of the historical occupation.

The same thing will happen in Israel that happened in South Africa during the apartheid regime. The question is whether it will be possible to talk sense into the Israelis, to make them willingly accept the end of their own apartheid state. Or if it has to happen against their will. No one can tell us when this will happen. The final insurrection will of course start from within. But emergent political changes in Syria or Egypt will contribute. Equally important is that, probably sooner rather than later, the United States will no longer be able to afford to pay for this horrible military force that prevents stone-throwing youths from having a normal life in freedom.

When change is coming, each Israeli has to decide for him- or herself if he or she is prepared to give up their privileges and live in a Palestinian state. During my trip I met no anti-Semitism. What I did see was a hatred of the occupiers that is completely normal and understandable. To keep these two things separate is crucial.

The last night of our trip was supposed to end in the same way that we had tried to start it – in Jerusalem. But the military and the police closed down the theatre once again. We held our event somewhere else.

The state of Israel can only expect to be defeated like all occupying powers. The Israelis are destroying lives. But they are not destroying dreams. The fall of this disgraceful apartheid system is the only thing conceivable, because it must be.

The question, therefore, is not *if* but *when* it will happen. And in what way.

June 2009

WHAT WE WITNESSED
Michael Ondaatje

What we witnessed in the Palestinian territories – in Hebron, in Jerusalem, in Haifa and other cities – during our time there with PalFest was an almost complete erasure of human rights – the rights of movement, the rights of ownership, of homes and land. The humiliations and limitations of Palestinians were so blunt and evident one cannot believe that they still exist in our twenty-first century, and still continue unimpeded and unprotested.

June 2014

STORIES FROM THE ARMENIAN QUARTER
Nancy Kricorian

G tells me that a few months after the Israelis conquered East Jerusalem he asked his father what he thought life would be like; would it be better or worse than under the Ottomans, the British or the Jordanians, all of whom his father had known? The old man told him that only the week before an American Jewish dentist had offered free dental care to all the kindergarten children at the Holy Translators School. They can't be all bad, his father said, if they want to look after our children's teeth.

Later G met the dentist himself and thanked him for his good offices. Yes, the dentist said, there was some discussion in the upper echelons of the Israeli government about whether the Armenians had intermarried with the Arabs. I went, he said, to inspect the children's teeth – you can tell from the jaw structure – and I was able to report that the Armenians were 100 per cent pure.

———

B, a priest I meet at a church supper in Virginia during my book tour, tells me that when he was a seminarian in Jerusalem in the early 70s the Haredi Jews spat on the Armenian priests on a daily basis – and on the seminary students. He says, One day I just got fed up with it. I called the other seminarians together – there were five of us – and we agreed that we'd undo our belts and keep the belts and our hands inside our cassocks. We walked out of the church and a man spat on us, and we pulled out our belts and gave him a thrashing. It might not have been the Christian thing to do, but I was young then and it was satisfying.

I say to B they still spit on the priests on a daily basis in the Armenian Quarter. Yes, he tells me, I know. I couldn't stay there. I might have risen higher in the Church if I had stayed, and the spitting I could have learned to tolerate, but watching the way they degraded the Palestinians was too much for me.

N says that everything is a problem in the Armenian Quarter. Getting a building permit is a problem. Having a regular travel document is a problem. Even finding a place to park your car is a problem.

The Patriarch signed a ninety-nine-year lease with an Israeli company that wanted to build a parking lot on Armenian Patriarchate land, she says. They built the parking lot, and we could park there, although we had to pay more than the Israelis did. And then one day they decided it was a 'Jews Only' parking lot, and we could no longer park there because we're Armenian even though it was on land belonging to the Armenian Church.

N says, They don't want us here, that's clear. They want the churches, they want the houses, the land, and they want the money from the Christian pilgrims and tourists. I think ideally they would like all the Christians to disappear, and then Jews could dress up as Christians like characters in Disney World.

K's family has been in Jerusalem for several generations. He outlines their entire trajectory – where his grandparents lived when they first arrived after the Genocide, where they took their children during the war in 1948, the house they returned to in 1950, how they managed in 1967 and how they live today with ever greater difficulty. K says, Just because I'm Armenian doesn't mean that I'm treated differently from other Palestinians. I think of myself as a Palestinian who is an ethnic Armenian. We breathe the same tear gas.

It takes some prodding, but S, the owner of a ceramics shop, finally tells me what he thinks of the occupation. They are chopping us like salad, he says. Everyone who has any means is leaving. They are slicing us like salami. First Gaza, then the West Bank. We are only hoping the machine breaks down before they get to us.

New York City, September 2016

A Scramble of Authors
Michael Palin

Although I'd travelled the world a fair bit, nothing in my experience quite prepared me for PalFest. For a start all my companions were writers. Poets, novelists, playwrights. And unlike many a book festival we were not brought together in one place for a day or two days' work. We were on the move together for a week (though I had to leave early to attend a more conventional literary book event in France) and we were travelling to a country of ancient culture and rich heritage which no longer officially exists but with which I felt powerfully familiar.

Palestine was where the Bible stories on which I was brought up were set, and as we crossed the Allenby Bridge I found myself looking out over the mythic waters of the River Jordan. And that was the first disappointment. The Jordan was little more than a muddy stream, its waters barely detectable.

For the first time in my life I found myself in Jerusalem, but with what an introduction. Before I could absorb much of this great city, our very first event was closed down by Israeli armed police. For some reason our stalls of books and tea and cakes were seen to be a threat to the authorities. In the wrong place at the wrong time. But the disappointment was short-lived and the see-saw of elation and frustration which marked our days together was established as we carried our wares, books, biscuits and all, down the street to the French Cultural Centre, where the first event of PalFest 2009 was able to go on undisturbed.

The next day we headed for Ramallah. I had the infinitely depressing experience of passing through the security wall separating Jerusalem from the West Bank, the most powerful physical reminder of the tensions that characterise what we were all taught to call the Holy Land. Once through however a high-light of the trip lay ahead. Raja Shehadeh (whose absorbing and inspiring book *Palestinian Walks* had been part of my prepara-tory reading) along with his wife Penny hosted a gathering at his house with the lemon tree in the courtyard. Then, followed by a scramble of authors, struggling to keep up with the diminu-tive Raja, he recreated one of his walks, down through the olive groves.

Raja was quietly informative, but I remember being surprised by his strong denunciation of the Oslo Accords, on the grounds that they had formalised a separateness between the Palestinians and Israelis which reduced contact and therefore obstructed any real chance of understanding between the two communities. Mind you, he also told me that Arabs love cats. The prophet was said to have cut off bits of his coat rather than disturb a cat sleeping on it.

We were all getting to know each other better, and the inter-action between Westerners and locals was celebratory and stim-ulating. Nervous as I was at my first panel I was fortunate to be 'onstage' in the gardens one evening with Raja and the force of nature that is Suad Amiry. Tall, strikingly beautiful and a terrific raconteur, with a rich head of hair and an even richer laugh, she showed it was possible to be passionate and very funny at the same time.

The next day I had a once-in-a-lifetime opportunity to work with the Swedish author Henning Mankell and the Freedom Theatre of Jenin. For two or three hours we took a workshop together. Something that would have been inconceivable without PalFest, it was a rare and valuable chance to use drama to air differences and confront problems.

And then on, through seemingly endless checkpoints, to Bethlehem, a pilgrimage site for centuries, now ringed by the security wall and refugee camps. And yet here too the panel discussions allowed us to learn how people lived with the situation and how they felt able to speak out fluently and fervently.

PalFest was one of the most concentrated periods of my life. Nothing had prepared me for the intense feelings and emotions in this crucible of religion and politics. There was so much to see, so much to discuss, debate, celebrate and deplore. PalFest created a team spirit which was always alert and alive. Though there were daily scenes that lowered the spirits, I've rarely laughed as much as with my companions on that tour. And above all else it was an affirmation that through writing and storytelling we could share universal values in a land where it is easy to give up hope.

We had flown in to Amman on a Saturday. As we were about to land, Suheir Hammad, one of the Palestinian writers in our group, had promised me, 'By Sunday you'll be shouting to get out. By Wednesday you won't want to leave.' She was right.

And what I learned in those few days will stay with me for the rest of my life.

London, 2016

Bethlehem

Sabrina Mahfouz

Next December
when nativity scenes
swamp school halls and high street corners,
ripped bedsheets
strung around children's shoulder bones
as they play three kings,
I will think of the shop where the Palestinian
let me charge my mobile phone for free.
Coaches were parked nearby
full of t-shirt tourists eager to touch the city
where Jesus was born.
They are told before they arrive
'the Christians here are hounded by the Muslims,
made to feel unwelcome'.
The Christian in the shop
where my iPhone charges says;
'but of course not, we are the same, it is Israel who hounds
      us all.
Israel covers itself with paper angels,
shepherding a concrete wall around us who live where
      Jesus did.
Mystery exists here, a virgin birth etcetera,
those buildings that appear overnight
so magical, so monstrous'.
O little town of Bethlehem.
My phone charged now, I tweet a picture of an old man
hunched over a walking stick, carrying white cheese and
      watermelon
as the unemployed smoke along the street
looking up at an illegal sky
clangorous church bells reminding everyone
that there is no such thing
as wise men.

CRUCIFIXION

Nathalie Handal

2013. I sit by the window and wait for her to finish her story. She has the posture of a ballerina. Her honey-coloured eyes against her hot magenta headscarf offer a striking contrast. We are on a bus at the Bethlehem checkpoint en route to Jerusalem. The anthology of Arabic verse I'm carrying inspired the exchange. She tells me that each time she enters Damascus Gate she recreates the day that changed her forever. Then adds that she has eleven versions so far. I don't know what she is speaking about and for a second the sky's paleness distracts us. She explains:

> I memorise. I'm addicted to memorising. I memorise the exact pitch in the voice of the cake seller, the gleam in my sister's eyes when she meets the sun by the window, the circumfer-ence of the circular window. I memorise al-Mutanabbi. I just memorised the face in the red Toyota Corolla that passed by us. I memorise street numbers, abandoned neckties, books. I memorise him. His charcoal eyes. His full lips. Square chin. White teeth. I forget him. I keep re-memorising him. Together we wrote poetry. Threw the fear into the mountains we never could get to.
>
> I forget he memorised with me. Once we memorised Jabra Ibrahim Jabra's work, and as we started Ghassan Kanafani's stories the half-moon insisted we memorise it first. We were

happy in our craziness. We ached. I memorise the way my
hands get cold and my heart beats aimlessly as if it's broken.
I forget I remember him. And his Lifta. Forget the rain caught
in the yellow light of night. I forget the pen he gave me. The
one I left with him so he could keep giving it to me each time
we met. I forget I never saw him again. Forget why he didn't
memorise the world and stay with me.

I just memorised the twenty-three cars that passed by since
we started this bus ride. I won't bore you with their colours or
the expressions on their faces. I'm not speaking of the drivers
or passengers. The faces beneath the faces. Everyone here is a
grave. And a pulse.

Once we get to Damascus Gate, I will begin a new version.
I will forget the version when I walked by the vendor selling
vine leaves and radios, dates and multi-cultured spices. When
the merchandise dangling above was like the colourful pages
of books of all sizes. When two girls were playing with their
ponytails and a boy was holding his father's hand. When a
man with a beaten wooden cart of lemons was heading out
as I moved towards the fork in the street. I will forget that
version. The version when he didn't come and the clouds clus-
tered together were a reflection of the bodies beneath them.
I will forget that version. I will memorise only the versions
that came after that one.

A year later. Four o'clock. Another blaze in the distance. My eyes
unable to close. It's unbearable to keep re-seeing the ruins of
small bodies. A roar under a cry. A sea beyond a heart. Shadows
beneath shadows. Boots pressing the air out of rooftops. The
threat is everywhere, even in the stack of papers in front of me.
I can't sleep because the fear and the vigour to resist it leave me
no time for caution, and time is outside of time here. We find
unusual ways to survive each scar as night tries to escape the
death it will awake to. The girl on the bus comes back to me. She

reminds me to wait for the *adhan*, the call to prayer. The sun to rise. The church bells to ring. I am in Bethlehem.

Jesus was born here. But I haven't seen Jesus for a while, something to do with not having a permit. It's summer 2014. The third Israeli war on Gaza in six years is going on. We want one minute to stop our hearts from racing. Just one minute. But here one minute is a lifetime. No one can reach grief on time to grieve properly. I'm sitting by the window where I've been sitting for hours. I lose track of how many. The stack of papers on the table in front of me is untouched. I feel what I once felt standing in the middle of a grove in Jaffa, holding two oranges, one in each hand: a feeling that turned into a voice, a voice that mapped a past. From the corner of my eye I glimpse the cloud flirting with the sun on and off my face. I start writing about Lifta.

It's one of my favourite places and one of the most stunning pre-1948 Palestinian villages in the District of Jerusalem. Lifta's inhabitants were expelled, or they fled. Earlier in the summer, before Israel's war on Gaza began, I asked a few writers and theatre workers to meet me there so we could think about a play about the pre-1948 Palestinian village. What remains of Lifta is under constant threat of being razed.

Not long before our meeting one of the Palestinian writers, currently living in London, was denied entry into the country. No reason given. Then the writer living in Haifa but originally from the hilltop village of Iqrit had clashes to deal with. For a few years now Iqrit descendants have been trying to reclaim their ancestral village in northern Galilee. They confront a colony of jarring obstacles. Iqrit's inhabitants were forced to leave their homes in 1948 when the new Israeli army alleged the area was dangerous. They were never permitted to return.

This left one other person. On my way to Lifta she called to say there were clashes in East Jerusalem so she couldn't join me. This is common in Palestinian life. There is no easy way to explain. The restrictions on freedom and movement are interminable and they're all down to Israeli law: checkpoints, the Green Line,

Areas A, B and C and whatever identity card or passport people hold. Gazans aren't permitted into the West Bank or anywhere. West Bank residents can't go to the 1948 territories unless given a special permit, and those are rare. Palestinians with Israeli citizenship can't live in the West Bank, and Palestinians in the diaspora are refugees and can't live in Israel, the West Bank or Gaza. And Jerusalem blue-card holders are under constant threat of losing their residency. Wherever Palestinians are dispersed in Israel, the West Bank, Gaza, in refugee camps in the Arab world, or displaced worldwide, they are confined to the particularities of whatever boundaries – national or physical, psychological or emotional – they were dealt after 1948. Can writers create in such a ceaseless twister of interruptions, barricades and heart-aches? For nearly seven decades Palestinian writers' oeuvres have contributed to Palestinian, Arabic and other literatures; they have left notable and cherished poetry collections, novels, plays and memoirs. But I can't help imagining how much more they could have created.

I don't actually make it to Lifta until the following year, when I hike the steep slopes with my friend from Jerusalem. We allow the stones, like cascades of stars, to guide us. We stay silent. What could be said amid such beauty, such horror, such grief, such love. The wild flowers speak to us. The jasmine and lavender speak to us. The empty old stone houses, gems of our heritage, our iden-tity, speak to us. The olive trees speak to us. The mill speaks to us. The ancient spring speaks to us. The ghosts roaming the village speak to us. The bride and the groom from 1947, who haven't aged a day, speak to us. And we listen. We mostly listen. What we hear: although there is nothing more to lose, no power has ever been able to steal memory.

Writers safeguard memories. We spot a Palestinian sunbird. It has orange tufts at the sides of its breast. My friend tells me as a child she would look for them, and that this one is a male sunbird because its black feathers are lustrous blue in the sunlight. A blue so electric it mystifies us like a poem does when it appears on the page. We sit under one of the arches of the old houses; we lean on the stones, cooling. The village is a perfect symphony of mystical green. The dry patches in between like sheets of hay, rough and songful. And the girl on the bus comes to guide me as I memorise Lifta.

My mind veers. I think of the expropriated Jerusalem houses not far away in the neighbourhoods of Talbiyah, Qatamon and Musrara, the ones that my sister so painfully researched and powerfully unfurled in her interactive web documentary art, 'Dream Homes Property Consultants'.

Then I stop. Beauty is a scar. History is a room. Longing is a gale.

Five o'clock. Summer 2015. A year has passed since the fifty-day hammering of Gaza and Israel's annexation, only a few days after the Gaza ceasefire, of nearly 1,000 acres of West Bank land in a Jewish settlement bloc near Bethlehem, which the international press called 'the biggest land grab in a generation'. The telephone rings; the voice says, 'Look outside your window.' I do. 'Look down,' he adds. It could have been a Romeo and Juliet scene except the tired lines on his face tell me he can't entertain even the illusion of our hearts. Who can, when seven miles is a long-distance journey? The once sister cities Bethlehem and Jerusalem are now separated by a wall, and love needs a permit issued by an occupying power.

We manage to smile and drive through the old city before it wakes. We pass through my mother's quarter, Harat Al-Tarajmeh. I see my grandmother's school, the former ateliers of the mother-of-pearl artisans and the stone houses of close and extended families. This is where I understand myself best, amid these lime-stones, these slender streets, in these courtyards, in these hundred stairs of the old city, under these arches, with Jerusalem before me and this person beside me.

We end up as we often do, having a conversation by the Nativity Church. Casa Nova, to be precise. Not long afterwards we exit our

217

hearts as we exit our bodies. We never reach our wounds nor get to our words on time. I memorise his hand instead of saying goodbye.

December. Every year Christians worldwide celebrate Christmas. Some will come to Bethlehem. They will be told not to buy anything in the birthplace of Jesus because the natives are dangerous and untrustworthy – even best to leave their wallets with their Israeli tour guide. While the faithful pray, the natives of Palestine will apply for permits to enter religious sites. Few visitors will discover what UNOCHA reports: that 'more than 85 per cent of Bethlehem governorate is designated as Area C, the vast majority of which is off limits for Palestinian development, including almost 38 per cent declared as "firing zones", 34 per cent designated as "nature reserves", and nearly 12 per cent allocated for settlement development'. That Bethlehem, along with Beit Jala and Beit Sahour, is surrounded on three sides by the segregation wall. That 'farmers in at least twenty-two communities across the governorate require visitor permits or prior coordination to access their privately owned land located behind the Barrier or in the vicinity of settlements'. That 'over 100,000 Israeli settlers reside in 19 settlements and settlement outposts across the governorate, including in those parts de facto annexed by Israel to the Jerusalem municipality'. While they pray the systematic and discriminatory policy of revoking the residency of Palestinians in Jerusalem will continue. While they pray writers will warn. Hearts will hurt. Rivers will be ruins. Words will be wounds. While they pray love will ask the Song of Songs for love. While they pray the daily, painful execution will continue. While they pray.

PAKISTAN/PALESTINE
Mohammed Hanif

MOHAMMED IN JERUSALEM

I met the only Jewish Pakistani in Israel by accident. It turned out he had also ended up there through a historic misunderstanding. I wasn't looking for him. He wasn't expecting me. In the last days of the last millennium, just before the millennium bug was predicted to wipe out all our computer memory, there were reliable rumours of peace between Israel and Palestine.

The proof of this impending peace was in my passport. I was given a reporting visa by the Israeli embassy in London on a Pakistani passport. They were understanding enough not to stamp the visa on the passport. I had grown up with a green passport which said in bold letters, 'Valid for travel to all countries of the world except Cuba and Israel.' I was convinced that peace was about to break out when I reported to the Directorate of Censors in Jerusalem and discovered all its staff was on strike. Having lived under various forms of censorship in Pakistan (from midnight knocks to what your uncle will think of what you are writing), I found it exhilarating: when your directorate of censorship goes on strike, who is there to fear?

Hours later, trying to score a drink, I was terrified. Like a naive tourist who believes that the best way to get to know a city is to get lost in the city, I tried to walk into random shops and cafes and bars. When I tried this in the upmarket district of West Jerusalem I was pounced upon at the doors. Your name? Your ID? And as I presented my passport with the hope of hearing, Oh where is Pakistan? What brings you to our country? I was told, We don't allow. I almost wanted to say 'But I am not Palestinian' but I realised it all probably sounded the same.

I retreated to the safety of the Jerusalem Hotel, where a tour operator with three mobile phones gave weary directions to lost souls like me. I decided to stick to East Jerusalem and observe peace from safe quarters. Here, the American Colony hotel could host an Iftar and put up Christmas decorations without being pelted by folks who don't approve of Iftar or Christmas. Al-Kasaba theatre could host rehearsals for an absurdist play and the actors could dream of taking their plays to international absurdist theatre festivals.

On Shabbat Israeli kids drove to Ramallah to have ice cream and drove back without killing anyone.

I went to late-night concerts in Ramallah. I had ice cream. I heard stories about the Palestinian Authority's corruption. When people start complaining about dug-out roads and traffic jams, you know that progress is on the march.

PAKISTAN IN RAMLA

After a few days of wandering around I decided to visit Ramla, where I had heard lots of Indians lived. This seemed like a story I could sell – a hey, look, Indian people living in the promised land type of story. I arrived in a synagogue on the evening of Hanukkah celebrations. There was a group of journalists from India on an official visit who arrived at the same time I entered the synagogue. Ramla seemed like one of those Gulf towns where men from the subcontinent go to live in semi-slavery so that their families can have WCs and LCD televisions. Inside the synagogue it seemed like a small-town Indian wedding. Or Pakistani wedding. You can never tell. Families dressed in shiny clothes, Indian sweets, incense.

I was taken for one of the Indian journalists' delegation and garlanded. Indians, I thought, can't help themselves; even if you arrive as a stranger in the middle of a Jewish shanty town, they will put garlands around your neck and expect you to make speeches. Indian delegates stood up one by one and lectured their audience about how lucky they were to have left Indian poverty and caste-ism behind, how they must stay faithful to Israel and the idea of Israel.

I was also asked to make a speech. I tried to clarify that I wasn't actually part of the delegation but I was glad to be here, thanks for the garland, thanks for the sweets; I was here to listen to their stories. And by the way I am not from India, I am from Karachi. I don't know why, but I didn't use the word *Pakistan*, as if that would make me sound like the enemy. As I uttered the word *Karachi* someone sobbed loudly in the audience. After the speeches a middle-aged man approached me. He was Daniel from Karachi. He was full of memories about places that didn't exist any more. That Irani restaurant? Gone. Minerva cinema? Demolished. He kept referring to his synagogue in Karachi as 'our mosque in Karachi'. He had nice things to say about the late dictator General Ayub Khan. He was very optimistic about our then current dictator, General Pervez Musharraf. He was pleased with his own leader, Ariel Sharon. 'Our nation needs strong man.' I assumed by 'nation' he meant the people of Karachi. His family had moved here in the late 60s. 'There was no trouble but our family moved because of better economic prospect.' I asked him if his family had done well. He took me aside and gave me a short lecture about the inner politics of Ramla. 'You see we are the only Pakistani family here. Rest are all Indians. Even my in-laws are Indian. But you know these Indians, they never accept us Pakistanis as their equals. They can never see us do well. So that's a big problem.' I was pleasantly surprised to see the Jewish diaspora divided along Indian–Pakistani lines. Some of us might go to the promised land but we are bringing our enemies with us.

PEACE IS COMING

I had seen the occupation only from a distance; in poetry, newspapers and very occasionally on TV. It was hard to imagine how you could have peace and occupation. I went to meet al-Aqsa's grand mufti and found some Israeli police officers sitting in his office. They were drinking tea and talking. Were they talking peace? I pestered my host for translation. He told me half-heartedly they were talking about archaeology. An archaeologist came in with a map and waved his hands in despair. My host told me that Ariel Sharon wanted to visit. And that would not be good for peace. The archaeologist kept pointing to the map and issuing warnings, the Israeli policemen kept having tea, the mufti kept smiling a benign smile.

Sharon wouldn't visit for a while and the illusion of peace would last a bit longer. You want proof? Count the number of new cafes coming up in the areas under Palestinian authority. You don't build cafes if you are expecting a war. He would come the following year, and all the peace-mongers would shut up.

In Bethlehem, right across from the Church of the Nativity, a Palestinian family was busy building the future. They had just migrated back from the United States and they had set up a posh restaurant. They opened days before Jesus Christ's 2000th birthday. It was a charming family enterprise; the owner and his teenage sons and daughters worked alongside other waiters. As young boys and girls balanced their plates amid the tourists who had flocked to this new establishment, I could imagine generations living off it. Peace means prosperity, I thought. When divinity meets commerce, everyone wins. Who would ever mess with Bethlehem? With the Church of the Nativity? They can mess with Palestinians but not with Bethlehem. It belongs to billions of Christians around the world. With so much optimism in the air my meal tasted divine.

Only about a year later, sitting at my desk far away, I saw the Church of the Nativity being shelled by Israeli forces. I didn't worry about the birthplace of Jesus, but I was heartbroken when I saw the restaurants and shops around it being reduced to rubble. Billions of Christians around the world couldn't save a little establishment that promised fine food for pilgrims.

And why stop at Jesus' birthplace when you can go and do the same with the last resting place of the grandpa of all prophets?

HOW TO EXILE THE PROPHET OF PROPHETS

A fact universally acknowledged, at least by those who believe in one god, is that Abraham was an uber-prophet. I am sure there is a religious sect somewhere which believes that he wasn't such a big deal, but for all Muslims, Christians and people of Jewish faith, he was the cuddly grandad loved by all. In 1999 I went to Hebron. As compared to the battle-hardened worshippers at al-Aqsa or the frenzy in front of the Wailing Wall, Hebron seemed like a large village festival.

There was an iron grille running through Abraham's last resting place though, neatly partitioning this grandest of graves. The massacre of the Cave of the Patriarch had happened and ostensibly to protect Abraham's grandchildren from each other the Israeli government had taken its favourite administrative measure: put in a partition so that Jews on the one hand, and Muslims and people of other faiths on the other, could come and pay their respects without having to stand in the same queue. A partitioned grave was a grim sign, but outside it was a non-stop shopping festival. Here shopkeepers didn't bother with your religion or ethnicity. I was reassured that despite having many children and spawning many religions the patriarch had united us in the pursuit of commerce. My faith was restored in the healing powers of haggling for cheap trinkets. For thousands of years people of all three faiths had been coming to his last resting place. It was one of those blessed places where a mausoleum is the centre of the economy. All you need to do is get a little shack, stuff it with vaguely religious stuff and wait for the suckers to come. In these shops you could find ivory crosses, figurines of the Son of God in a dozen poses, little phials of holy water, little phials of holy earth, daggers, swords, freshly antiquated urns, and for some vague reason those jingly belts that belly dancers wear.

With such a grand variety of merchandise and a spectrum of potential buyers that covers two thirds of the world's population, Hebron would never go out of business.

Ten years later I visited Hebron with PalFest. Not only had it gone out of business, but for the first time I saw a proper ghost town. Once a living, throbbing centre of spirituality and commerce, Hebron was completely locked down. The mosque and the partitioned grave were locked up. The area around the mosque was completely locked up. Most of the residents of the area evicted. All the glorious little shops shut down. God's own economy in a meltdown.

This was all to calm down a few hundred Jewish settlers who had descended from the United States and Canada. Israeli kid soldiers patrolled the streets in full battle gear. They trained their guns at any visitor who managed to come near the mosque. These kids had come to wage a battle against their long-dead grandpa and predictably won. I have never seen a more scary bunch of teenagers.

A COUNTRY RUN BY TEENAGERS

The irrepressible urge to slap an Israeli teenager in uniform waving a gun at your head is only repressed by seeing his or her finger on the trigger. I had encountered them at every border crossing, at every checkpoint. The first thing you want to ask them is why aren't they in school. But then you look at their baby fat and their automatic weapons and keep your inquiries to yourself.

One of them, who was not even wearing a uniform, made me sit on a bench at the Jordan River crossing under a blazing sun. He took away my sunglasses. There was nothing to look at so I looked at him while he looked at me. He kept his sunglasses on. I focused on his gun. He had an extra magazine taped to the original magazine on his gun. I had seen some Karachi gangsters do that to their guns, presumably for extra firepower. Why else do you tape an extra magazine to your gun? How does that extra magazine even work?

'What do you do?' another teenager later asked me at immigration.

I am a writer.

What do you write?

Stories.

What kind of stories?

Love stories, I said, hoping to have my exit expedited.

What kind of love stories? And it went on and on till I realised I was creating a whole fictional character about myself, someone who believes that Israeli kids are actually literary critics who need to be engaged in the nature of fiction. And then you are passed on to a second and third interrogator till you completely submit to the tyranny of teenagers.

PALESTINE'S PAKISTAN PROBLEM

With PalFest I taught a creative writing workshop in Ramallah. Ramallah was full of entrepreneurs and people who hated them. The place meant for the writer-in-residence wasn't ready yet so I was hosted above a newly opened posh cafe and bar. It really was posh; some weeks they had Spanish nights. What time do you close? I asked the owner and my host. Half an hour after the last client leaves. The young man had chucked his flourishing career in New York to bring a taste of the world to Ramallah. Some nights there was confusion if I was the last client – would he wait for half an hour after I went upstairs?

It turned out that the workshop that I was teaching consisted entirely of girls. There was one boy who had registered. He came on the first day and then disappeared. The students, despite their forced isolation from the outside world, were worldly-wise, sharp and keen. And wanted to learn. I had a feeling that I was faking it. I tried to encourage them to write about what they knew. In our writing exercises an F16 would appear outside an apartment window, a woman baking a cake would get shot in the head by a stray bullet, an olive grove would get sprayed with acid. They weren't trying their hands at magical realism. They were writing about their family lives. In most writing exercises a family elder was humiliated, sometimes stripped, sometimes slapped by the Israeli kid soldiers as the family watched. They wanted to write and get published. Their stories started out about love and sibling rivalry but bullets would start flying. Or someone would get slapped by a kid soldier. After the first few days I didn't feel too fake. I have started countless stories set in Pakistan promising myself to keep it happy and shiny, and by page six someone has died a horrible death. We kept returning to basic questions. Should one write what one knows? What if nobody wants to read what I know? What if I hate what I know? There was anger over occupation, but more anger over why we must always be telling this story.

Many of my students had a family elder who had studied in Pakistan in the 70s. They had heard good things about Pakistan. What is wrong with it now? they would ask me. Why so many bomb blasts? Why was Pakistan always in the news, always for the wrong reasons? I felt defensive. I tried hard to explain that we were better off in an understated kind of way. We don't live under occupation; in fact parts of Pakistan claim that we are the occupiers, we have a democracy of sorts, we have voters' lists and elections and we have a free press although we routinely kill journalists for exercising that freedom. You don't need an Israel to mess you up, you can be your own Israel. You can kill your own children, you can build your own ugly walls.

One of the students had been lucky, the only one in the class to have travelled to Europe. 'When we travel abroad they ask us where are you from. We say Palestine and they say what – Pakistan? Easy mistake to make, I know. But then they subject us to extra checks; they have started treating us like Pakistanis.' I wasn't sure if I should be pleased that in the crazed-out world of airport security Pakistanis have beaten Palestinians. Or was there something deeper going on?

226

I was travelling in a Palestinian minibus from Bethlehem to Ramallah. An Israeli traffic police car chased us and stopped us. They fined the driver and all the passengers for not wearing safety belts. None of us were wearing safety belts, I wasn't sure if we were supposed to wear safety belts in a minibus. All the passengers chipped in to pay the fine. They refused to take my contribution as I was a stranger from Pakistan, how was I supposed to know? We all wore our safety belts. As the minibus resumed its journey and the Israeli traffic police car receded, all the passengers without looking at each other removed their safety belts. I waited for a few seconds and then I did too.

HEBRON
Sabrina Mahfouz

In Hebron, once-heaving streets of silent shops
shadow our path with shuttered rust,
we walk quiet, throats full of unanswered bulldozers.
Soldiers block off neighbourhoods
to those whose bones have carbonised the ground.
Children playing chicken over machine-gun motorways
the size of two pairs of khaki-covered conscripted teenage
    thighs.
The price for their game might be a sigh
or a slap or a shout or perhaps one day
a bloom from the stem of the gun
held by hands that haven't yet learned their lines.
We scatter ourselves around on tarmac
two shades darker than the overcast sky,
lean against concrete blocks to take in
the scaffolding of dismantled existence.
A settler approaches with a video camera
(the kind that used to be called handy before they
    actually were).
We ask if he's filming because he appreciates our dress sense
or if he's making a documentary
about the few who come to Hebron to witness the apartheid,
tell of it what they can to the outside, and he says,
with spit spinning around the hooves of his words,
'I'm filming you for god'.
He won't elaborate, I guess that says it all really.
In the middle of that now-sunlit midnight street
I began to daydream about god
watching our group of writers on a flatscreen TV –
once the settler sends it via courier or however it is
they do this kind of thing.
I wonder if god would have HD or even 3D?
Would this supreme being need
those rubbish blue and red cardboard glasses?
Would god have a remote or would it all work via mind
    control?

Would the back of the TV get dusty all the way up there?
Would god watch it alone? With popcorn?
With pick-and-mix sweets that send torrential downpours
of eaten-too-much-too-quick
sick down to the ground a few hours after,
the world having no idea what caused this
strangely coloured sticky covering to tumble down in lumps
  one morning.
Then I was wondering
what else would be included on this exclusive home video
  for god?
Would it show certain settlers filling plastic bags with bleach,
throwing it down onto the Arab marketplace to mark clothes
  unsellable?
Or how about a little cameo from the settler school
built on top of the Palestinian one,
literally crushing its core,
which now requires a 1.5-hour detoured walk
to get to and from every day,
since the army blocked the entrance alleyway
that used to get the local kids there in ten minutes?
I'm sure that would make for scintillating TV.
But the really juicy stuff, I assume the filmmaker settler,
who directs movies for god,
will leave until last.
Close-ups on the roads Palestinians can't drive on
but are certainly encouraged to die on,
ambulances included in the ban
so stretchers held in hands that have outlived their lives
rush people to what care they can get.
Sunken canvas pulsing muscles
doing what wheels were invented for.
Perhaps a fitting finale
would be the six-year-olds arrested
for allegedly
throwing stones against thunder.

Held under military law until fines take them home
to a place that's allowed a lock
only because light has been forced to languish
under metal permissions and permits.
Here they will count their tears to the age of twelve –
The legal age for pebbles they touch
to become army slabs of rock they will be tied to,
pecked like Prometheus
but before they grow old enough to give fiery gifts.
And the credits for this movie?
A disturbing number of worldwide names
mainly American and European.
It's doubtful god would be able to watch all the credits roll,
as being god requires strict time management, I imagine.
In conclusion, we turned our own cameras on the settler,
    saying;
'We'll be sending this to you once god's had a preview.
You won't be invited to the cinema screening,
but we have a feeling you'll steal someone else's seat
    anyway.
Good day.'

THE STRANGLEHOLD

Victoria Brittain

GAZA CITY, APRIL 2016

A breakfast invitation in Gaza brought us to a table laden with warm cheese and spinach pastries, laban, za'tar, olive oil, cheeses, eggs, fruit, juice, mint tea, after the scent of coffee led us up the stairs to a smiling hostess. We had parked in her small garden under flowering trees, next to a few old roses and a sleepy cat stretched out in the sun. Gazans can lull visitors into a recognisable normality as when eating a relaxed huge breakfast and listening to a teenager's everyday preoccupations with music, friends, teachers, exams, clothes, selfies and social media. You could be anywhere in the world.

Except that you couldn't. Every detail of life is unpredictable. Choices can only be hopes.

Within minutes we heard that the smiling mother – a medical technician – had an offer of a short training course in Jordan which would radically change her career prospects. But she was worried that she would not get an Israeli permit to leave through the Eretz crossing; the Rafah crossing into Egypt was closed; and even Jordanian permits for Gazans to transit through Jordan to catch a flight were being refused. She was braced for disappointment. (Months later I heard she had not been allowed to go.)

Her cheerful teenager told the story of her recent first visit to the West Bank. She had set off early in the morning in a minibus of business studies students invited by the US embassy to a conference in Ramallah with successful Palestinian businesswomen. At Eretz everyone on the US embassy list passed through except her. The Israeli border official told her they had read her tweets and she could not enter. After much phoning to the US embassy by her teacher, and a very long wait, she was finally allowed to join the others, but by then they were so late that they only had half an hour in Ramallah and saw nothing of the conference. They had to turn back for Gaza before Eretz closed. 'It was really disappointing – all I saw was how nowhere is like Gaza,' she said.

Eretz with its turnstiles, steel gates, disembodied voices ordering you where to stand with your arms up to be scanned, and its half-mile walk through a fenced-in tunnel across a no-man's-land of scrub into the almost empty $60 million ten-year-old border terminal is a glaring symbol of the inhumanity of the Gaza blockade. Twenty years ago the crossing was just a walk to an armoured watchtower where a soldier examined a foreigner's passport without much interest.

Nowhere is like Gaza now – the young woman was right. It is not just the UN reports which detail how Gaza will be unliveable by 2020, or the twenty-hour power cuts, the lack of drinking water, the sewage lakes, the blackened precarious shells of bombed tower blocks, the miles of rubble that were houses, the Israeli surveillance balloon hovering constantly, the regular shelling of fishermen and farmers or the living in constant fear. Nowhere but in Gaza is the entire population living in prison. Only foreigners know they can leave.

In just one day I met a prize-winning poet/professor, a surgeon, a doctor, a would-be graduate student, a journalist, all with professional invitations from prestigious institutions in Europe or the US which they, like my breakfast hostess, could not take up because Israel refused them permission to leave Gaza.

Life is lived here in an intellectual and psychological stranglehold. But it is part of the will to survive of Gazans that so many of them make their voices resonate so far outside.

One of these men with a stream of invitations was Ziad Medoukh, head of the French Department at al-Aqsa University, a poet with degrees from universities in Algiers and Paris, the first Palestinian to be honoured as a chevalier de l'ordre des palmes académiques de la République Française (2011) and the coordinator of a peace centre in Gaza. In April Medoukh should have been in France to speak at two universities. He had the necessary Jordanian and French visas and the French consulate in Jerusalem made every effort to get him the Israeli permit to go through Eretz. There was no response – as had been the case for three years. But his situation, as he put it, 'is nothing compared with patients who are in danger of losing their lives, the hundreds of students in Gaza who have lost their scholarships and places in universities abroad, and the dozens of university lecturers who cannot participate in conferences and scientific meetings abroad because of this blockade which violates international law with the complicit silence of the international community'.

Another was Mohammad, a soft-spoken idealistic student with perfect English learned on the Internet. 'Where is my human right to study, to live my life in the wide world, to know other people? What do they think will happen for me here, where they know there is no work, no future?' he asked. A friend broke in with the story of one of their friends who had recently tried to commit suicide because he thought he would never have a chance of a job so would never be able to marry the girl he loved. 'His sister found him hanging and screamed, so her mother came and he was saved.' But there was no saving him from his despair.

The statistics back such new stories of suicide which have accelerated fast in the last year, though no one knows how many go unreported. The general attitude to suicide, as to mental illness, is one of shame. At a conference in April to discuss psychological needs in an unprecedentedly hard time, Gaza's doctors, psychologists, researchers and social workers presented a bleak picture of anger, depression, anxiety, violence against women, hopelessness in the face of international complicity with the crushing siege. Teachers spoke gloomily of new levels of aggression among schoolboys, and doctors of patients with out-of-control violent demands for instant attention. 'I don't recognise this generation, I don't recognise our society,' said one experienced teacher. And a professor said flatly, 'Our whole psychological being has been destroyed.'

One young doctor told me, 'I don't want to hear any more about Gazans' special resilience – why should our children have to be especially resilient in this way; psychological exhibits? They are normal children with all the normal needs for love and safety and life's chances. Gaza is made abnormal.'

On this frontline of Gaza's despair is Dr Yasser Abu Jamei, a gentle soft-spoken psychiatrist. He is head of the Gaza Community Mental Health Programme, which organised the conference I was attending. The German, Swiss, Swedish and Norwegian governments helped GCMHP to host 800 people, including a dozen old associates of GCMHP from the US, Europe and South Africa given permits to enter at Eretz. Mainly it was an all-Gazan affair, and a rare meeting on this scale that was not a funeral. Guests from all over Gaza listened and discussed the sombre assessments of their society all day. But in the evenings, in the brand-new Qatar-built hotel, where the electricity does not fail and the taps run clean water, people relaxed and chatted overlooking a moonlit sea, and one evening the young men danced a dabke. Hundreds of selfies were taken on phones and circulated on social media, showing the world that Gazans were something different from the tragic victims of a thousand UN and charity reports.

Everyone in Gaza knows that Dr Abu Jamei himself lost twenty-eight people in his family to an Israeli missile strike in 2014. When he spoke to the conference of his vision of keeping the hope of peace alive he moved even the most depressed and cynical among his listeners. 'Mental health means mothers who can see their children sleep, farmers who can plant, fishermen who can sail, youth who can study abroad, people who can plan, detainees who are free . . . it means breaking the siege, ending the occupation,' he said. 'Planting hope is our main duty.'

Many of the next generation keep hope alive day to day in a multitude of modest, vibrant projects, not waiting for the breaking of the siege by politicians at home or abroad. In a kindergarten in Nuseirat camp young graduates lead the Afaq Jadeeda programme with storytelling, dance and relaxation games, as a young psychologist watches carefully and picks out the most traumatised children who may be referred to GCMHP or the Palestine Trauma Centre for treatment. This cheerful, outgoing group, on tiny salaries, has gone from one camp and one kindergarten to another every day for years.

Meanwhile Professor Medoukh's French language and literature students regularly go into schools for play sessions with small children, helping them to relax from the war traumas which are such a big part of their little lives. They lead discussions with adolescent girls in school about family and societal problems special to them; some join villagers to work in ruined farm areas. Every Sunday some of them do a live TV discussion in French, which can be watched on a computer. They are living in the world well beyond Gaza.

And there are others. In a small neat office in Gaza City an impressive team of young researchers, many still at university, are part of the independent Geneva-based Euro-Med Monitor for Human Rights network, an initiative of Palestinian youth in Europe. They live on the Internet. Their most recently published report is *Strangulation Twice: Oppressive Practices of Palestinian Security Services*. It well illustrates the independence of thought that lives on in this many-faceted society under unimaginable pressures. Another of their initiatives, called We Are Not Numbers, is for young writers. Here are the words of one, Doaa Mohaisen.

APOLOGY FOR BEING ALIVE

I feared I wouldn't be able to go back to my former life after
the war ended, but I did.
It felt so awkward. Everything was normal and people were
acting as usual.

How did I go back to my life, loaded with the guilt of being
   alive, of breathing?
I apologise for being alive. I apologise to the son who asked
   his dad to bring him some chocolate, but he got neither
   chocolate nor his dad. I apologise to the boy who wanted
   to see the sky, but it was the last thing he saw. I apologise
   to the people who went to an UNRWA school believing it
   was safer, a haven, but it was their graveyard.
I apologise to the girl who thought her father had abandoned
   her when her mother couldn't tell her they didn't find
   the body.
I apologise to Gaza, my love. I apologise that it must carry
   such a burden.

Young people in Gaza, like these writers or Mohammad or
the bouncy teenager at breakfast, are living an unprecedented
experiment – and some of them wonder aloud about its results.
Where is people's breaking-point from relentless fear, stress and
deprivation? From eight years blockaded in a tiny, crowded
enclave, where whole neighbourhoods and infrastructure were
destroyed by three wars in just six years?

Walking the devastated streets of Shujaiyya, where sixty people
died in Israel's 2014 Operation Protective Edge, then standing
in a home where half the building is rubble and half the family
died in the Israeli onslaught, was to see life without hope. No
normality was recognisable in the world of Namer Monsabah
in Shujaiyya. Here, in a house with half its rooms yawning open
into heaps of rubble, Namer lived with his eight-year-old son
Mohammed, his ten-year-old daughter, his cousin and his wife
and their three-year-old, Nisreen. Namer's wife supported them
all, he said, with a stall selling chocolate in the playground of a
nearby school. He took out of his pocket a two-month-old slip
of paper stamped by a French aid group – the latest foreigners
to see his living conditions and promise to return, but who never
did. 'We have talked so much – all in vain. People came and gave
promises, and nothing happened . . . we tried to apply to Qatar,

to Kuwait, to the government, to anyone, for materials to rebuild the house.'

Namer hesitated before talking to us. He was thirty-eight and seemed decades older, worn and angry, his eyes dark pools without expression. The four rooms the household used were on the first and second floors, with gaping holes in the walls, showing the ground floor below filled with rubble from the collapsed other half of the house. His cousin's wife Fadwa was twenty-three. She spoke of her constant anxiety for little Nisreen, who had twice recently fallen through the open walls into the rubble. Fadwa cooked for the household what little food they had on an old black stove using wood the two unemployed men collected among the broken homes; their water was in a blue plastic barrel on the stairs filled from a neighbour's roof tank; their toilet was behind a sack curtain by the stairs.

This is what life without hope looks like.

THE SOUND OF A FESTIVAL
Chinua Achebe

I was deeply moved to learn of the initiative of those writers who decided to do something about the world in which we live; to replace the sounds of war with the sound of a festival – even for a short while. To switch off, even for a moment, the noise of violence and death and bring back the voices of literature and of peaceful conversation.

I am deeply honoured to be a patron of the Palestine Literary Festival [sic]. May this quiet event grow and resound with peace in Gaza, the West Bank, in Palestine, in the Middle East and around the world.

April 2008

South Africa and Israel: A Familiar Geography

Rachel Holmes

'I've never met a nice South African.' So rang the chorus of a famous musical sketch featured in the 1980s British satirical TV puppet show *Spitting Image*. A mirthful popular political intervention, it went on to be released as the B-side of the chart-topping 'Chicken Song'. So I, like all my fellow English school-kids, was exposed to its campaigning message. But unlike them I was half South African, had grown up there during the 1970s and now spent half the year there with my South African mother and extended family. From the perspective of most of my British peers and teachers, I was a racist and fascist. From my own perspective, I was confused.

British television was one of the great revelations. Apartheid South Africa suppressed the introduction of – fully state-controlled – TV until 1976. Thanks to state propaganda, everyone knew that this new technology was *the divil's own black box for disseminating communism and immorality*. Unlike the rest of the world, no one at the southernmost tip of Africa – which has some of the most spectacular night skies on the planet – was able to watch the moon landing live. Responding to popular demand at the time, the government arranged some restricted viewings of the landing, showing fifteen minutes of edited footage. When those few grown-ups and older cousins who had the opportunity to see one of those screenings told us about it, it sounded like movie folklore. No wonder a generation of children grew up, like me, extremely dubious about the truth of reports that men had in fact landed on the moon back in 1969.

Somewhere along the equator that marked the geographical division of my life by my parents into perpetual crossings north and south, scepticism flared and dissent smouldered. There were many, many reasons, but two stand out starkly. Firstly, my boy cousins, who I'd grown up with as brothers, going off to do their military conscription for the SADF, returning with quiet, distracted stories about bush wars we weren't supposed to be fighting over borders we weren't supposed to be crossing. Secondly, the rows over the rebel English cricket tours in the early 1980s. In white South Africa there was fevered excitement at the unexpected news of the arrival of an English team captained by Graham Gooch, scheduled to make a one-month tour of our republic. The government and press celebrated the return of official international cricket. Springbok colours flew; three one-day internationals were met with the excitement of an Olympics. Crossing the equator to visit my father, I discovered that these self-same England cricketers were decried as 'the Dirty Dozen' and regarded as pocket-filling mercenaries and a national disgrace. Around the same time I was beginning to wonder why interesting British TV series and period historical dramas were never available to us back home in South Africa, where the only international programming imports were shows from America about wildly rich white Texan oil barons or professional black families living in huge houses with lives unlike any of the black people we knew.

In those years of increasing isolation in the 1970s and 80s, Israel was our only trusted international friend. When I was eleven, the apartheid government's yearbook reminded us, 'Israel and South Africa have one thing above all else in common: they are both situated in a predominantly hostile world inhabited by dark peoples.' Family friends went to work in government jobs in Israel, taking with them the children I had played with. In whispered conversations I self-importantly advised on the pleasures and pitfalls of going to school abroad, reassuring them that it would not be freezing cold like England. I was fairly certain of this advice, imagining as I did that Israel was situated somewhere between Mozambique and Kenya, since I had seen a picture of my mother on a beach in Tel Aviv that looked very much like Durban.

These were some of the memories that surfaced, randomly, while we were held up at the King Hussein/Allenby Bridge border crossing on my first PalFest. Divided and separated by name and supposed race – whatever our passport or citizenship – we were held at the unhurried pleasure of the IDF for over six hours. I realised that I was returning to somewhere I had never been before. I knew exactly where I was. The recognition was instinctive, intimate and sickening. We traced the familiar irrational geography of the separation wall, filed through cattle-pen checkpoints, were physically ejected from theatre venues by military units of armed IDF soldiers, or grasped tightly on to raw onions to try and alleviate the tear-gassing and intimidation deemed proportionate to the threat posed by a group of young rappers performing in a tent.

In 1937 Nancy Cunard sent a questionnaire to 200 writers, inviting them to state their position on the civil war in Spain. Cunard's call required writers to take a stand in a struggle between fascism and democracy: 'It is clear to many of us throughout the whole world that now, as certainly never before, we are determined or compelled, to take sides. The equivocal attitude, the Ivory Tower, the paradoxical, the ironic detachment, will no longer do.' The responses were overwhelmingly in support of the Spanish Republic, demonstrating strong anti-fascist sentiment. A few, like T. S. Eliot, did not agree with being forced to 'take sides'.

In April 2016 Nathan Linial, professor of computer science and engineering at the Hebrew University of Jerusalem, son of an immigrant from Nazi Germany and a Holocaust survivor, gave a speech on receipt of a Rothschild Prize.

> I'm sorry, I am going to darken your mood a bit . . . But I hope that you will see what I am saying . . . In every historical text one reads about fascism, one finds this one insight repeated time and time again. Fascism succeeded exactly in those places where decent people did not find it within themselves to stand up against it – be it from laziness, weakness or just cowardice . . . As Dante taught us, there is a special place in hell for those people who, at times of a deep moral catastrophe choose a neutral stance. I swear I would have preferred a thousand-fold to share the joys of science with you today, to praise the good teachers from whom I have had the privilege to learn . . . I could have told you all about the happiness to be found in daily work alongside brilliant, enthusiastic young students and about the things I provide them with that no one can take away. But during times like these one cannot fall silent. It is the duty of every decent person to stand forth proudly and say in a loud clear voice what the anti-fascist fighters said during the Spanish Civil War, No pasaran. 'They shall not pass.'

Linial's speech, in Hebrew, was posted widely on social networks and political blogs in Israel. The speech did get a mention in *Haaretz*, but in no other local news sources. It became available to the wider world only recently thanks to a translation by Breaking the Silence posted on their YouTube feed.

A few months later, in July 2016, celebrated Palestinian-Israeli writer Sayed Keshua refused an honorary doctorate from Ben-Gurion University. Keshua left Israel after the Gaza incursion in 2014 but still maintains a large persona in Israeli cultural life and writes for the Israeli press. 'I don't support a boycott of Israeli academia. But Ben-Gurion University's decision not to honour Breaking the Silence, an NGO whose crime is to remind people of the occupation, leaves me no choice but to decline the honorary doctorate it has offered me.'

Sajid Javid, while British minister for culture, media and sport, ignored the call by Palestinians and Israelis for an international cultural and academic boycott of Israel; instead he celebrated the current state of Israel as a nation offering the 'warm embrace of freedom and liberty'.

The Israeli government is turning anti-occupation activists into dissidents. In 2016 the Knesset passed the so-called NGO Transparency Law, legislation targeting 'left-wing' NGOs and human rights organisations as agents of foreign powers. The law requires NGOs that rely on funding from foreign governments to plaster FOREIGN AGENT next to their name on every report, website, document or publication. It also requires NGO representatives to wear special identifying tags when meeting with state officials or attending sessions in the Knesset.

Culture Minister Miri Regev has been working hard to suppress political dissent in the arts, culture and sport. Israeli artists received questionnaires asking them to declare whether they perform in West Bank settlements. Regev explained that 'institutions that delegitimise the State of Israel will not receive funding'. The questionnaire prepared the ground for what Regev calls her 'cultural loyalty' law, which, she stated, aims 'for the first time, to make support for a cultural institution dependent on its loyalty to the State of Israel'. She plays heavily on inter-ethnic relations between Mizrahi and Ashkenazi Jews. In a recent initiative she released 'modesty' guidelines for appropriate dress for women appearing at government-funded events, a decision taken following the Celebrate August Festival in Ashdod, in which a female singer dressed in shorts, a bikini top and open shirt was removed from the stage. 'Festivals and events funded by public money will respect the general public, which includes different communities,' a ministry official said, adding the further helpful clarification, 'this is exactly the difference between freedom of expression and freedom of funding. Therefore, a proper directive to all production bodies working through the Culture Ministry will be issued to ensure that this policy is implemented in all events.'

In 2015, Israel's Education Ministry rewrote the teachers' guide for high-school civics, and issued new guidelines warning teachers to beware the 'dogmatism of democracy' and to stress the 'Jewish nation state'. According to the guide, 'An ethnic-cultural nation state is a basis for strong solidarity among a majority of citizens because of the national connection between them.' A democratic political culture, the guide goes on to state, 'does not exist to an equal extent in all democracies and is not a necessary condition for defining a state as democratic'. Moreover, pupils should be taught that there is 'tension between the values of pluralism, which encourages multiple opinions, and the value of agreeing, which strengthens unity'.

The Israeli State Attorney's Cyber Division has sent numerous take-down requests to Twitter and other media platforms in recent months, demanding that they remove certain content or block all Israeli-based users from being able to view it. In August 2016, for example, Twitter's legal department notified American blogger Richard Silverstein that the Israeli State Attorney claimed a tweet of his, published in May, violated Israeli law. Silverstein breaks stories that Israeli journalists are unable to publish due to internal gagging orders. Two days later the California-based company announced, 'In accordance with applicable law and our policies, Twitter is now withholding the following tweet(s) in Israel.'

Today, BDS features almost daily in the Israeli news and is referred to as 'the new anti-Semitism'. Yet some of the most anti-Semitic cartoons that I have seen in recent times come from an extremely surprising source. A German called Herr Stürmer is masked by a newspaper parodying *Haaretz* headlines. At periodic intervals the voice of a housekeeper shrieks that a character referred to as 'ze Jew' has arrived at the door. A hideous racist stereotype of a man with a hooked nose appears and reappears to be tossed shiny gold euros by Stürmer in exchange for stories critical of Israeli policy: BOYCOTT ISRAEL! KILLING INNOCENT TWENTY-YEAR-OLD PALESTINIAN BABIES! IDF ABUSES HAMAS'S HUMAN RIGHTS; GAZILLION PALESTINIANS

STUCK IN ISRAELI BORDER CHECKPOINT. At the end, when Herr Stürmer has no further use for him, 'ze Jew' obligingly hangs himself. This animation was not produced by a far-right group in Europe, where an increase in anti-Semitic hate crimes is a real cause for concern. No, it was made and promoted by the Samaria Settler Council, an organisation representing Israeli settlements in the northern West Bank.

Unsurprising that the girl who could once only communicate with one parent or the other by letter grew up to be a writer. Unsurprising too that the white South African learned to listen out for the dissident voice. Such people can be seen as oppressors by unknowing strangers and branded as self-loathing traitors by their own. Yet if we do not allow them to be heard no country on earth can become its better self, democracy is stifled and the wars go on and on.

PalFest enabled me to hear these voices.

September 2016

The Gaza Suite: Rafah

Suheir Hammad

there is a music to this all
the din has an order of orders
a human touch behind all arms
all of it manufactured stars above all

something melting a dove molting mourning through dusk

one child after another gathered if possible
washed where possible wrapped there is always cloth
all the while prayed on then pried from the women
always the women in the hot houses of a winter's war
the cameras leave with the men and the bodies always
the women somehow somehow putting tea on fire
gathering the living children if possible
washing them when possible praying on them
through their hair into their palms onto dear life

something fusing into dawn feathers shed eyes

people in a high valence state
that's when breathing feeds burns
that's where settlers take high ground
that's how villages bulldozed betwixt
holidays before your eyes
high violence holy children lamb
an experience no longer inherited
actual
earth in scorched concrete
heart in smoking beat

Shujaiyya Dust
Molly Crabapple

'We accepted the sorrow, but the sorrow didn't accept us.'

Ibtisam sat in the dust, laughing, her witty broad face framed by her flowered hijab. In her forty-five years living in Gaza she'd seen so much sorrow that laughing was the only real response.

Her husband had died during the second Intifada from a stress-induced asthma attack she believes was triggered by the sound of a tank firing. He'd left her with four children to raise, which she did in a four-family home surrounded by olive trees, chicken coops and a garden where she grew thyme.

That home is gone now – along with the rest of the Shujaiyya neighbourhood – due to Israeli shells and bulldozers during Operation Protective Edge, which hit Gaza in the summer of 2014.

Operation Protective Edge was Israel's third full-scale military incursion into the Strip since Hamas took control in 2007. During their bombing campaign and ground invasion Israeli forces killed over 2,100 Palestinians, according to the United Nations, 70 per cent of them civilians, including nearly 500 children; 11,000 more were injured. A June 2015 UN report found evidence of war crimes.

While all Gaza suffered during the war, Shujaiyya endured a unique decimation. One Gazan translator, a thin sarcastic man in his thirties, struggled for words to describe what he'd seen there. He finally settled on one: 'Hell.' *Will I die here?* he remembered wondering during Protective Edge. *Will I be left in the sun, swelling like a balloon, with no one able to pick up my corpse?*

The devastation extended to industry and infrastructure. Israel destroyed water networks, universities, sewage pumping stations and over one hundred businesses, according to a report initiated by the Association of International Development Agencies. The main fuel tank of the Gaza power plant lay in ruins, and lack of spare parts left 25 per cent of the population without power. Hospitals sank into darkness. Gazans could not locate their loved ones, and food and water grew scarce.

The war destroyed 18,000 housing units, leaving 108,000 Gazans homeless.

Nearly a year after the end of Protective Edge little had changed in Shujaiyya. A few houses had been patched up but many more were nothing but rubble. Piles of prescriptions fluttered in front of the destroyed Ministry of Health. Everywhere homes lay collapsed like ruined layer cakes, the fillings composed of the flotsam of daily life: blankets, cooking pots, Qur'ans, cars. In one pile of dust I saw a child's notebook, abandoned. 'My uncle collects honey,' the nameless child had written on the first page.

Graffiti adorned many houses: I LOVE GAZA scrawled next to a heart pierced by a rocket, I'M STILL HERE, AK-47s sketched by a fighter, a mural of a bleeding man pulling down the barrier between the West Bank and Israel to look at al-Aqsa Mosque. For all the attention Banksy won painting on Gazan rubble, this art is far sharper. Banksy can come and go, but these artists are trapped here in what many call an open-air prison. Defiance bleeds from their every line.

I watched as construction workers straightened rebar in front of the bombed-out el-Wafa Hospital, once a rehabilitation centre for paralyzed adults. During Protective Edge the Israeli army shelled the medical facility, knocking out the power and forcing nurses to carry disabled patients down pitch-black stairwells.

Rafiq, thirty, is an engineer working for one of the companies hired by the United Nations Development Programme (UNDP) to clear rubble. Clearing bombsites is always a technical challenge, but Israel's blockade, which limits the importation of construction equipment and materials, has made it much harder. Donkeys hauled loads of rubble. Workers straightened rebar with crude hand tools and rocks. Sometimes Rafiq's crew found unexploded bombs, which they had to call the police to disarm. Worse were the bodies. Once Rafiq stumbled across a dead boy still clutching his school bag. Another time his crew dug out a mother whose head had been crushed while she was shielding her baby, her long hair tangled in the dust.

Shujaiyya wasn't supposed to be like this. After Israel and Palestinian armed groups called a ceasefire in 2014, donor countries gathered in Cairo and pledged $3.5 billion to rebuild Gaza. But the high of good PR fades fast, and by April 2015 donors had only given a quarter of what they promised.

To deal with the lack of funds, the UNDP divided ruined homes into three tiers, depending on the amount of damage. According to sources working in rubble clearing, only owners of homes with minor damage have seen cash or materials. According to Gazans I spoke to, the help offered was rarely enough to fix what had been destroyed.

Ibrahim Abu Omar, fifty-seven, is one of the many Gazans who has taken rebuilding into his own hands. He served my translator and me tea in the concrete shell of what would be his new house. The grey box took ten months for his family to build and cost the $15,000 he had saved working as a truck driver. He recently took out a $12,000 loan. Despite this, the home is nowhere near finished. Its shell sits next to a twisted pile of rebar left by a private company he'd paid to clear his land.

Ibrahim remembers every conflict going back to the 1967 Six Day War. He remembers the lemon trees his father planted when he was a boy. He remembers 2006, the year of Hamas' election and Israel's subsequent blockade. 'Everything was destroyed after that,' he said with a sigh.

During Protective Edge he had to flee his home with nothing but the clothes on his back, running with his family through the streets to the UNRWA school, where they stayed for weeks. He returned to find both his home and his son's neighbouring house completely gone. So that Israeli soldiers did not have to move through the streets, where they would be exposed, their tanks cleared paths by firing into houses. What shells started, bulldozers finished. Ibrahim's house lay crushed under the rubble of his son's.

After the ceasefire was declared, Hamas' charitable arm gave Ibrahim's family $2,000. The money quickly disappeared on food and other essentials. When he began to rebuild, Gaza's munic-ipal government demanded $2,500 to register the new house and connect it to the power grid. This was one of many stories I would hear of the municipal government using the destruction of people's homes to extract fees or back taxes.

At least Hamas had given him some money initially. Ibrahim said that none of the NGOs swarming Gaza gave him a shekel, though UNRWA did stop by to take photos.

I asked him what he thought of Hamas. He laughed, then looked nervously to the side. 'If you're with Hamas, you have a good life. If you're not . . .' Ibrahim had been employed by the Palestinian Authority, whose dominant Fatah party has spent the last decade in an occasionally violent struggle with Hamas. Even now employees of the PA living in Gaza told me that, despite receiving salaries, they don't show up for work, though they nervously declined to spell out the reason.

Meanwhile, Israel maintains its blockade on building mate-rials coming into Gaza, claiming that it wants to prevent them from being used by Hamas to create tunnels. According to Israeli human rights group Gisha, Israel has only allowed into Gaza about a fifth of the amount of construction materials experts esti-mate are needed to repair the war's damage. This trickle is so inadequate that Oxfam has estimated it will take a hundred years to rebuild the Strip, assuming Israel doesn't invade it again in the intervening century.

According to Israeli politicians across the spectrum, Hamas is the cause of all Gaza's woes. Because Gazans elected Hamas in

2006, and its government later pre-empted a coup in 2007, they are fair game.

Hamas itself isn't much of a threat. It has ineffectual rockets – since 2007 rocket and mortar attacks have killed forty-four people within Israel, and many of these attacks are claimed by militant groups outside Hamas control. Hamas' municipal government is so broke that many civil servants have gone months without pay. The besieged residents' economic life-lines were the smuggling tunnels – before most of them were destroyed.

But Israeli politicians are more concerned with Hamas as a PR construct, one that lets them recast aggression as self-defence. Israel invokes Hamas to justify its hundreds of ceasefire viola-tions, its restrictions on Gazans' movement and the blockade that devastates Gaza's economy, grinding the residents' futures as fine as Shujaiyya's dust.

On my last night in Gaza I saw that sort of misattributed revenge take place on a smaller scale.

A jihadi group opposing Hamas shot three rockets into Israel. They landed in a field where they burned a small circle in the grass. Israel holds Hamas responsible for any rocket attack coming from the Strip, even those launched by Hamas' enemies. The drones buzzed more loudly than usual above our heads that night.

I sat on the balcony of my apartment overlooking Gaza's beach, where during the day little boys hawked boat rides and couples smoked shishas. A year before, Israeli soldiers had killed four children on that beach. A week after my visit an Israeli internal investigation would absolve the army of any wrongdoing.

The drones grew louder. On the horizon out to sea I could see gold pinpricks – the lights of Israeli gunships. Then I heard the growl of fighter jets. These were common sounds on a common night in that uncommon, besieged and defiant city. By midnight the shells had begun to fall.

GAZA

Sabrina Mahfouz

Let's be the protectors of poetry
let's pull bricks down
with the tricks of words
and build them up again
when the sky no longer burns shadows
where we once spoke.

Let's spill dark ink on the sand
use the forgotten fingers of our hands
to fight with tides
that try to wash us away.

Let's mark walls with the blood of our tongues
to know our lives will be heard
even when they are reduced to nothing
but reddish-grey rubble.

Let's displace sentences
until they are so at home
in every metal-doored house
nobody is able to tell where they came from anymore.

Let's throw darts dipped in vowels
so when they pierce skin they bring not only pain
but the ability to begin at the beginning of language again.

Let's put out our cigarettes on full stops
allow the ash-drowned letters
of doomed love to look through glassless windows
with shards of a hope made whole.

Let's stare at the sea
until similes sting our eyes
until we agree
standing on a rock older than poetry
that this land can only ever belong
to those who love.
No matter what the checkpoints say

or how loud the rockets scream
we know that love is enough
because there is nothing more
and we learned that through words
when touch was disallowed
so read me the poems as I drown

my love.

A DECADE OF WRITERS' WALKS
Raja Shehadeh

The night before I was to take the authors participating in the Palestine Festival of Literature on a walk through the West Bank hills I woke up in a sweat.

The festival, launched in 2008, describes itself as a 'cultural roadshow' that travels around historic Palestine. Its chair, Ahdaf Soueif, felt that it would not be complete without experiencing the land through taking a walk. As the author of the book *Palestinian Walks*, it fell upon me to accompany the writers on this walk.

At first I asked for a slot of five hours. But they were pressed for time. The whole festival was one week, with many areas to visit, panels to conduct, workshops and performances to deliver. We bargained and settled on a maximum of two and a half hours. I had to give a lot of thought to the best representative route for so brief a walk. I found it near my house.

Were this walk to have taken place twenty years earlier we could have done without the drive. Close to my house is the start of an ancient trail that cradles the hill and slopes gently down to the valley. Once there we would have walked along the dry riverbed. We would have found ourselves in a wide valley with terraced hills on both sides and could have examined the various features of the land: the terraces, the springs, the old stone structures – qasrs – built by farmers to store their produce, where they slept on the roof during the hot summer months. (The Arabic word qasr literally means palace or fort.) It would have been possible to get the feeling of being entirely away from any urban development – roads, houses and walls. But in the past two decades the speedy and unplanned expansion of Ramallah has destroyed those ancient paths. To start the walk we now had to drive several miles down the hill to where the last building stands.

But where Palestinian construction stops, Area C begins; this is the largest area, comprising the majority of the land of the West Bank, and the Oslo Accords put it entirely under Israeli jurisdiction. Here Israel is rapidly expropriating Palestinian land to build new and expand existing Jewish settlements. Technically Palestinians cannot walk there without permission from the Israeli military authorities. As I planned the walk I considered the risk that a busload of mainly foreign writers would attract the attention of Israeli soldiers or settlers. We would then be stopped, questioned and eventually asked to leave. But then most areas where it is still possible to walk are classified as Area C, and so the risk is unavoidable.

If nature is an open book on which humans continuously write their script then there are few areas in the world where they have scribbled more avidly than on these hills. With seemingly unlimited financial means, the Israeli settlers have been the most active. Since the beginning of the Israeli occupation of the West Bank five decades ago they have never stopped scribbling.

When I started these walks, for the first few years I would begin by briefing the PalFest authors about the land law applicable in Palestine and how Israel had amended it to make it possible to seize land for the settlements. I would be so involved in my task that I would not notice how bored the writers were getting until I saw my wife Penny gesturing to me to stop. By the time I finished, a precious half-hour had passed out of the two and a half designated for the walk. In later years I came to realise that nothing compares to being physically on the land, walking it, brushing against the dry herbs – the sage, thyme and oregano – smelling these and seeing with one's eyes the ruined paths and the encroachment by buildings and roads, and realising the tragedy of these places – unchanged for centuries – that are now vanishing.

The plan was to walk a short distance along the valley then climb up the hill and get to one of the qasrs. From there we would continue to the next village, Ayn Qenia, where we would meet the bus that would drive us back to Ramallah.

The first brief stop along the drive down was where the outpost of Yad Yair had once been. This small settlement was evacuated by the Israeli army in 2009, leaving behind reams of the concertina wire that used to surround it and blocks of concrete. Otherwise nature was taking over, as nature always does, with weeds and shrubs growing again on the land. As I explained how the settlement and the military outpost that were placed there to protect it had prevented us for ten years from using this road I wondered how many of my companions could imagine how the place had looked and what it meant to live next to this fledgling illegal Israeli presence so close to Palestinian homes. The day may come, after the settlement project is abandoned, when it will take a strong imaginative effort for visitors to a Palestine free from illegal Jewish settlements to realise what it had meant to those of us unfortunate enough to have lived through it all.

After this short stop we began a drive along a narrow, pockmarked, winding road that has only recently reopened. Down we went and I had to deal with the complaints of the bus driver: 'Is the road like this all the way? How will I be able to make it up again with such narrow spaces to make turns?'

Soon after we began our descent a few of the authors asked whether the housing project they could see on the next hill to our right, east of Ramallah, was a Jewish settlement. I picked up the microphone (which made me feel like a tour guide) and explained that it wasn't.

'But it looks like one,' I heard someone say. I had to agree. In the past Palestinians built individual homes surrounded by gardens. Now large construction companies are spending huge sums borrowed from banks, aiming for large returns on their money by building as many units as possible on a single plot of land. The gardens are gone and uniformity is in. No wonder the Palestinian houses built in rows look much like the settlements, displaying the same ugliness and causing an equal degree of destruction.

I gave the authors the best clue to recognise Israeli from Palestinian housing. The former can do without water tanks on the roof because they are assured a constant and steady supply of running water. Not so the Palestinians, who need to store water in the tanks that identify every Palestinian house.

Soon we came to a crossroads close to the valley. The bus found a place to park and we started on our walk.

Once in the valley, the hills spread out on either side with their terraces and olive groves. We walked for a short distance and started our ascent along barely discernible trails up the hill heading to the qasrs. The land was extremely stony so the possibility of someone falling or spraining their ankle was strong. I worried about this. How then would we be able to carry them down? And what if someone was bitten by a snake or scorpion or tripped and fell or collapsed from exhaustion or heat?

There were two qasrs on the same level. These were left over from when the residents of Ramallah lived off the land and left their houses in the village for the summer, tending their vegetable plots and caring for their olive trees and vines, using ancient tracks to transport the produce on donkey-back or if they were more affluent on a mule. I decided the qasr to the north was the more interesting and headed to it. When we got there I realised my mistake. But now there was no visible track to the other one, so we had to plunge into thorny bushes to get through. I feared we might come across a wild boar, who would rush out at us and frighten the visiting authors, but none were around that day.

A number of the writers during the walk got their legs scratched. Some were wearing the wrong kind of shoes, too soft for the stony fields. However, J.M. Coetzee, the oldest in the group, straight-backed and strong-legged, kept up with me and continued to ask questions about the occupation and the laws governing it. 'Do you have resort to the Israeli High Court?' he asked. I told him that we did but it has constantly proven futile. He also said that Ramallah struck him as affluent, which surprised him. The economy of the occupation never ceases to surprise me.

We arrived exhausted, this time at the right qasr. It looked dark and forbidding inside and no one was prepared to venture in. I threw a few stones to scare off any animal that might have been sheltering from the sun and entered. The others were at first reluctant but then began to stream through and up the circular stairs to the next floor. Fortunately I was the first to arrive at the top because just as I entered I saw a snake politely slide away through a hole between the stones. I did not announce this previous visitor to the others.

It was indeed cool and atmospheric inside the stone structure. I could see the relief in my guests' eyes, but some were clearly worried about the way down. We sat on the windowsills. Some, like Coetzee, kept standing, and I began to read.

There was no time to walk to the village of Ayn Qenia near the settlement of Dolev, so I chose to read a section from *Palestinian Walks* about my first encounter with the hill in 1979, before the establishment of this or any other settlement in the area – when indeed the land had been untouched by cement. During that walk I had decided to run up to race the setting sun. For someone who had just lost his way in these familiar hills perhaps this bravado was out of place, but the writers listened politely. My only saving grace was when I produced the cold watermelon slices I had been carrying on my back up the treacherous path.

What the writers heard me describe was a completely different reality from the present state of these hills. Several roads have now been built through them, and Jewish settlements dominate the tops of most of the hills around where we had taken our short walk. Only by looking through the narrow window of the qasr, from which none of the buildings, roads or settlements could be seen, could they get a glimpse of the unspoiled hills and imagine how the entire area had once been before the onslaught on this precious land. That is what it now takes to experience the land as it used to be: selective looking through a narrow window from one of its remaining stone structures.

As I think back over the different walks I have taken over the past nine years in these Palestinian hills with some of my favourite writers: Kamila Shamsi, Gillian Slovo, J.M. Coetzee, Henning Mankel, Colum McCann, Michael Palin, Teju Cole . . . I remember how much I have enjoyed their company and the talks we had as we walked. Some years the weather was agreeable and we were able to amble up and down and through the valley to the next village; other years it was hot and we were pressed for time. Many of their comments still ring in my mind, and if there was space I would include all of them here. But the words of Claire Messud stand out: 'We scrambled up rocks among terraced olive groves to a stone shepherd's hut, from which we could see the green and gold hills interlaced to the horizon. We picked our way along a dry riverbed, surprising a tortoise, and on to a small village, where a mangy donkey gazed balefully from its tether and ruddy-faced children demonstrated their tree-climbing prowess.' With an aching heart she concluded, 'What is a world where you cannot go for a walk, cannot assemble to read and discuss literature in public, cannot be certain of visiting your grand-mother in a neighbouring city?'

Fortunately no one on any of these walks over the past nine years has sprained an ankle or collapsed from exhaustion or heat. No one was bitten by a snake or scorpion. Many shared my anger over the destruction of the spectacular land of Palestine with new roads and thousands of tons of cement; illegal homes for Israeli settlers, who have not only spoiled the landscape but also contributed to complicating and prejudicing the chances of peace in this tortured land.

LET YOUR LIVES SPEAK
Linda Spalding

At eighteen I made a pilgrimage that was unusual for a Kansas girl raised up to be Episcopalian. My fellow travellers were strangers to me, birthrite Quakers from many countries, travelling by bus in England to visit historical Quaker sites. It all came back to me forty years later when I was travelling with a different group of strangers in another bus, one that moved by slow degrees through Palestine. In England, in 1961, we teens roomed in a Manchester schoolhouse and made daily trips to old Quaker meeting houses. I had a crush on Ramsey, a boy from Lebanon. *Where is he now?* I wondered, looking out on the winding roads of the West Bank. I remembered an elderly woman who'd sat with us in the chilly Manchester schoolroom and unfolded her theory of resistance. Passive because she was Quaker, but fierce and dedicated to right living. Her name was Elfrida Vipont Foulds, and I was electrified by her passion, her insistence. No adult had ever spoken so fervently in my hearing and yet the message was basic and simple. She said, *Let your lives speak,* and the words struck me then with such force that they may be the reason I found myself on a bus in Palestine.

In spite of that insistence on making my life matter, I could not, in Palestine, imagine how to address the wounds we saw around us. How does one find words to speak of such unfairness, such horror? How abstain from complicity? We were writers, adults of various ages and countries, each of us mindful, each attentive. We looked out on a land mythical to a person of Christian or Jewish or Muslim background. Didn't we cross the River Jordan? Weren't the people we met familiar? But they are cut off now from the rest of the world by a vast enclosing wall. They are surrounded by soldiers holding weapons and by barricades and turnstiles and hostile faces shouting orders and insults. They are surrounded by the illegal occupiers of their land.

To the occupiers we were suspect. Writers who wanted to visit the West Bank, we were kept waiting for hours at Passports in spite of the authorisation letters we carried. We were interrogated about one thing and then another – about where we live, about where we were born, about what right or need we might or might not have to travel in the West Bank, where no one should want to go. There are certainly things better left unseen. In Hebron, Banksy has made a beautiful message out of the ugly wall, but the streets are empty, and an Israeli ambulance is painted with black silhouetted guns along with the names of the Americans from Minnesota who paid for it. There are police cars too, and tanks, all given, all funded and sent with blessings from afar. Whole streets in the old Hebron marketplace are condemned by locks and bolts on every shop door. The few stores still open are mainly on the street directly under apartments taken over by illegal Israeli occupiers who sometimes throw buckets of bleach on the shirts and shoes below. Shit too and urine, because along with the buckets, the Israelis hold the wanton power of victors. 'Are you Jewish?' is the question we were asked on an empty street. 'Because you cannot walk here if you're not.' And so it goes for the man who cannot get to his olive trees because the roads are forbidden to him while settlers in big American cars go speeding past to their vast Soviet-style settlements, and we remind ourselves that they too carry guns. No use appealing to the Israeli soldiers as a car swerves towards us menacingly. The soldiers are girls and boys with bigger, heavier guns than any child ought to carry and an attitude too merciless to be challenged. O Israel what are you doing to your children? Do you not see what they become?

In the West Bank we went from one town to another. Hebron, Ramallah, Bethlehem, Nablus. We gave little performances of our skills and invited participation from local residents. We visited a camp created out of tents and boxes and bits of wreckage. We watched children dance. We each of us, on both sides of the fence that separates those who are free from those who are not, entertained the other as we could. We shared a meal around long tables and joked and sang. I remember flirting with a man of my generation who was dignified and sexy. I do not remember his name as I do not remember names well any more, and he is probably like me in that way, thinking only of the hour so mutually pleasant.

Kafr Bir'im is a place of low rock walls that show the outlines of what were once homes. It was a flourishing village before its residents were required, nearly seventy years ago, to leave for two days in order to register in a census. In that ruined place we had tea with a group of people who have come back with tents to reclaim the land that was bombed while their parents and grandparents walked towards the next town as ordered. Seeing a small plane moving in the direction of their homes they must have turned as one and then stood on the dusty road and watched as those homes were destroyed in minutes. Eradicated. Disappeared. There is a pretty Christian church still standing. There is the graveyard with its stones inscribed. But the people acting their Right of Return are not permitted to live on the land that holds the bones of their families. They may not build there, and the planting they do in their fields is clandestine.

Although planting is not what it used to be in Palestine. We learned this from Raja Shehadeh, who has walked the hills for decades. He knows the ridges and the valleys and the plants and streams, and one afternoon he led us up a steep incline and into a grove of old olive trees. Each tree had been watered by hand for generations, but now the great Jordan is being drained to water thirsty Israel and the life-giving trees are shrivelling.

There are a thousand ways to genocide.

At the Qalandia checkpoint we waited in a long line to enter Jerusalem. Everyone else in the line was Palestinian on the way to a job on the other side of the wall. They wait for such savage lengths of time after their early-morning commute. Then they are interrogated and harassed before being allowed to go off to work for their overlords, whether doctoring or digging ditches. This is where we heard the story of two young soccer players, Jawhar (nineteen) and Adam (seventeen), shot in the feet by Israeli soldiers because – because? They were going to play for Palestine in the World Cup. I took a photograph of our surroundings with my iPhone but inside, having made it through the turnstile, they took me to a room behind a steel door and commanded me to delete the photograph. After all, there are things that must not be seen. We were surrounded by turrets and guns and razor-wire fences very like the Nazi death camps, and that is not the image Israel wants to project. A people walled in, without rights, without freedom to move, without protection of the law, are prisoners. The guns and turrets belong to the jailors as usual.

'I don't know how to delete things on this phone,' I said to the young soldier.

'I'll show you.' And he did.

In Jerusalem the stone-covered tomb can be visited in a great hollow and echoing church. And the little alleys through which it is said Jesus walked on his last walking day are there too, but I had no will to follow. Instead I went into a neighbourhood of stacked dwellings cut off in the way Palestinian homes are cut off from the rest in this supposedly shared city, where in so many places the star of David announces that one more Palestinian resident has been ousted. Generations may have lived here in peace, and yet there are Israeli flags fluttering all over the city boasting of ignoble victories. I WILL NOT MOVE read a banner over a doorway. But it was a fine dwelling near a fine market-place, and it had already been emptied and given to a Jewish family.

Well, they are losers, my father said of the Palestinian people after a trip to Israel. He said Israel should never return the territory it stole in the Six Day War. He and my mother, good Kansas Episcopalians, went to visit the Wailing Wall in 1968. They did not go to London or Paris. They did not travel to Europe even once. They went to Israel and touched the wall where Mohammed is said to have tied his wondrous steed Al-Buraq, before he was taken up through the seven heavens and into the presence of God. A year earlier and the Moroccan Quarter of Jerusalem would have been at their backs, but now even the great plaza is forbidden to anyone with a Palestinian ID. One of the first acts of the Israelis, upon occupying East Jerusalem during the 1967 war, was to give the Palestinian inhabitants of this neighbourhood a few hours to evacuate their homes. Then the bulldozers came in to make of the place a clean enough slate to accommodate Jewish pilgrims. And tourists, like my parents, who could not see or understand what had been taken away. *Let your lives speak.* But first know the truth. I have a vivid memory of an old Quaker woman leaning towards me with her hand upraised. I wonder, though, was she really old, or did she only seem that way because of her glow and the challenge of the words that sent us on into our lives?

A BUS STOP IN LONDON
Najwan Darwish

At the bus stop in the morning
you think of a small house in a town by the sea
that you claim is the mother of all the cities of the world.
You reflect
as you walk in the funeral of pulsing capitalism
where each step is sold by the square centimetre.

At the bus stop in the morning
you say that life is late
or that its bus has gone
but still you stand there thinking of a small house
hidden by the wind,
given away by the trees at the foot of Mount Carmel.

Translated by Kareem James Abu-Zeid

THE SCATTERING

Claire Messud

The cicadas sing without let in the olive grove beyond the lip of the hill, and the dry leaves clatter softly in the hot breeze. Dust rises in small clouds with each step, and settles upon her sandalled feet, greying her toes. Shading her face with her hand, the young woman turns to look back, towards where the sea ultimately lies; but between her and the water are too many hills and valleys. She sees instead the rows of gnarled trees and the golden cairn of a shepherd's hut with its hollow black eye. Rock and no water and the sandy road. The others have gone on ahead.

That evening back at the hotel she listens to the men speak. Distant cousins, they too have come from far away; they too have histories in this place that they know only partially. They speak about the houses of their grandfathers, merchants of Haifa and Jerusalem lawyers, about ways of life and worlds now extant only in sepia photographs, plastic-coated in albums in Oklahoma City and Detroit. She has no photographs, neither here nor at home; no known grandfather's house to lament.

Her grandmother Mona, the youngest of four, the afterthought, was transplanted first to Beirut then to Columbus, Ohio, a child of seven then for whom memories of home were already myth. The details the young woman hears now, over sweating Cokes in the hotel bar – other people's family fables, of deeds and rusting keys carefully handed down through generations; of the spreading swallow-tailed willow and the carpet of vermilion pheasant's eye in a summer garden; of long-legged boys splashing along the grassy banks of the al-Zarqa River – loom vivid and dream-like. Her inheritance instead is a grandmother's American immi-grant stories: of a childhood in Columbus, trailing through snow behind an older sister and two brothers chattering between them-selves in Arabic; of a mother prone to migraines who required quiet and a darkened room, and a laconic father wizened by care, scrabbling to rebuild his family's life in middle age. These, her grandmother's stories, include dinner plates stored for years in their packing crate, carefully returned each night after washing (just in case the family had to move again); a little girl's shame in the mid-century Midwestern playground at the blackness of her glossy braids, the wrongness of her home-made skirt and her mother's inability to speak English; the loneliness of not-belonging, of being at home nowhere but in an imaginary land, its topography gleaned second hand from sister and brothers, because her mother and father could not speak of it.

This means, the young woman reasons, that her own Palestine is born out of the mists of myriad imaginations. In life her grand-mother never returned; nor has her mother made the journey: she blesses but does not understand her daughter's pilgrimage. The past is the past, she says, your life is here; with a gentle stamp of her sneakered foot on the plush sod outside the family house in Natick, Massachusetts (built 1989). But why, then, are the trees on this hillside so familiar? Why does the shaft of light that falls through her dust-streaked hotel-room window soon after dawn strike her as a summons?

Over four days she listens to the others, to their stories; she listens to the guide, a young man from a village not far from Ramallah who will take them wherever they ask to go – within of course the constraints of the possible and the strictures of the Israeli maps. They visit Jenin, Nablus, Jericho, Bethlehem. She speaks little; asks questions, but few. She notices: the rattling exhaust pipe of their white minivan; the fluttering keffiyehs arrayed outside the shop next to the hotel; the way the old man at the corner cafe cups his cigarette inside his palm against the wind, and his avian face, reddish like modelling clay, etched by time. His tattered suit jacket hangs from his shoulders as if on a hanger, as if he had no body at all. She buys a set of coffee mugs for her mother, glazed dark blue like the night sky, and wraps them for her suitcase in her laundry. At bedtime she writes down what she has seen and heard each day in a small notebook, and sleeps with it under her pillow.

On the last day the group returns to walk in the countryside. They set out straight after breakfast, before it gets too hot. This time their guide parks the van on a ridge, half off the road, and they pick their way across a tufted valley to clamber up the winding rutted road to a village, the guide's village, in the gnat-whine wake of a moped. A goat sidles out to greet them, emitting its sceptical bleat. Two little boys squatting in the dust look up from their game as the party passes; an older woman pauses in her cleaning, duster aloft. Not an insignificant number, they are manifestly foreign. The young guide has friends here, calls out to a man his own age and the youth with him. The young woman, who speaks no Arabic, cannot understand what is said. Laughter is exchanged, shoulders slapped. Two of her fellow travellers who speak some Arabic join haltingly in the conversation; all the young men crowd in a circle. A few more emerge as if magically from the buildings around. The old woman, her duster on her shoulder, steps up the road to join the group, smiling now. A rooster, pecking his way across the junction, crows, jubilant.

It is easy to slip back down and around the bend, away from the people. She doesn't have to go far to be alone. *Parched*, she thinks, is the word for it. If there were the sound of water only. She longs for a drink but can wait. There is a bottle in the minivan, but instead she walks beyond its shadow, above her on the ridge, and out into the valley.

She can no longer hear the villagers, the handsome young guide, her fellow travellers, the dyspeptic goat. Instead the cicadas shriek against the whispered clatter of the olive leaves. She removes from her pants pocket a large linen handkerchief, neatly folded, and from within it a small clear plastic bag, of the sort now used at airport security for toothpaste and deodorant.

The young woman listens carefully; her eyes scan the green, grey, gold, dun of the landscape before her. She can't see anyone, anything. Hasty nevertheless, she fumbles to open the little bag's seal and tilts it gently earthwards. A silvery spray flies into the morning air, spreading, rising, falling, dispersing. With a shake of her shoulders she tips the bag further; the rush of cinereal dust intensifies, floats and settles. When she looks down at her feet, grey-coated in their sandals, she cannot tell whether her skin carries particles of the path or of her grandmother. That is fine.

She is almost content: Mona, or at least a small part of her, is home at last, or not too far. Her grandmother was born in Jaffa, by the sea. The young woman would have wished, ideally, to scatter this small portion of her ashes there, over the water; but – as with the others' family photographs – the place where her grandmother was born is no longer. This place – this vast sky in its naked light, this earth, this sandy road, these rocks, these bent trees, this hidden village above – will serve.

As she turns to climb back to join the others – they will fly back to New York tomorrow – she is stayed by the music of a bird close by. The rock thrush sings in the olive trees. For a few moments she listens, eyes closed. The air feels different then, gentler: perhaps she has granted Mona the unreachable wish. Swiftly she bends and grasps between her fingers a handful of the pebbled soil, releasing it into the empty plastic bag. She wipes her hand on her pants, seals the bag, wraps it in the napkin, slides the napkin back into her pocket. Her own name is Nadine, which in another language means hope.

It is time to go. She can hear the others coming down the hill. The rock thrush sings in the olive trees.

HOW TO SURVIVE EXILE
Sabrina Mahfouz

'Keep your heart warm and your body won't rust',
trust that things will get better, you will not be bitter.
Accept that bits of you won't ever look the same again,
when they were how they were you just complained anyway,
    so let it go.
With each change reshape your name with your tongue,
find that syllables don't only soar through falling leaves when
    you're young.
Rummage through the luggage of your life,
pull the treasures out by their hands and hold them tight,
dance around the storage boxes you've blocked your
    veins with,
sieve the heavy grains away,
feel the lightness of lace light up the places you've yet to go.
Because it's far from over,
even if it can't be lived over.
It's knowing it can be lived until it's gone and you've become
    something else,
touching the air in a new form, but before that –
find a morning that spreads butter on your toes,
let the sauce of a storm levitate whatever hair you have left,
ride the wind's broken tracks to a triangle of glass you've
    never slid on before,
sunbathe your core until your insides are so nicely heated they
    could be eaten,
then lay your star-warmed body down,
your origamied skin meeting what it once was
and now
close your bruised eyelids,
let the masks make their own way,
give your liver to the birds,
they will sing to us all the things you've heard.

WHAT WE TALK ABOUT WHEN WE TALK ABOUT PALESTINE

Jamal Mahjoub

Surreal is the word that springs to mind when I fly into Tel Aviv late at night, surrounded by a planeload of excited tourists returning from their holiday in Spain. An hour later I am in a taxi driving along a narrow strip of motorway that cuts deep into the surrounding darkness. Rows of sodium lights stand sentinel over the deserted road. A high chain-link fence topped by scrolls of razor wire runs along each side. It is not so much a road as a charmed corridor, a magical path through hostile territory. Against the glare you cannot see what lies beyond the glow of the lights.

Palestinian vehicles are not allowed on these smooth, modern roads. The West Bank proper begins beyond the penumbra. Once you leave the highway, skirting concrete barriers, the road begins to wind, rising and falling, as it passes along unlit roads that thread their way between dark, silent villages. It is as if you have fallen off the edge of the known world and passed into another dimension.

So much of what is now said is merely the regurgitation of established tropes. Time, like the accumulation of sediment at the bottom of a river, has made movement so sluggish as to be imperceptible. Progress of any kind has become intractable. We are bogged down by the very weight of history the issue has accreted over the years.

It's an issue that raises hackles, brings out furious, irrational responses, often founded on nothing less than a personal sense of moral outrage, an ill-perceived duty towards righteousness, a repressed, unspoken disgust. Palestine has become a metaphor, a postmodern deconstruction of past episodes of annihilation. Unlike the Holocaust, whose memory has been sanctified by time and the knowledge that what the Nazis did was a crude expression of the disdain that Europe as a whole felt towards its Jewish population, for Europeans the suffering of the Palestinians is seen as remote and disconnected from the notion of *our* history.

To most it is simply an awkward inconvenience. Nobody wants to think too hard about the fate of a people who appear to be doing their best to undermine their own cause. Suicide bombs, rocket attacks, stabbings. None of it plays well on the global media stage. And history has a habit of fading, allowing us to forget the parallels between this relentless process of destruction and the persecution of the Jews. The deception is aided by the fact that this is happening not in an instant but in slow motion. Palestine is being dismantled, turned into a jigsaw puzzle so complex that eventually it will be impossible to see the pieces for the lines between them.

For Israel what is at stake is the national conscience, the moral compass of the people. Putting aside the civilian casualties for a moment, a fraction of those whom the Palestinians have lost, what Israel has lost in the past forty years, since 1967, is the innocence it believed it had, best symbolised perhaps by the sun-bronzed kibbutzer that Amos Oz holds up in admiration in his memoirs. Today that is a fond memory, a dangerous delusion. Violence corrupts the violent, and it does so absolutely.

As a child growing up in Khartoum in the 1970s I was familiar with the heroic Palestinian images that appeared on television every night: of fedayeen, freedom fighters, leaping over trenches or crawling under barbed wire to a stirring soundtrack of martial music. It told us that there was a battle going on somewhere. Where exactly, we could not say, but it was a struggle between good and evil, justice and injustice. For decades martyrdom has been the role of Palestinians in the Arab world, their suffering a cover for all its failings – nationalism, despotism, corruption. We watched the pictures of refugees: forlorn, ragged people, the world's conscience. And we saw them, the women who gathered around our garden gate asking for help. We would give food and clothes, leftovers, cast-offs, to a people who had nothing left to lose.

Once when I refused to eat the peanut soup that was set before me I was lectured about children starving in camps. I can recall the shame I felt but also the resentment at being made an example of, at the absurdity of the idea that my not eating this soup somehow dishonoured the suffering of those people. I knew my soup would never reach them, and so it wasn't about that; it was about reconciling this life of privilege I had, where there was food on the table and clothes on my back, where I slept peacefully in my bed, with a world in which children just like me were starving and had no home to give them shelter. I resented being reminded of their existence.

The persecution of the Jews in Europe still exists in living memory. The Nazis marched through the city where I now live. Some eighty thousand were deported to the camps. Sixty thousand never returned. What do we learn from that history? Surely the only lesson we can take away is that such persecution, humiliation and destruction should never happen again? At times it seems as if we are not seeing the world clearly, but looking at it through a two-way mirror. The people on the inside see only themselves; from the outside you see them watching their own reflection but not seeing you.

How many times have I made the mistake of speaking my mind? Once, in Sarajevo, over dinner with an expert on Céline, the conversation took a turn and I got into an argument about Amos Oz. I made the observation that I didn't understand his support for the security wall, or separation barrier, as it is also called. For most of its length the barrier is a barbed-wire fence with surveillance cameras and towers; in built-up areas it rises into a concrete wall, eight metres high. As a security measure it fails miserably. There are so many weak points that a determined suicide bomber or terrorist would have no difficulty walking across it. Oz had quoted from Robert Frost: 'Good fences make good neighbours,' he'd said. It had struck me as paradoxical that a writer seen as a voice of reason, a voice for peace, would defend the idea of segregation. And besides, as he must have known, the wall is not about security; it is, like so much else, about seizing land. You see that when you watch Israeli soldiers uprooting olive trees, cutting off farmers from their crops, from their water.

The wall also has a symbolic role. It tells Palestinians that they cannot even touch their own land, draw water from their wells. In this way their Palestine has already ceased to exist. The physical separation is about deprivation, prising away contact between a people and the land they hold dear. The issue here is not security but the prevention of contact. It carries with it the idea of contamination, so clearly and casually depicted by Hollywood in the zombie movie *World War Z* – the notion that Palestinians are not human beings at all, not even animals, but germs or a virus that must be isolated and destroyed.

Aside from the land it seizes, the real impact of the wall is psychological. Eight-metre-high walls turn the West Bank into a gigantic prison. It makes residents into inmates, their crime being their existence. It is a logical extension of the checkpoints around Bethlehem and Jerusalem, which are an exercise in humiliation. People pass along cattle runnels, separated from one another by high metal bars. Soldiers bark commands in Hebrew. Keep moving. Stop. Start. Go. Do not go. The humiliation is reinforced by the fact that the guards are kids barely out of their teens. To live with such monstrosity would be unbearable for most.

Why is none of this alarming or familiar to the world? How can rational, intelligent, educated people look at this and feel it is justified. By what twisted algorithm have they arrived at this conclusion? How is it that we accept this irrational fear of an entire people, a minority most of whom are not violent but oppressed, not fanatical but resigned, not the aggressor but the aggrieved? Yet to speak this aloud is, in many quarters, considered an obscenity. Gentle, sensitive souls become apoplectic when speaking of the clumsy, pathetic rockets launched by Hamas, the children dressed up as jihadis, the young women who dream of martyrdom. It is a rationale based on incomprehension, on fear of the other taken to the extreme. In Sarajevo it wasn't even an argument, just an awkward silence. The blank stare, the shake of the head, the silent, unforgiving look which says, How can you possibly feel sympathy?

The context has changed, of course. When I was a child the struggle of Palestinians was regarded as a war of liberation. PLO stood for the Palestine Liberation Organisation, with the emphasis being on liberation. On freedom. In those far-off days terror had a finite, political aim. There was an ideology which argued that the use of violence was justified in the pursuit of the final outcome: freedom for the homeland. Looking back now, that kind of thinking seems almost quaint. Time. Betrayal. Deception. It all adds up. One could argue that there are no ideologies today, only faith and sacrifice. The perversion of politics means that the scope for negotiation has been whittled down to nothing. The limits of what is achievable have been eroded to the point where all that remains is martyrdom or the belief that one's actions are guided by a divine hand.

Meanwhile, the outside world looks on, numbed by guilt and prejudice, bowing to self-interest and the will of partisan lobbyists. Where does this passivity stem from? In Europe a blend of tolerance and guilt gives rise to a plea for parity; the plight of Israelis and Palestinians must be understood as equal in order to avoid any accusation of anti-Semitism. This discomfort is a moral one. It is produced by the awareness that the line drawn between the genocide suffered by the Jews in Europe and the fate of Israel today is not as straightforward as it might seem. It also acts as a blindfold. Perhaps this goes some way towards explaining the difference in attitude between those brought up in Europe and those, like myself, whose experience on the outside allows them a different perspective.

In the West the conviction persists that sympathy for the Palestinian cause is synonymous with anti-Semitism, as if the two were bound together by a simple equation that is not only unquestionable but almost sacred. Yet as long as we refuse to distinguish criticism of the Israeli state from racial hatred we will continue to labour under the deception that we understand what is actually happening. And perhaps the point is that this is no longer about Israel and Palestine, it is about who *we* are and what kind of world *we* want to live in. The 9/11 attacks broke a taboo, they crossed a line, touching American bodies on American soil. And the actions of a handful of men unleashed cataclysm on the entire region: from Iraq and Afghanistan through Guantánamo and Abu Ghraib to drone strikes and civil war, societies have been shattered and the region devastated in ways that we are only just beginning to comprehend. The world is drifting further apart and yet, of course, we have nowhere else to go.

Perhaps the conflict works best at the metaphorical level. Without a belief in a unifying common humanity, in something that can allow us to rise above our differences and bring us together, we are left with nothing more and nothing less than a world that is a gated community. This is what lies ahead: a world in which we all live in fear of difference, of the other, of those whose appearance and beliefs differ from ours. That is what apartheid was and that is what the separation wall is today. It is a symbol of what the future holds for all of us, unless we change course.

Once we let go of our belief in the greater good that holds mankind together we become prisoners of fear, the same rabid delusion that propelled the Nazis to become an ugly footnote in history. This is what you see when you pass through the Israeli checkpoints, when you look into the eyes of the Israeli soldiers on patrol in Hebron, the protective nets the Palestinians have strung over their market, the Israeli settlers stoning schoolchil-dren, Israeli joggers bearing M16s, Israeli watchtowers sprouting cameras like cactus spines, the ruins of Gaza City, the dusty, desolate landscape around the tunnel lifeline, the Klieg lights marking the open sea with fishing limits, the buzz of drones overhead, the despair of hunger strikers, the concrete noose thrown around Rachel's Tomb, the golden Menorah surveilling al-Aqsa Mosque, the apartment buildings crumpled like accordions, the names and faces of the martyrs that turn refugee camps into memorials for the dead.

PalFest gave me the chance to see all of this and more. It gave me the opportunity to talk to people, to students and civilians, ordinary people trying to live their lives in the midst of this imposition of insanity. Not only to live, but to dream, to work towards something. What struck me was the sense that I would not have survived had I been born in Palestine. The anger, frustration, humiliation. There are of course those who succumb, who feel that violence is the only possible response, even when that has to take the hopeless form of suicide. This is not a surprise. To live under such conditions year in, year out, generation after generation, would be enough for most people. It would be enough for me. And yet it is not. The wonder is that there is not more violence. The remarkable thing is to see that there are many who still believe in working towards a peaceful outcome through unarmed protest, through theatre, art, poetry. Lawyers and civil rights workers, farmers and students, NGOs, actors, writers, booksellers and singers, all those who have chosen not to take up the gun but to believe, against all the odds, that peace with justice is still possible. This is the true miracle of Palestine. This is the real miracle. For all our sakes, we should believe in it.

The Gaza Suite: Tel El Hawa

Suheir Hammad

what day is it
alkaline of neck alley base
of musk alcohol top note

what the night was like
blooming sky white smoke black out
a dawn flaming life

so long this winter
so cold this shadow
what day is it

a woman dreams a baby years
embroiders wishes names angels
a future onto cloth the people carry her
child shelled streets shaheed
what day is it

a father works hours to bone to feed
seed dress them bless them buries them
his pain a sonic collapse
who can imagine

today the first day
last night the worst night

Exit Strategy

China Miéville

So we should ask Mohammed al-Durra. He isn't dead again.

Recall his face. Even from a government one of the chief exports of which is images of screaming children, his was particularly choice, tucked behind his desperate father, pinned by fire. Until Israeli bullets visit them and they both go limp. He for good. *Pour encourager les autres.*

Now though, thirteen years after he was shot on camera – one year more than he lived – he has been brought back to life. But wait before you celebrate: there are no very clear protocols for this strange paper resurrection. Mohammed al-Durra is a bureaucratic Lazarus. After a long official investigation, by the power vested in it the Israeli government has declared him not dead. He did not die.

There was another boy at the hospital, there were no injuries, it was a trick. A blood libel to suggest he was killed by Israelis, the same day as were Nizar Eida and Khaled al-Bazyan, one day before Muhammad al-Abbasi and Sara Hasan and Samer Tabanja and Sami al-Taramsi and Hussam Bakhit and Iyad al-Khashashi, two before Wael Qattawi and Aseel Asleh, three before Hussam al-Hamshari and Amr al-Rifai, but stop because listing killed children takes a long time. Keep his name out of that file.

Jamal al-Durra will open his son's grave. Is that enough? he asks with a unique exhaustion. To prove that this thing we saw happen happened, that the boy we saw die died?

The task is complete. Wheels are spinning. A new pass law. The IDF has been sent, a checkpoint set up at the border of the land of the dead. And Mohammed al-Durra has been hard-stopped by the guards because he does not carry the right papers.

Undesirable life is ended, and unauthorised death is banned. Where is Mohammed to go now, the victim of this necrocide, this murder of the killed?

Between wire runnels, tangled chains, cages, again. Again, again. Maybe that's where the shot-again newly unkilled boy will kick his heels. A purgatory not for the unshriven but for the troublesomely Arab, for the death-contested.

In Jerusalem the government decrees that Palestinian deceased sublimate after seven years, to be absent, to go to the nothingness that their recalcitrant bodies, living then dead, resist. They absent themselves finally from the real estate they hog, and at last it can be where a cable car touches down. It can be a foundation for engines.

Peace is a corrupt business in Palestine, he says.

Driving in from Allenby, the rock gorge has been hacked ruthlessly out of the mountains, and protruding from one part is a jagged fringe of metal where some once-submerged and hidden corridor has been exposed and left to weather and dangle from its housing.

Yes, we know the Holy Land is now a land of holes, and lines, a freak show of topography gone utterly mad, that the war against Palestinians is also a war against everyday life, against human space, a war waged with all expected hardware, with violent weaponised absurdism, with tons and tons of concrete and girders. This is a truism, and/but true.

Settler is an odd term for these vectors of the unsettling, government-sponsored agents of government-desired permanent crisis, for whom stability and everyday life are anathemata to be fought unstintingly, with bullets and beatdowns and strategies of berserker spite.

The low mesh sky of al-Khalil market is pelted with its own grotesque microclimate. Hebron. These low clouds are piss bottles, concrete slabs, storms of trash, a suspended weather of race hate. Stand between stallholders whose dogged sales patter become heroics in the shadows of bags of shit, stand by a ledge where a ginger kitten picks intrepidly through razor wire and look up. There's something brewing.

They used to play games, she explains. She and her friends were told to behave or else the settler would come and get them. They knew his name, they knew he had a wooden leg, they convinced each other and themselves that they could hear him coming. *Clack drag clack drag clack*. They knew the scary rhythms and covered their mouths. Those sounds he made. They pantomimed the terrible things he would do if he caught them. Much later she read a newspaper, and of course he had been real.

In Jerusalem the flags on the stolen house metastasise. They jut vertically, and horizontally, but then they protrude at all ludicrous angles in between, as if any sough of Palestinian air unruffled by the white and blue is an outrage. They must not leave a breath unclaimed.

There is a mannequin in al-Khalil, in the market, a plastic woman with very pale skin and outdated hair, modelling a long black dress with red trim. She stares stupidly ahead, as if she would like you to join her in ignoring the hole in her forehead, almost exactly in the centre, only a little to the right, where her eyebrow ends. It is just like the hole a bullet would make if this placid woman were targeted by a sniper. Move to the side: the right rear of her head is gone. Yes, that's where the exit wound would be, and it would pass through much like that, yes, leaving a hole like that one, shaped, I swear to God, like that one, like something big and familiar.

The young Jewish woman turns and gasps as you follow her into Qalandia, through steel runs that are too narrow. She says, 'I can't believe this was designed by people with these memories.' An entrance to discourage entrance in the first place, but, like a pitcher plant, to make it impossible, once entered, to change your mind.

There's a place where the wall incorporates a house. If you hang a picture up you decorate the inside of that dorsal ridge, the scales of that rising concrete animal.

And in its wedge of shadow the long stupid zigzag of the checkpoint between Bethlehem and Jerusalem is indicated with a sign, there on the Bethlehem side. ENTRANCE, it says, white on green, and points to the cattle run. Inside are all the ranks of places to wait, the revolving grinder doors, green lights that may or may not mean a thing, the conveyor belts and metal detectors and soldiers and more doors, more metal striae, more gates.

Finally, for those who emerge on the city side, who come out in the sun and go on, there is a sign they, you, we have seen before. White on green, pointing back the way just come.

ENTRANCE, it says. Just like its counterpart on the other side of a line of division, a non-place.

No exit is marked.

The arrows both point in. Straight towards each other. The logic of the worst dream. They beckon. They are for those who will always be outside, and they point the way to go. Enter to discover you've gone the only way, exactly the wrong way.

ENTRANCE: a serious injunction. A demand. Their pointing is the pull of a black hole. Their directions meet at a horizon. Was it ever a gateway between? A checkpoint become its own end.

This is the plan. The arrows point force at each other like the walls of a trash compactor. Obey them and people will slowly approach each other and edge closer and closer from each side and meet at last, head on like women and men walking into their own reflections, but mashed instead into each other, crushed into a mass.

ENTRANCE, ENTRANCE. These directions are peremptory, their signwriters voracious, insisting on obedience everywhere, impatient for the whole of Palestine to take its turn, the turn demanded, until every woman and man and child is waiting on one side or the other in long long lines, snaking across their land like the wall, shuffling into Israel's eternal and undivided capital, CheckPointVille, at which all compasses point, towards which winds go, and there at the end of the metal run the huge, docile, cow-like crowds will, in this fond, politicidal, necrocidal, psychecidal fantasy, meet and keep taking tiny steps forward held up by the narrowness of the walls until they press into each other's substance and their skins breach and their bones mix and they fall into gravity one with the next. Palestine as plasma. Amorphous. Amoebal. Condensed. Women and men at point zero. Shrunken by weight, eaten and not digested. An infinite mass in an infinitely small space.

In the bowels of that hangar where the lines of those arrows meet are advertisements. ISRAEL, one says in that no-place, on the line in the sand, WHERE IT'S VACATION ALL YEAR ROUND.

Please understand that there is nothing unthinking about that joke, that these are exactly the posters a Palestinian is supposed to see at this point, that this is information she needs, now move on, keep going on this time out of time, time off, this vacation you have been given on the sand. You are beached. Get out.

There is no out. The signs are very clear. Everything is an entrance, and it all leads here.

In Hebrew, Arabic and English, in black on yellow: PREPARE YOUR DOCUMENTS FOR INSPECTION. And below that another of the posters. Under the smiling, piggy-backing couple: ISRAEL: FOR THE TIME OF YOUR LIFE.

It's not intended to be a surprise. So that is the plan, and there it is. Here is time, and your life. Have everyone shuffle forward for all time on this bad, bad holiday, into this eternity.

You are supposed to follow the signs. Here is the idea. It will be explained again, as often as it takes. The end is not to be three strangers in a room alone but a nation, two near-unending lines of broken living and the authorised dead, ordered forward and pushing and pushed and becoming nothing. What is lawfully inscribed here is not NO EXIT; it is ENTRANCE–ENTRANCE.

THE GAZA SUITE: ZEITOUN
Suheir Hammad

where from here
a ribbon of land smoking
within the girl's hair smoking
wire wood word smoking
there are bodies here
micro mosaic children
a triptych exile against wall
my dead are rescued
a closing of crossings
a scatter vapor of earth
a trance of metal
where from here

i am all tunnel

The End of Art Is Peace
Omar Robert Hamilton

The bus stops outside Bethlehem. The reverend lifts the microphone. We are returning from the Cremasin Monastery, a palazzo of elegant stonework standing above a terraced valley of vineyards. The monastery's Salesian monks make the best wine in Palestine. 'See the wall?' the reverend says, and the group looks out the window to see the concrete future coming down the hill. 'And see it on the other hill there?' Heads turn, eyes follow the bulldozer's tracks. 'The wall is coming. This might be the last time we ever drive down this road.'

'They are digging underneath the houses.' Youssef, our host, is calm; he's told this story before. The sun presses down on the Jerusalem streets, but the air is cooler in his Mameluke atrium. 'A settler broke through my kitchen wall last year. They are tireless, the Jerusalem settlers. They are digging.' I translate for the authors, the transmitters to the outside world. Some take notes.

We sit on our balcony in Cairo, my mother, Yasmin and I, and we plan the coming festival's route. Will we try a new city this year? Or are we fixed with the regulars? Ramallah, Jerusalem, Bethlehem, al-Khalil, Haifa and Nablus. Should we drop Haifa and go to Lydd this year? But we have such a strong audience in Haifa. Maybe this is the year we perform in Jaffa? But there are no Palestinian hotels in the city. Can we go to Qalqilya, Tulkarem, Jenin? We only have five days – what would we drop? And what about the Golan, the Bedouin, the border with Gaza? How can you understand Palestine without them? Five days is so little time.

Cement blocks sever the road, a grey town in the distance of this scrubland of bowed heads and silences and soldiers' large guns hanging heavy off their shoulders. The second Intifada still smoulders. Sunglasses keep all possible violences alive. We show our passports. The soldier doesn't move. We walk on. Years later I come to know that they call this place Qalandia.

Get on the bus. Our annual catchphrase. Every day our festival troupe packs its bags, changes city, changes hotel, checks in, unpacks, listens, performs. Five days, seven cities, twenty-two authors, five public events, five walking tours, twenty-nine hotel rooms, two universities, two thousand posters, thirty-six flights, two checkpoints, no free time.

Get on the bus. Get off the bus.

The bus drives up from the Dead Sea. The festival begins at the lowest point on earth. The bus drives up into the mountains to Ramallah, the Heights of God, away from the border and the long wait for the Arab names to be waved through. The audience waits in Ramallah. Nowhere to go but up.

The first time I breathed tear gas was in al-Khalil. We were sitting in Hajj Yahya al-Ja'bari's garden behind the Ibrahimi Mosque. The gas arrived invisible, and when our eyes began to burn our host cut up onions and told us to breathe them in. I didn't ask any questions. I think it helped.

Each year has its standout moments, its public triumphs and private crises. Scenes hold close to me: scouring downtown

Ramallah for a fax machine, Mahmoud Darwish's letter of welcome in my hand, the *Guardian*'s phone number written out on the back; the spotlight on Suheir Hammad, the brutal electricity of her suite of Gaza poems, tonight five short months after Operation Cast Lead; the crowds hanging off the rooftop of the Qassem Palace to get a view of the night's poets; our logo on a bag hanging off a random shoulder in London; the timbre of Mohammed Bakri's baritone reading China Miéville's words; our first poster by Muiz; Maya Khalidi's soprano soaring in improvised perfection in the beats of Gillian Slovo's breaths; Najwan Darwish's poetry in the dark of Silwan:

> The earth is three nails
> and mercy a hammer:
> Strike, Lord.
> Strike with the planes.

It's dark and tear gas hangs low in the air and a dumpster is burning in the middle of the road. The bus pulls to a stop. I get out. The houses in the valley above are all shuttered. The skirmish – the Jerusalem kids with rocks and Israeli soldiers with assault rifles – has moved up the hill. Our venue is up the hill. The tear gas stings. We have no onions. I stand looking at the blazing trash, no idea what to do, when I hear my mother, the Boss, declare that she's walking. She marches past the smoking trashfire into the darkness and for a moment I think she's insane, but then someone else starts walking behind her, and another person, and soon the whole troupe is marching up the hill and into the tear gas and up to our venue, and before long the mics are plugged in and Gary Younge is reading and Najwan is performing and DAM are booming their bass lines out at the soldiers watching us in silence from the darkness of the hills.

The settlers in al-Khalil watch us from above too. One drops a cement block from four storeys up. It misses, destroys itself on the ground. We carry on into the city. The deeper you go the older it becomes, the walls of houses binding to one another:

no endings and no beginnings, an interconnected hive of shared space and mutual fortification. Each step takes you deeper inside, deeper into the city's physical memory, into its trauma. House by house this battle is fought. Some have fallen, the flags of the victor plunged deep in their chests. The Palestinian colours are nowhere to be seen, long outlawed by the martial government. The streets are nearly silent. Shop after shop is shuttered. Again and again graffiti – stars of David, graffiti in Hebrew: GAS THE ARABS. The settlers are above, watching, building a new network of watchtowers and sight lines and access points. Another people, another history taking shape above, pressing down on those below, working, waiting, watching.

When we stand in the Ibrahimi Mosque I point out the bullet holes. I say the word *massacre*. Some stop to look at them, some authors understand what that word, that fracture in the marble, really means. I can do no more than point.

They are digging underneath the houses, they are watching from above.

Another language is forming above us, around us. A settlement is a civilian community, a village, an expression of Israel's natural growth, a fact on the ground, a negotiable asset, a military outpost, a political provocation, a colonial expansion.

It's not a wall. It's a security barrier, a separation fence, an immigration control, a complex collection of cement and barbed wire and ditches and patrol roads, it's an apartheid wall of racial segregation.

Words are important in Palestine. Nowhere is it more important to call a wall a wall. To call apartheid, apartheid.

Archbishop Desmond Tutu calls it an apartheid state. What more should anyone need to know? Archbishop Desmond Tutu calls it an apartheid state. Repeat it like a mantra.

Get on the bus. Each day you will understand more. Each day we cross lines drawn by soldiers in the sand, cross lines that millions of others cannot. Tomorrow we will go to Jerusalem. Tomorrow we will go through Qalandia. Tomorrow we will walk through the razor wire and the cattle runnels and the steel gates that they call Qalandia. That first time I was forced through the metal humiliation I was so angry I cried. It was the first festival. Suheir Hammad squeezed my hand. Sometimes I think that was the first time I felt that I was an Arab. But I had an EU passport in my pocket. I drove on to Jerusalem.

We cross Qalandia and drive along the long wall towards Jerusalem. On the other side is al-Ram, once a suburb of the capital, now a smuggler backwoods cast out of the demographic fold. The wall stretches on. It's not a wall, it's the cumulative effort of dozens of international corporations earning billions of dollars for cement from Ireland and barbed wire from South Africa and construction vehicles from Caterpillar, JCB, Volvo and Bobcat and patrol vehicles from Humvee and General Motors and dogs from K-9 Solutions and biometric IDs from Hewlett-Packard and X-ray machines from Rapiscan and guards from G4S. The wall stretches on.

We arrive in Jerusalem, a city of soldiers' guns and victors' flags and intricate alleyways, French tourists carrying replica crosses along Jesus' footsteps and sweating white soldiers and armed settlers in sunglasses carrying provisions up to their urban fortresses above the simmering, taciturn population, who have held on to their houses through fifty years of military dictatorship and night patrols and arbitrary arrests and increasing taxes and municipal neglect and brutalised children and administrative detentions and destruction orders and travel restrictions and offers of millions of dollars and passports to those who will leave quietly in the night.

They are digging underneath the houses, they are laying siege with new settlements, they are choking you with the wall.

317

When you enter the gardens of al-Aqsa decades of pressure fall away. Families sit under the trees, children kick footballs around the ancient arches, the elegant but firm stonework of the city rises to protect you from what lies beyond, to hold you in contemplation and calm togetherness. The Dome of the Rock stands in magnificence at its centre. This is the grand prize. This is the eye of the storm.

In the Jerusalem of 2003 a small shop stands in the Jewish Quarter with a strange architectural model in the window. A settler with an M16 dangling off his shoulder hurries past me. I lean in to read the label: THE THIRD TEMPLE. There is a fringe millenarian movement who believe the Third Temple must be raised in the place of the Dome of the Rock to help bring us to the End of Days.

In the Jerusalem of 1966 650 people lived in the Moroccan Quarter, the Wailing Wall the neighbourhood's boundary to the east, the Golden Dome high above it.

In the Jerusalem of 1967 the Moroccan Quarter is no more. What had stood for 770 years is bulldozed in a moment by the occupying Israeli army. Three days after the invasion the Wailing Wall Plaza stands in its place: 120 square metres of prayer area becomes 20,000.

In the Jerusalem of 2013 every gift shop in the Jewish Quarter sells images of the Third Temple, a tourist attraction features an enormous architectural model of the Dome of the Rock cracking open as the temple births itself from the mosque's ruins. The Jerusalem of 2013 is a hyper-segregated city of techno-piety, of rabbinically blessed metal detectors and biometric databases of God's preferred people. Red cows are genetically engineered to fulfil ancient prophecies. Priests who can prove a patriarchal bloodline from Aaron should apply for jobs at redheifer@templeinstitute.org. Every day armed settlers march into the gardens of al-Aqsa demanding 'equal prayer rights'.

They are digging under the houses, they are digging under al-Aqsa, they are digging for the End of Days. You can feel it, feel the rumblings underneath, underground, the new city being hewn, unseen and unheard, a city of secret tunnels and sinister archaeologies, an underground city for a fanatical few. The settlers, the government, the City of David Corporation, the Temple Institute, the Jerusalem Municipality – tunnelling and digging and pulling away the foundations of the old city, waiting, working, praying for a collapse, for a war, a purging, a new beginning for their new history of archaeological parks, education centres, historical tours, school trips, PhDs and Lonely Planets – a new mythology being carved out of the foundations of the old, an underground city that will yawn and swallow the upper world. The keepers of al-Aqsa Mosque sit by the doors of their charge, waiting. For houses to crumble, for a tunnel to appear, for a wing of the ancient mosque to collapse into the valley. For the spark. We are all waiting for the spark. The End Times are being built for. The siege grows deeper. The Red Cow must be sacrificed. The Third Temple must be raised. The people must be purified.

Lead must be cast.

The spotlight is cold on Suheir Hammad:

a bell fired in jericho rings through blasted windows a woman
carries bones in bags under eyes disbelieving becoming
numb dumbed by numbers front and back gaza onto gaza
for gaza am sorry gaza am sorry she sings for the whole
powerless world her notes pitch perfect the bell a death toll

Richard Ford pauses to catch his breath. The poem is by Seamus Heaney. The lights are down, the audience holds its breath with him. 'I'm sorry,' he says. He was friends with Heaney, he says. He reads on:

> The end of art is peace
> Could be the motto of this frail device
> That I have pinned up on our deal dresser—

I have been nervous around him all week. But, in this moment, I think I understand him.

In Cairo I cut an onion in two halves, wrap them in newspaper and put them in my bag. When the tear gas is too much I take them out, offer one half to a boy choking next to me. He looks at me incredulously. 'It's what the Palestinians do,' I say. He breathes it in. I think, for a moment, of al-Ja'bari and his garden.

Get on the bus.

I spend the evening in the cool comfort of Ramallah, in a garden bar shaded by azkadenya trees. Friends are thirsty for stories from the revolution, keen to tell me how they stayed up all night watching Al Jazeera, willing the barricades to hold, how they took to the streets in tears when Mubarak fell. They tell me their plans for Palestine, for the spark, the start, the next revolution, the continuation of what Bouazizi started.

Two hundred people crowd into the top floor of the hotel to sing along to Eskenderella's pop-up concert. The chief of police of Gaza City is sitting downstairs with a man in fatigues. A man they call the Butcher. The Butcher does not look happy. The Butcher looks furious. He stares coldly ahead as the chief of police apologises for our event being shut down. It was a misunderstanding, he says. It's 2012, and this year's festival is mostly Egyptian writers and activists and we've forced the stuttering post-revolution government to open the border and have brought daily antagonisms of the newly liberated with us: incendiary words are spoken on television, there are calls for revolution on the local radio, teenage audiences are left unsegregated, we keep shaking our security detail. The Butcher clicks through his prayer beads, staring ahead.

Six months later I watch the bombs fall on streets I now know. I check the lists of the dead for the names of new friends. Friends I have abandoned to Israel's bombs, to the Butcher's blades. I have an EU passport. I cross the borderlines. I do not return to Gaza.

The wall can be cruised through. The wall is incomplete. There is still more money to be made. The wall waits above the Cremasin Monastery.

The festival finishes, and we collapse with exhaustion and we sit and debrief in a cafe in Ramallah and we take notes on what to change and in September we begin again: the annual report, the emails to funders, the invitations to new authors, the bus climbs from the Dead Sea, the audience waits in Ramallah.

I have an EU passport. I hand it to the border guard at Allenby. I hold it up for the soldiers in Qalandia. I feel it in my pocket when I am taken into an interrogation room.

J.M. Coetzee strides up to the stage. The audience is full to overflowing, not even standing room at the back. The world holds its breath. Will he say it? In the moment nothing matters more. It is the final night of the festival. He has seen all we have to show him. Will he call it apartheid or not?

Words are important here.

Words tell you who's on your side, tell you who understands and show you who wants to hide. Words can cling on to a reality slipping out of comprehension. Disrupt the language and you

disrupt reality. If you have no word for it, how can anyone understand? How can anyone even listen?

The bus pulls away from al-Khalil. We are all in silence. There
are no words for the things being done here. We drive north. That
night Nancy Kricorian reads from a passage about the Armenian
genocide.

> My grandfather trailed behind us, hobbling along with a cane.
> My mother called back to him, 'We'll see you at the resting
> place.' He would arrive after dark and fall down to sleep
> without even eating. One morning he didn't wake up. My
> grandmother slapped her face and called out to God in a loud
> voice. She sat in the dust and wouldn't get up until my mother
> pulled her to her feet. The next day Grandmother sat down
> in the dirt by the side of the road and begged us to leave her.
> She said she couldn't take another step. My mother kissed my
> grandmother's hands and said a prayer. Then she wrapped a
> scarf over my head so I couldn't look back.

When she wipes away a tear the audience cries with her.

They are digging underneath the houses, they are watching
from above, they are building a new language, a new reality.

How can anyone understand it all? How can anyone, in one
week, understand the segregated roads and the weaponised
agriculture and the stolen aquifer and the tactical topography
and the five different legal systems and the psychology of the
oppressor and the medieval history and the economics of blood
diamonds and their own complicity and the Holocaust industry
and the EU trade deals and settlement profiteering and the Soviet
diaspora and the Oslo Accords and Sabra and Shatila and the
tunnel industry and the ethnic cleansing of Jerusalem and ID
cards and Camp David and the collaboration of the PA and the
one-state solution?

The bus climbs from the Dead Sea. The audience waits in Ramallah. Get on the bus.

Years pass.

The land changes as you drive out of the West Bank. The lands conquered in 1948 are subjugated again with six-lane highways. Israel does not go round the mountain, it goes through it. The message is clear. The fertility is breathtaking. The sea is a perfect blue. They chose a beautiful place to conquer.

From Haifa we drive east, back into the West Bank. One day, in 2014, I understand it. The low coastal plain falls away behind us as we start our ascent back up into the mountain, up towards Nablus. Up, up, the fields disappear and the brown rocks and olive terraces begin. It's 1948 and the villages are ablaze, the Hagganah are coming, more massacres are coming, everyone is fleeing the militias, their guns and grenades chasing relentless through the lands of Raml Zayta and Khirbat Zalafa, through the ruins of Qaqun there is only flight, only running – until the mountain. The mountain breaks the assault. The villagers have gathered themselves, they hold the elevated position. The Zionist militia cannot penetrate the mountain. A line is drawn. A land is divided.

And now?

If Israel can't go through the mountain, it will grip into it with settlements. They dig and tunnel and build. Every day they grow, every day a little more mountain is conquered. If Israel can't go through the mountain, it will dig into it. Every day people arrive, new settlers, new lives. They arrive from Russia, Ukraine, France – 150,000 new settlers since the festival began ten years ago.

Thirty-nine per cent of the Russian settlers in Palestine do not read Hebrew.

A fifty-year plan is unfolding, built brick by settlement brick, body by colonist's body the mountain is subdued, the elevated position is usurped for the coming war.

They are always watching us. One year they shut us down in Jerusalem. The rest, they just watch. The wall still looms over the road to the Cremasin Monastery. It's been ten years now. Why don't they finish it? What are they waiting for? Is something slowing them down? Or is this part of the plan?

They don't google me. Every time at the border it's the same questions. What's your father's name? Have you ever been to Syria? What is a writing workshop? If they googled me they'd see I'm not telling them the whole truth. But they don't. Or they do, and they don't care. Or they do, and they like what they see. Maybe a little literature festival once a year is good for their image. Don't they know that words are important?

Coetzee calls it apartheid. He doesn't say 'this is apartheid' but he says this is apartheid. Another battle won in the culture war. We send the press release to our mailing lists. J.M. Coetzee, South African Nobel laureate, talks about apartheid in Palestine. Surely the world will pay attention?

Culture might be a weapon, but is it a gun?

The BBC refuses to carry an emergency appeal for Gaza during Operation Cast Lead.

There are Mustangs in Ramallah now. Red convertibles without licence plates and rumoured to be stolen from a Romanian cargo ship. The banks grow stronger. Everyone can get a line of credit. The land belongs to the last century.

'On your right' – the microphone, in 2016, is heavy in my hand; the group looks to the right – 'is the Beitar Illit settlement.

Those lower structures – the trailer-park containers – they're new. If you come back next year they'll have turned into full houses.'

It is a certainty.

Inch by inch, the land is conquered. House by house, Jerusalem is surrounded.

'Underneath us is the West Bank aquifer. Israel takes 80 per cent of the aquifer's water each year to fill the swimming pools of settlers.'

Drop by drop, the underland is conquered. The elevated position is parched. Wells are sealed with cement.

'On your left was a field of trees. Olive trees. You can see the stumps. They were hundreds of years old. They'll likely replace them with northern pines.'

Tree by tree nature is conquered. Divinity is engineered. The Red Cow must first be born if it is to die.

So many have died since we started doing this. Harold Pinter, Chinua Achebe, Seamus Heaney, Mahmoud Darwish, John Berger – our festival patrons who never got a chance to come with us. Taha Muhammad Ali, Henning Mankell, Radwa Ashour, Rawda Bishara Atallah – who will take your places?

Edward Said. Incredible how much that still hurts.

They are digging underneath the houses, they are watching from above, they are building a new language, they are draining the mountain, they are breeding the Red Cow, they are building for the coming war.

I see a name I know on a list of the dead. Al-Batsh. See it repeated again and again. Twenty-one times. The Gaza police chief's name. His entire family are killed in a targeted strike. Except him. He was only wounded. They found a fate worse than death for him.

Targeted strike.
We need new words.
Familicide. Mass murder. War crimes.

We need new words if we are to feel again. The bus climbs from the Dead Sea. The audience waits in Ramallah. Our host in al-Khalil is dead. I don't cry going through Qalandia any more. I don't feel anything.

I stand at a bar in Ramallah. We don't talk much. Just some heavy words about where it went wrong, the things we failed to see, the reasons all revolutions fail.

The bus climbs. A bullet punctures a lung on Mount Calvary.
We have seen this all before.
The bus climbs. A body hangs limp from a tree above Abraham's tomb.
Strange fruit.
The fire burned the inside of his lungs.
A mother buries her child in Jerusalem.
They made him swallow the gasoline.
Mohammed Abu Khdeir was sixteen years old.

Get on the bus.

The Maghrebi Quarter was razed in three days – 120 square metres of prayer area became 20,000. We need new words. And to remember old ones.

Lebensraum.

KKK.
They are digging underneath the houses.
They are building for the coming war.

Get on the bus. We will drive to Qalandia. The horror they have named Qalandia. The name they have stolen for the new horror. Qalandia – a land, an idea, a land dies here.

Cast
Lead

They are watching from above.
You listen for them in the night, for the scratch of metal against rock, for the night-vision goggles and the click of a flashlight standing over your bed, they are watching, building, every day.

White
Phosphorus

An incendiary gas, a highly efficient smoke-producing agent, burns fiercely and can ignite cloth, fuel, ammunition and other combustibles.

And flesh.
White phosphorus.

The night lights with a flare and six burning stars fall to the ground and one lands on you, you're running but it's on you and your skin and you smell it burning smell your flesh singeing and water won't help water won't put it out it just burns and burns deeper burns through you.

No.
We need a new language. The old one has been corrupted.
They have engineered the Red Cow.

Burning gas falls from the sky.
They are building.
We need a new language.
Negotiated settlement, natural expansion, security barrier, internal refugees, defence forces, seam zone, blockade, conflict, humanity, democracy, dialogue, peace.

Peace.
We need –

Peace. Peace Now. Seeds of Peace. A Lasting Peace. Children of Peace. Comedy for Peace. Peace Oil. Combatants for Peace. Peres Centre for Peace.

We need a new language.
Peace.
Peace?
I hate the word.
Give me justice.
Get on the bus.
Justice.
They are digging underneath the houses.
Get on the bus.
They are building for the coming war.
Get on the bus.

AUTHOR BIOGRAPHIES

Susan Abulhawa is a novelist, poet and political writer. She is also the founder of Playgrounds for Palestine, a children's non-profit organisation dedicated to upholding the right to play.

Chinua Achebe (1930–2013) was among the most influential authors of the twentieth century and a key figure of post-colonial literature. He was the author of over twenty books, most notably *Things Fall Apart*, which became an international best-seller and a modern classic. He received numerous honours and honorary doctorates, including the Nigerian National Merit Award and the Man Booker International Prize for Fiction. In 2008 he became a patron of the Palestine Festival of Literature in its inaugural year.

Suad Amiry is a Palestinian writer, an architect and a social activist. She is the author of numerous architectural and non-fiction books. Her acclaimed *Sharon and My Mother-in-Law* was translated into twenty languages and won the prestigious Italian Premio Viareggio in 2004. Amiry is also the author of *Nothing to Lose But Your Life* and *Golda Slept Here* which won the Premio Nonnino in 2014. *My Damascus* (2016) is Amiry's most recent book. Amiry is the founder of RIWAQ, the Centre for Architectural Conservation in Ramallah. She and RIWAQ are winners of many international awards including the Prince Claus Award (2011), the Curry Stone Design Prize (2012) and the Aga Khan Award for Architecture (2013). She has served on the board of PalFest.

Victoria Brittain is a journalist and author and a founding member of PalFest. She has lived and worked in Saigon, Algiers, Nairobi, Washington and London, and travelled frequently in the Middle East and Central America. She worked at the *Guardian* for twenty years and writes for several French- and English-language publications. Her books include *Death of Dignity: Angola's Civil War* and *Shadow Lives: The Forgotten*

Women of the War on Terror. She is on the Council of the Institute of Race Relations and a trustee of the annual Palestine Book Awards.

Jehan Bseiso is a Palestinian poet, researcher and aid worker. Her poetry has been published in *Warscapes*, the *Electronic Intifada*, *Mada Masr* and the *Palestine Chronicle* among others. Her book *I Remember My Name* (2016) was the creative category winner of the Palestine Book Awards. Bseiso is co-editing *Making Mirrors*, a new anthology by, for and about refugees. Bseiso has been working with Médecins Sans Frontières / Doctors Without Borders since 2008.

J.M. Coetzee was born in South Africa in 1940 and educated in South Africa and the United States. He is the author of sixteen works of fiction, as well as of memoirs, essays in criticism and translations. Among awards he has won are the Booker Prize (twice) and in 2003 the Nobel Prize for Literature. He lives in Australia, where he is professor of literature at the University of Adelaide.

Teju Cole, novelist, essayist and photographer, was born in the United States and raised in Nigeria. His work has been recognized with the PEN/Hemingway Award, the Internationaler Literaturpreis, and the Windham Campbell Prize, among other honours. He is photography critic of the *New York Times* Magazine.

Molly Crabapple is an artist, journalist and author of the memoir *Drawing Blood*. She has drawn in and reported from Guantánamo Bay, American prisons, Abu Dhabi's migrant labour camps, and in Syria, Lebanon, Gaza, the West Bank and Iraqi Kurdistan. Crabapple is a contributing editor for *VICE*, and has written for publications including the *New York Times*, the *Paris Review* and *Vanity Fair*. Her work is in the permanent collection of the Museum of Modern Art, New York.

Selma Dabbagh is a British Palestinian writer of fiction. Her first novel, *Out of It* (Bloomsbury), set between Gaza, London and the Gulf, was a Guardian Book of the Year in 2011 and 2012. Her short stories have been published by *Granta*, the British Council, *Wasafiri*, Al-Saqi among others. In 2014 her play *The Brick* was produced by BBC Radio 4 and nominated for an Imison Award. She regularly writes for the *Electronic Intifada* on Palestinian culture and has written for the *Guardian*, the *London Review of Books*, *GQ* and other publications.

Mahmoud Darwish was born near Akka in 1941 and died in Houston in 2008. He had been the Arab world's pre-eminent poet for a quarter of a century, with more than 20 published volumes, numerous awards, and thousands filling stadiums at his readings. Darwish was also at the heart of the political struggle for Palestine, joining both the Israeli Communist Party and the Palestine Liberation Organisation. Darwish wrote Palestine's Declaration of Statehood announced by Yasir Arafat in Algiers in 1988, but resigned from the Executive of the PLO five years later over the Oslo Accords.

Born in Jerusalem in 1978, **Najwan Darwish** is one of the most prominent Arabic-language poets of his generation. In 2009 he was on Beirut's Hay Festival list of '39 best Arab authors under the age of 39'. Darwish's poetry has been translated into twenty languages. In 2014 US National Public Radio (NPR) listed his book *Nothing More To Lose* (New York Review Books, translated by Kareem James Abu-Zeid) as one of the best books of the year. Currently he is the chief editor of the cultural section of *Al-Araby Al-Jadeed* newspaper, and serves as literary adviser to PalFest.

Geoff Dyer's many books include *But Beautiful* (winner of the Somerset Maugham Prize), *The Ongoing Moment* (winner of the ICP Infinity Award for Writing on Photography) and *Otherwise Known as the Human Condition* (winner of the National Book Critics Circle Award for Criticism). His latest book is *White Sands: Experiences from the Outside World*. His books have been translated into twenty-four languages. He currently lives in Los Angeles, where he is writer in residence at the University of Southern California.

Adam Foulds is a poet and novelist from London. He has been the recipient of a number of literary awards, including the *Sunday Times* Young Writer of the Year, the Costa Poetry Prize, the Somerset Maugham Award, the South Bank Show Prize for Literature, the E. M. Forster Award, the Encore Award and the European Union Prize for Literature. He was named one of *Granta* magazine's Best of Young British Novelists in 2013 and of the Poetry Book Society's Next Generation Poets in 2014. His latest novel, *In the Wolf's Mouth*, was published in 2014.

Ru Freeman is a Sri Lankan and American writer whose work appears internationally, including in the *Guardian*, the *New York Times* and the *Boston Globe*. She is the author of the novels *A Disobedient Girl* (2009) and *On Sal Mal Lane* (2013), a *New York Times* Editor's

Choice, both appearing in translation, and editor of *Extraordinary Rendition: American Writers on Palestine* (2015). She is a contributing editor of the *Asian American Literary Review* and *Panorama: The Journal of Intelligent Travel*, has won the Sister Mariella Gable Award for Fiction, and the Janet H. Kafka Prize for Fiction by an American Woman, and blogs for the Huffington Post on literature and politics.

Omar Robert Hamilton is an award-winning filmmaker and writer, and a co-founder of the Palestine Festival of Literature. He is the author of the novel *The City Always Wins*, and has written for the *Guardian*, the *London Review of Books, Mada Masr* and *Guernica*.

A poet raised in Brooklyn, New York, **Suheir Hammad**'s poems have been widely anthologised and reinterpreted on to stage and screen. She is the author of *Born Palestinian, Born Black, Drops of This Story, ZaatarDiva* and *breaking poems*. Reading her poems in Palestine with PalFest was a dream come true.

Nathalie Handal's recent books include *The Republics*, lauded as 'one of the most inventive books by one of today's most diverse writers' and winner of the Arab American Book Award and the Virginia Faulkner Award for Excellence in Writing; the best-selling *The Invisible Star*; the critically acclaimed *Poet in Andalucía*; and *Love and Strange Horses*, winner of the Gold Medal Independent Publisher Book Award. Handal is a fellow of the Lannan Foundation, the Centro Andaluz de las Letras and the Fondazione di Venezia, and the recipient of the Alejo Zuloaga Order in Literature, among other honours. She is a professor at Columbia University and writes the column 'The City and the Writer' for *Words without Borders*. She serves on the board of PalFest.

Mohammed Hanif is the author of novels *A Case of Exploding Mangoes* and *Our Lady of Alice Bhatti*. He wrote the libretto for the opera *Bhutto* and is a contributing columnist for the *International New York Times* and BBC Urdu. He lives in Karachi.

Jeremy Harding is a contributing editor at the *London Review of Books,* where the pieces in this anthology first appeared. His translations of Rimbaud are published in Penguin Classics. He is the co-translator of *Modern French Philosophy* by Vincent Descombes. His memoir *Mother Country* is about the discovery of parents, absent and present. He has reported often on refugees and migrants in Europe, North Africa and the US. *Border Vigils: Keeping Migrants out of the Rich World* appeared in 2012. He has also reported from sub-Saharan Africa and run non-fiction and editing workshops in Palestine.

A PalFest veteran, **Rachel Holmes** is the author most recently of *Eleanor Marx: A Life*. Her previous books include *The Hottentot Venus: The Life and Death of Saartjie Baartman* and *The Secret Life of Dr James Barry*. Holmes curated many programmes with Palestinian artists while Director of Literature at London's Southbank Centre. From 2009 to 2014 she was tutor and writer in residence at the Palestine Writing Workshop in the West Bank, a PalFest initiative. She is currently writing a book about Sylvia Pankhurst.

John Horner was brought up in Kenya. He began his advertising career in London in 1965. After twelve years he started his own agency. He sold the business and worked in various marketing roles before buying into one of the most successful model agencies in the world, Models 1, where he still works today. His entrepreneurial spirit involves him in businesses as diverse as children's clothing, costume jewellery and per-fume. He is a trustee to the Jaipur Heritage Trust and a mentor to the Prince's Trust and the Jack Wills Young Entrepreneurs programme and is PalFest's treasurer and a member of its founding board.

Remi Kanazi is a poet, writer and organiser based in New York City. He is the author of two collections of poetry, *Before the Next Bomb Drops: Rising Up from Brooklyn to Palestine* and *Poetic Injustice: Writings on Resistance and Palestine*, and the editor of the anthology *Poets For Palestine*. He is a Lannan Residency fellow and an advisory committee member for the Palestinian Campaign for the Academic and Cultural Boycott of Israel.

Ghada Karmi was born in Jerusalem, but grew up in England. She is a leading Palestinian academic, activist and writer and her publications in-clude *In search of Fatima: A Palestinian Story, Married to Another Man: Israel's Dilemma in Palestine*, and, most recently, *Return: A Palestinain Memoir*. She is a Research Fellow at the Institute of Arab and Islamic Studies, at the University of Exeter.

Brigid Keenan has worked as an editor on *Nova* magazine, the *Observer* and the *Sunday Times*. She has published two fashion histories as well as *Travels in Kashmir, Damascus: Hidden Treasures of the Old City*, the best-selling *Diplomatic Baggage* and its sequel, *Packing Up*. Her most recent book, *Full Marks for Trying*, is a memoir of her childhood in India and her days as a young fashion editor at the dawn of the 60s in London. She has spent most of her life in far-flung postings with her diplomat husband. Keenan is currently fashion editor of *Oldie* magazine. She is a founding member of the PalFest board.

Mercedes Kemp is writer and director of community and research for WildWorks Theatre Company and senior lecturer in fine art at Falmouth University. She was born and grew up in Andalusia. For the past forty years she has lived in Cornwall, UK. She travels with WildWorks, developing text for site-specific theatre. Her method involves a kind of eclectic ethnographic research into a variety of sources: archives, libraries, cemeteries, bus stops, town gossips, old photographs, conversations and, above all, a close observation of the process of memory and its effect on the value that people place on their environments.

Omar El-Khairy's plays include *Burst, Sour Lips, The Keepers of Infinite Space* and *The Chaplain: or, a short tale of how we learned to love good Muslims while torturing bad ones*. His latest play *Homegrown* was published in 2017. El-Khairy is a former Leverhulme associate playwright at the Bush Theatre and a founding member of Paper Tiger, a collective of theatre and film-makers, working collaboratively and autonomously. His short film *No Exit* received its world premiere at last year's Dubai International Film Festival. He holds a PhD on sociology from the London School of Economics and Political Science.

Nancy Kricorian is a New York City-based writer and activist. She is the author of the novels *Zabelle, Dreams of Bread and Fire*, and most recently *All The Light There Was*, which is set in the Armenian community of Paris during World War II.

Sabrina Mahfouz is a British Egyptian playwright, poet and screenwriter. Her 2016 plays are *With a Little Bit of Luck* (Paines Plough), *Slug* (nabokov), *Battleface* (Bush Theatre), *Layla's Room* (Theatre Centre) and *The Love I Feel Is Red* (Tobacco Factory Theatres). Her TV short *Breaking the Code* was produced by BBC3 and BBC Drama earlier this year. Her play *Chef* won a 2014 Fringe First Award, and *Clean* was produced by Traverse Theatre and transferred to New York in 2014. She has been the Sky Arts Academy scholar for poetry,

Leverhulme playwright in residence and associate artist at the Bush Theatre.

Jamal Mahjoub was born in London and brought up in Khartoum, Sudan. His literary novels include *Travelling with Djinns* and *Nubian Indigo*. His fiction and non-fiction have appeared in numerous publications. He also writes crime fiction as Parker Bilal: The Makana series takes place in Egypt in the decade prior to the Arab revolutions. He has lived in Denmark, Spain and currently Amsterdam.

Henning Mankell (1948–2015) was a crime writer, children's author and dramatist, best known for his series of mystery novels featuring Inspector Kurt Wallander. He was a committed political and social activist and after attending PalFest in 2009 he took part in the following year's Freedom Flotilla to Gaza and was arrested and deported to Sweden.

Claire Messud is the author of four novels and a book of novellas, including *The Emperor's Children* (2006), an international best-seller which was translated into over twenty languages. Her most recent novel, *The Woman Upstairs*, was published in 2013. She writes regularly for the *New York Review of Books*, the *New York Times* and the *Financial Times* (London). She teaches at Harvard University and lives in Cambridge, Massachusetts. She visited Palestine as part of PalFest 2009.

China Miéville is the author of several novels, including *The City & the City* and *Embassytown*, the short-story collection *Three Moments of an Explosion* and the novella *This Census-Taker*. His non-fiction includes *London's Overthrow* and *Between Equal Rights*, a study of international law. He is a founding editor of the journal *Salvage*.

Pankaj Mishra is the author of several books, including *The Romantics: A Novel* and *From the Ruins of Empire: The Intellectuals Who Remade Asia*. He writes political and literary essays for the *Guardian*, the *New Yorker*, the *London Review of Books* and the *New York Review of Books*, and is a columnist for *Bloomberg View* and the *New York Times Book Review*. His most recent book is *Age of Anger: A History of the Present*.

Deborah Moggach has written eighteen novels, several of which she has adapted as TV dramas. Her novel *The Best Exotic Marigold Hotel* was made into a hit movie starring Judi Dench and Maggie Smith, and her novel *Tulip Fever*, set in Vermeer's Amsterdam, is to be released in early 2017. She also wrote the BAFTA-nominated screenplay for *Pride and Prejudice*, starring Keira Knightley, and adapted Nancy Mitford's *Love in a Cold Climate* for the BBC. She lives in London and Wales, and her latest novel, *Something to Hide*, was published in 2015. She is on the council of the Royal Society of Literature, is a past chair of the Society of Authors and was on the executive committee of PEN, the writers' organisation which campaigns for freedom of speech.

Muiz is a visual communicator who specialises in bilingual art direction of Latin and Arab scripts. His visual explorations of the historical, cultural and political legacy of language through typography and graphic design have been published in four continents and were featured as art in a solo exhibition in the Nour Festival of Arts, London (2012). Muiz continues to explore identity by de-colonising and de-constructing heritage arts through radical experimentation, in an effort to honour the legacy of master crafts-men whose work defied the separation of the arts from science.

Maath Musleh is a Palestinian journalist and academic from Beit Safafa in Jerusalem. He obtained his masters in political journalism from City University in London and is currently head of the Humanities/Arts Division at Al-Quds Bard College. He has worked with PalFest as a social media specialist and general consultant since 2014.

Michael Ondaatje was born in Sri Lanka and has lived in Canada since 1963. His books include *The Cat's Table*, *Anil's Ghost*, *The English Patient*, *In the Skin of a Lion* and *Coming Through Slaughter*, a memoir called *Running in the Family* and *The Conversations: Walter Murch and the Art of Editing Film*. His collections of poetry include *The Cinnamon Peeler* and *Handwriting*.

Michael Palin established his reputation with *Monty Python's Flying Circus* and *Ripping Yarns*. His work also includes several films with Monty Python, as well as a BAFTA-winning performance as the hapless Ken in *A Fish Called Wanda*. Palin has written books to accompany his eight very successful BBC travel series and he has also published three volumes of diaries. In 2014 with his fellow Pythons he performed a ten-night sell-out show at the 02 Arena in London. Between 2009 and 2012 Palin was president of the Royal Geographical Society. In 2013 he was awarded the BAFTA Fellowship.

Ed Pavlić is the author of six collections of poems and two critical books. His most recent works are *Who Can Afford to Improvise?: James Baldwin and Black Music, the Lyric and the Listeners, Let's Let That Are Not Yet: Inferno* and *Visiting Hours at the Color Line*. He lives in Athens, Georgia and teaches at the University of Georgia.

Yasmin El-Rifae joined the PalFest team in 2013. She worked as a journalist and human rights researcher in Cairo and New York. She is writing her first book, inspired by a civilian group that combated sexual assaults during protests in Cairo's Tahrir Square.

Atef Abu Saif was born in Jabaliya refugee camp in the Gaza Strip in 1973. He has published six novels and two collections of short stories. His novel *A Suspended Life* (2014) was shortlisted for the 2015 International Prize for Arab Fiction. His account of the 2014 war on Gaza was published in English as *The Drone Eats with Me: Diaries from a City under Fire*. He studied at the Universities of Birzeit and Bradford and at the European University Institute in Florence and has written several books on politics, his academic speciality.

Kamila Shamsie is the author of six novels, including *Burnt Shadows* (shortlisted for the Orange Prize) and *A God in Every Stone* (shortlisted for the Baileys Prize). Three of her novels have received awards from Pakistan's Academy of Letters. She is a fellow of the Royal Society of Literature and in 2013 was named a Granta Best of Young British Novelist. She grew up in Karachi and now lives in London.

Raja Shehadeh is a writer and a lawyer who founded the pioneering Palestinian human rights organisation Al-Haq. Shehadeh is the author of several acclaimed books including *Strangers in the House, A Rift in Time: Travels with my Ottoman Uncle, Occupation Diaries* and *Language of War, Language of Peace* and the winner of the 2008 Orwell Prize for *Palestinian Walks*. He lives in Ramallah in Palestine. His latest book is *Where the Line is Drawn, Crossing Boundaries in Occupied Palestine*.

Gillian Slovo is a South African-born novelist and playwright. She has published twelve novels including her latest, *Ten Days*, her Orange Prize-shortlisted *Ice Road* and *Red Dust*, which won France's Temoin du Monde prize and was made into a film starring Hilary Swank and Chiwetel Ejiofor. Her family memoir, *Every Secret Thing*, tells the story of her activist parents Ruth First and Joe Slovo. Gillian has written three verbatim plays: *Guantanamo: Honor Bound to Defend Freedom* (with Victoria Brittain), *The Riots* and *Another World: Losing our Children to Islamic State*, which played in London's National Theatre in 2016.

Ahdaf Soueif is the author of the Booker Prize-shortlisted *The Map of Love* as well as the memoir of the January 2011 revolution, *Cairo: A City Transformed*. She co-founded the Palestine Festival of Literature and is based in both Cairo and London.

Linda Spalding was born in Kansas and lived in Hawaii before migrating to Toronto in 1982. Her non-fiction work *The Follow* was shortlisted for the Trillium Book Award and the Pearson Writers' Trust Non-Fiction Prize. *Who Named the Knife* is an intimate portrait of her relationship as a juror with the defendant in a murder trial. She has written five novels, including *The Purchase*, which won the Governor General's Award for fiction and, most recently, *A Reckoning*.

William Sutcliffe is the author of seven novels, including the international best-seller *Are You Experienced?* and *The Wall*, which was shortlisted for the 2014 CILIP Carnegie Medal. His work has been translated into twenty-six languages. *We See Everything*, set in a reimagined London which has been reduced to the condition of Gaza, will be published by Bloomsbury in September 2017.

Alice Walker is an internationally celebrated writer, poet and activist whose books include seven novels, four collections of short stories, four children's books, and volumes of essays and poetry. She won the Pulitzer Prize for Fiction in 1983 and the National Book Award. Walker has been an activist all of her adult life and believes that learning to extend the range of our compassion is activity and work available to all. She is a staunch defender not only of human rights, but of the rights of all living beings. Alice Walker was awarded the Mahmoud Darwish Literary Prize for Fiction 2016.

CREDITS

Grateful acknowledgement to the following original publishers and rights holders of the pieces listed below: 'Welcome' by Mahmoud Darwish, reprinted by kind permission of Tania Nasir, translation by Ahdaf Soueif; 'Through the Looking-Glass' by Adam Foulds, first published in the *Jewish Quarterly*, 23 July 2010; 'Once Upon a Jerusalem' by Susan Abulhawa, a shorter version of the text that appears here was originally published in *Elle* India, July 2016; 'Sleeping in Gaza' by Najwan Darwish, first appeared in English in *Nothing More to Lose*, published by New York Review Books, April 2014 (© Najwan Darwish 2000, 2012, 2013, 2014; translation copyright © Kareem James Abu-Zeid, 2014); 'In the Company of Writers' by Kamila Shamsie, features Kamila Shamsie's translation of Faiz Ahmed Faiz's poem, 'Falastini Bachay Kay Liye Lori', published with kind permission of the Faiz Foundation Trust, Lahore, and © Moneeza Hashmi, Salima Hashmi. The lines from Mahmoud Darwish's 'Guests from the Sea' are taken from the *Anthology of Modern Palestinian Literature* (ed. Salma Khadra Jayyusi) © Columbia University Press, 1995. Lena Jayyusi and WS Merwin's translation of Mahmoud Darwish's 'You Will Carry the Butterfly's Burden' first appeared in *Poetry East* Issue 27, Spring 1989; 'An Image' by Geoff Dyer, first published in the *New Republic*, 6 August 2014; 'Exit Strategy' by China Miéville, first published in *Guernica*, 1 November 2013; 'Shujaiyya Dust' by Molly Crabapple, is an abridged edit of the piece that first appeared in *Vice* (https://www.vice.com/en_uk/article/shujaiya-dust-molly-crabapple-456), 30 June 2015; 'Gaza, from the Diaspora – Parts One and Two' by Jehan Bseiso, were first published on *The Electronic Intifada* (https://electronicintifada.net/), 28 July and 14 August 2014 respectively; 'The City of David' by Ghada Karmi,